MATRIMONIAL PROCEDURE IN THE ORDINARY COURTS OF SECOND INSTANCE

THE CATHOLIC UNIVERSITY OF AMERICA
CANON LAW STUDIES
No. 253

Matrimonial Procedure in the Ordinary Courts of Second Instance

BY THE

REV. LORAS T. LANE, B. FOR. COMM., A.B., S.T.L., J.C.L.
PRIEST OF THE ARCHDIOCESE OF DUBUQUE

A DISSERTATION

SUBMITTED TO THE FACULTY OF THE SCHOOL OF CANON LAW OF THE CATHOLIC UNIVERSITY OF AMERICA IN PARTIAL FULFILLMENT OF THE REQUIREMENTS FOR THE DEGREE OF DOCTOR OF CANON LAW

THE CATHOLIC UNIVERSITY OF AMERICA PRESS
WASHINGTON, D. C.
1947

Nihil Obstat:

LUDOVICUS MOTRY, S.T.D., J.C.D.
Censor Deputatus
Washingtonii, die 16 maii, 1949

Imprimatur:

✠ HENRY P. ROHLMAN, D.D.
Archiepiscopus Dubuquensis
Dubuquii, die 20 maii, 1949

PRINTED BY
LORAS COLLEGE PRESS
DUBUQUE, IOWA

RESPECTFULLY DEDICATED
WITH
REVERENCE AND GRATITUDE

TO

THE MOST REV. HENRY P. ROHLMAN, D.D., LL.D.
ARCHBISHOP OF DUBUQUE

TABLE OF CONTENTS

PART TWO

CANONICAL COMMENTARY

CHAPTER V

CHAPTER VI

CHAPTER VII

FOREWORD

The increasing disregard for the sanctity of Christian wedlock[1] has made it imperative that the Church maintain a system of well organized diocesan courts to take care of the mounting number of cases in which the marriage bond has been called into question. It has been committed to these tribunals to assist in seeing that the injunction, "Quod Deus coniunxit, homo non separet," shall, according to the powers granted, be maintained.[2]

Various causes are at times alleged in an effort to prove that the nuptial union was not joined by God at all, with the consequence that the bond is said not to exist. It pertains to the Church to decide whether or not a just cause for such a claim is present, and to that end an elaborate judicial system has been developed. A very important tribunal in that hierarchical system of courts is the ordinary court of second instance. It is the purpose of this dissertation to present a historical synopsis of the development of the methods of procedure used in that tribunal in the centuries past, and then to give a commentary on the organization and procedure in such courts according to the legislation now in force. This treatise will be limited to a consideration of that procedure relating to formal trials in cases of nullity.

It is logical that the historical synopsis should begin with an outline of appellate procedure in Roman law, as found in the Justinian compilations. In the latter collections, as well as in the new laws promulgated by Justinian himself, is to be found a system so well developed that the Church incorporated it almost bodily into her own judicial system. After consideration has been given to the Roman sources, a survey will be made of the development of ecclesiastical appellate procedure from the beginning up to the time of Gratian. It will be shown that in the eleventh century, with the rediscovery of Justinian's

1 Pius XI, encycl. *"Casti connubii,"* 31 dec. 1930— *AAS,* XXII (1930), 539.

2 Matth., XIX: 6.

Code and the freeing of ecclesiastical courts from secular control, there began a new period in procedural development. The Decretals of Pope Gregory IX, along with the *Liber Sextus* of Boniface VIII and the Constitutions of Clement V, will be the main sources consulted in this period up to the time of the Council of Trent.

The historical synopsis will then reveal that the greatest development of procedural law in courts of second instance before the promulgation of the Code of Canon Law is to be found toward the middle of the eighteenth century. It was at that time that the renowned canonist Pope Benedict XIV ascended the throne of Peter, and enacted legislation regarding matrimonial procedure that has undergone few substantial changes since his day. The chief source of that legislation is contained in his celebrated Constitution *"Dei miseratione,"* promulgated on November 3, 1741.

The canonical commentary will comprise the second part of the dissertation. The general principles that govern matrimonial trials are found in the fourth book of the Code. While it is true that the procedure in the court of second instance is the same, *congrua congruis referendo,* as in the court of first instance, nevertheless it is no small task properly to adapt the one process to the other. Inestimable aid was given in that regard by the Sacred Congregation of the Sacraments when it issued an Instruction on August 15, 1936, dealing with matrimonial procedure in diocesan tribunals. Its purpose is to facilitate the application of the procedural law of the Code to matrimonial causes. The regulations contained in the Instruction are to be observed as universal law, and obedience to them may be enforced by proper sanctions if necessary.

The introductory decree of the Instruction makes it clear that the regulations set forth are not intended to abrogate or derogate any part of the Code. It states: "In hisce regulis iudices ipsi et tribunalium administri praecipuos canones de processibus agentes accurate apteque dispositos reperient, necnon brevem facilemque eorundem explanationem, ex iurisprudentia praesertim erutam atque ex Normis S. R. Rotae, quo plenius ipsis iidem Codicis canones, quibus derogatum non est, sint perspecti, eosque expeditius singulis aptare possint matrimonialibus causis."

Thus, if there is any seeming discrepancy between the Code and the Instruction, the clear law of the Code is to prevail.

One of the most helpful and practical sections of the Instruction is that which treats of appellate procedure. It has been instrumental in greatly clarifying many points of law concerning appeals which previously were vague and obscure. It has likewise served to correlate those canons whose reciprocal relationship to other parts of the Code was not always clear. In bringing together under one unified treatment those canons which relate to appeals in matrimonial procedure, the Instruction has given a most valuable contribution to procedural law.

It is beyond the scope of this dissertation to make a study of the complete process of the court of second instance, and thus it presupposes at least a fundamental knowledge of the principles of procedure as followed in the court of first instance. The principal aim has been to select for thorough treatment only those procedural norms which are peculiar to the appellate tribunal. Reference will be made to the procedure common to both first and second instances only when clarity and unity of treatment demand it.

The writer welcomes this occasion to express his sincere gratitude to the Most Reverend Henry P. Rohlman, D.D., Archbishop of Dubuque, for the opportunity to pursue a course of graduate studies in Canon Law; to the Faculty of the School of Canon Law at The Catholic University of America, Washington, D. C., for their kind guidance and assistance; and to all others who have aided in any way in the preparation of this work.

PART I

CHAPTER ONE

APPELLATE PROCEDURE IN ROMAN LAW

Appeals in civil cases, in the sense of an application to a higher court to retry or review the proceedings of a lower court, were unknown in Roman law before the period of the Empire. [1]

What was called an *appellatio* in the *Legis Actio* and Formulary periods had an entirely different judicial effect. [2] Every decision of a magistrate was formally a manifestation of his sovereign *imperium,* and was, legally considered, not a sentence, but an imperative order. On the other hand, the decision of a *iudex privatus,* a private citizen chosen by the litigating parties to decide their case, was a sentence. The twofold stage of the law of civil procedure in Rome prohibited the magistrate from deciding the case himself; it was within his province to hear only the preliminary proceedings up to the *litis contestatio* (proceedings *in iure*), and then to award the decision of the case to the *iudex privatus* (proceedings *in iudicio*). [3]

Inasmuch as the latter was only a private citizen and not an official of the government, an appeal to a State court was impossible. An appeal was also precluded by the fact that the litigating parties agreed that the decision of the *iudex privatus* was final.

[1] Wenger, *Institutes of the Roman Law of Civil Procedure,* revised edition, translated by Otis H. Fisk (New York: Veritas Press, 1940), p. 27; Jolowicz, *An Historical Introduction to the Study of Roman Law* (Cambridge: University Press, 1932), p. 406; Buckland, *A Text Book of Roman Law from Augustus to Justinian* (2. ed., Cambridge, 1921), p. 665; Costa, *Profilo Storico del Processo Civile Romano* (Roma, 1918), pp. 178, 179.

[2] The *Legis Actio* system of procedure in the early Republic lasted from the time of the XII Tables until about 150 B. C. The Formulary system, having its inception around the latter date, continued until about 300 A. D.

[3] For a detailed treatment of this procedure, cf. Wenger, *Institutes of the Roman Law of Civil Procedure,* pp. 94-230.

The remedy referred to as *appellatio* could be invoked only against an order of an official of the government. It had the effect, not of modifying the order in question, but of vetoing it. Entitled to exercise this veto were, in the first place, all magistrates equal or superior in authority to the ordering official, and, secondly, without reference to the question of rank, the Tribune of the people. Thus, if a private citizen sought to set aside a magisterial order which he considered unjust, he had to invoke the aid of some official vested with the veto power. The interceding official had no power to substitute an order of his own. It was this remedy that gave rise to the system of appeal as developed in the later Roman law, one magistrate being "appealed to" to intercede against another. [4]

It was not until the Imperial period, when the *iudex* became an official of the State, that there was a disappearance of the obstacle which had hitherto stood in the way of allowing an appeal against the sentence. Because of his official position it now seemed imperative to provide for an examination into the question whether or not he had applied State-willed law. Accordingly the Emperor, since he was invested with supreme power, permitted appeals to be brought to him, which he at first decided in person. The multiplicity of these appeals led to an arrangement of courts of higher and lower instances, a higher court trying the case over again with a view toward pronouncing a new sentence. [5]

Although the term *appellatio* was also used in conjunction with this procedure, its meaning was radically different from that in earlier Roman law. Then it meant the laying aside of a magisterial order; now it meant the trying of the case again in a higher court resulting in a new sentence. The date of this important procedural reform cannot be assigned with any degree of certainty. [6] It is known, however, that in the

[4] Sohm, *The Institutes of Roman Law* (translated by Leslie, 3. ed., Oxford: Clarendon Press, 1907), pp. 228, 229.

[5] Englemann and Millar, *History of Continental Civil Procedure* (Boston: Little, Brown and Co., 1927), p. 368.

[6] Wenger, *Institutes of the Roman Law of Civil Procedure*, p. 211, note 13.

time of Paulus and Ulpianus it had already become the subject of detailed scientific study.[7]

Throughout the Imperial period the appellate process underwent many modifications. It is not within the scope of this dissertation to enter into any detailed account of these changes. For this reason a survey of appellate procedure in Roman law will be restricted to that which obtained at the time of Justinian. It was then that it reached its fullest development, and it was this more perfected form that the Church was to use as a basis for its matrimonial procedure in its own ordinary tribunals of second instance. Having survived the test of the centuries, the basic principles of Roman law procedure have proved themselves as fundamentally sound.

ARTICLE I. INTRODUCTORY STAGE OF THE TRIAL

1. The Right to Appeal

Usually appellants were not heard unless they had an interest in the case, or had been properly commissioned by others to act, or were conducting the business of another in such a way that their acts were ratified immediately.[8] Those under twenty-five years of age were looked upon as minors, and had to be represented by another.[9]

One who promised not to appeal from the decision of a judge lost the benefit of the right to appeal.[10] The same was true of a party against whom a judgment had been obtained by default, *contumax non appellat*. An appeal was likewise denied to a party whose oath or refusal to take an oath had been the basis of judgment.

An appeal to a superior judge was generally admitted against any definitive sentence. Although appeals were admitted from interlocutory sentences in the early Empire, they were, with few exceptions, forbidden by Justinian.[11]

7 Most of the works of Paulus and Ulpianus date from the early part of the third century. About one-half of Justinian's *Digest* owed its origin to their writings.

8 D. (49.5) 1.

9 D. (49.1) 27, 28.

10 D. (49.2) 1, 3.

11 C. (7.62) 6; (7.45) 16.

According to Roman law, one attorney could not appoint another. It was permitted, however, that when a case was defended in the court of first instance through an attorney, the latter, being the master of the case through the joinder of issue, could appeal through another attorney.[12]

2. The Petition to Appeal

At the conclusion of a trial in the court of first instance the litigants had the right to an immediate oral appeal. For this it was sufficient merely to say *"Appello."*[13] If it was not done then, ten days were allowed for the filing of the *libellus appellationis*. This period began with the rendering of the judgment, and was computed *a momento ad momentum.*[14] The appellatory document was to contain the names of the parties by whom it was filed, and of those against whom it was lodged. It was also to indicate from what decision it was being made.[15]

The petition of appeal was given to the judge who pronounced the sentence, and he could not ordinarily refuse to allow it, unless it was based on futile or unreasonable grounds, or was made against a sentence that was unappealable by law. In case the judge did refuse it, he had to give to the appellant a copy of his reasons for doing so. If it happened that a judge refused on insufficient or improper grounds to permit the appeal, his action was punishable with a fine, and the aggrieved party could appeal such an unwarranted refusal directly to the appellate court.[16]

If the appellant did not mention in his petition against what adversary he appealed, he could not be barred by an exception based on that omission.[17]

It belonged to the judge to notify the defendant that an appeal had been taken, even when the appellant did not request

[12] D. (49.1) 4, 5. The right to representation and counsel was fully provided for. Cf. C. (2.12) 10; (2.12) 22; (2.14); D. (3.3) (40.4); (43.4) 49; C. (2.6) 7.

[13] C. (7.62) 14.

[14] Nov. (23.1).

[15] D. (49.1) 1.

[16] D. (49.5) 5.

[17] D. (49.1) 3. Likewise an exception was not permitted against a litigant merely for the reason that he did not name all the adversaries, in the event that action was taken against a group.— D. (49.1) 3.

it, but the former was not required to furnish security to conduct his side of the appeal.[18]

The next step was to send the appeal to the proper court of second instance.[19] A report was made out by the judge of first instance, which was called *litterae dimissoriae, libelli dimissorii,* or merely *apostoli.* Although these letters were addressed to the superior judge, the transmission of them was a matter for the appellant.[20] This record was to be taken to the appellate court within a period of thirty days. A judge could be held liable to perpetual infamy if all the matters submitted by the litigants in the examination and evidence were not inserted in the documents accompanying the appeal.[21] Special rules prescribed that these documents were to be expressed in concise language, and were not to contain any new matter. It was not allowed to make any additions in order to supply what had been omitted. A succinct statement of the facts and an abridgment of the opinion of the judge of first instance were considered as sufficient.[22]

ARTICLE II. PROBATORY STAGE OF THE TRIAL

The purpose of the proceedings in the court of second instance was not merely a re-examination of the trial, but a new examination of the whole status of facts and law. In this trial the appellee could also obtain a judgment in his favor, and not merely a dismissal of the appeal.[23]

Cases were to be decided in conformity with the laws in force at the time the judgment was rendered in the inferior court, and not according to those subsequently promulgated.[24]

It was the effect of the appeal ordinarily to suspend the previous sentence until the appeal was decided and a new

18 C. (7.62) 6.

19 The different instances of appeal were prescribed in such a way that they were to take place *gradatim.* One could not, for instance, pass over the Governor and appeal directly to the Emperor.— D. (49.1) 21.

20 Wenger, *Institutes of the Roman Law of Civil Procedure,* p. 307.

21 C. (7.62) 15.

22 C. (7.62) 39.

23 Wenger, *Institutes of the Roman Law of Civil Procedure,* p. 308.

24 Nov. (16.1).

sentence pronounced, and during this time the principle *appellatione interposita, nihil innovari* was observed, and the judge of the lower court could do nothing to hinder the appeal or to weaken the case.[25]

From the time of Diocletian (284-305) the moment for the assertion of dilatory exceptions was fixed at the beginning of the proceedings, and later advancement of them availed nothing.[26] Peremptory exceptions could be made any time up to the giving of the sentence.[27]

With the consent of the judge new witnesses that had not been heard in the court of first instance could be introduced at the appellate trial.[28] A litigant was permitted to take exception to the person or the testimony of his opponent's witnesses.[29] New documentary evidence was also permitted. Exception could be taken against the credibility or genuineness of these documents.[30] The burden of proof rested on the plaintiff who asserted a right or fact. It was not required of the defendant to disprove the claim in order to be released.[31]

The judge had the right to compel necessary witnesses to appear, or, if they were beyond his jurisdiction, he could request a competent court to take their depositions. It was possible to recall witnesses two or three times for reexamination

[25] C. (7.62) 3.

[26] C. (4.19) 19: "Exceptionem dilatoriam opponi quidem initio, probari vero, postquam actor monstraverit quod adseverat, oportet."

[27] C. (8.35) 8.

[28] C. (7.62) 6.

[29] A general fundamental duty was imposed on witnesses to testify, and provision was made for a preliminary oath of the witness. There was also a varied estimation of the credibility of the witness according to his higher or lower rank. Due to supposed liability to corruption, the testimony of the poor carried little or no weight. Witnesses were excluded on numerous grounds. Convicts, adulteresses, perjurers and children under fourteen years of age were absolutely incompetent to act as witnesses. Consanguinity, intimacy, dependency or common interest with the party in favor of whom the witness appeared, or enmity to his adversary, were sufficient reasons to exclude a witness as suspect.— C. (4.20) 16; Nov. (90.1).

[30] C. (7.62) 6. Rash challenging of documents carried special penalties. A characteristic mark of the development of the law of proof is shown by the change in the method of estimating testimony and documents. During Constantine's reign, witnesses and documents were admitted to establish proof on an equal basis. In the time of Justinian, however, greater value was given to written over oral evidence.— C. (4.20) 1. Cf. Wenger, *Institutes of the Roman Law of Civil Procedure*, p. 294.

[31] C. (8.5); (4.19) 23.

in the same trial.[32] In the period of the *cognitio extraordinaria* the judge was given the right to question the parties *ex officio*.[33]

ARTICLE III. CONCLUDING STAGE OF THE TRIAL

1. The Sentence

The appealed case was to be settled decisively within one year from the time it reached the court of second instance. If a reasonable interruption occurred during that period, another year was permitted, but if the case was not decided within two years it generally became a *res iudicata* and the sentence was ordered to be executed.[34]

The appellate court had the power to reverse as well as to confirm the sentence of the lower court, but the superior tribunal was not to remand the cause to the inferior court for a new trial.[35] The judge evaluated the probative force of the evidence according to objective rules of proof, and then gave his decision.[36]

For validity the sentence had to be put in writing,[37] and then was to be read in the presence of at least one of the parties.[38]

Wilfully unreasonable appeals were usually punished with a fine, and there were also instances of imprisonment for such rashly lodged appeals.[39] The party losing the suit was, as a rule, condemned to pay all the expenses of the trial.[40]

2. Legal Redress against the Sentence

From an unjust sentence the parties had the right to a further appeal, but more than two appeals on the same issue were forbidden.[41]

32 Nov. (90. 4-5); C. (4. 20).
33 C. (3.1) 9.
34 C. (7.63) 2.
35 C. (7.62) 6.
36 Cf. Wenger, *Institutes of the Roman Law of Civil Procedure*, p. 293.
37 C. (7.44) (3.1).
38 Nov. (16.2)
39 C. (3.1); (13.6).
40 C. (2.1) 4.
41 C. (3.1); (13.6).

In Roman law the plaint of nullity as a means of attacking a sentence was unknown. However, a declaration of nullity could be obtained for preventing the execution of the sentence.[42] The sentence was null and void if it was pronounced by an incompetent judge, if it was contrary to a positive law or judgment already given, if it decreed what was impossible of execution, if the basic rules of procedure were not observed, or if one of the parties lacked the capacity of bringing suit.[43]

The sentence could also be opposed by means of the remedy of the *restitutio in integrum,* as, for instance, when the judge had been bribed, or when there had been presented false testimony or documents upon which the sentence was based. In Roman law the distinction between *restitutio in integrum* and appeals was this: an appeal was used as a remedy against the injustice of a sentence, whereas *restitutio* was employed in a case of error on the part of the judge or because of deception on the side of one of the parties.[44] In this sense *restitutio in integrum* became a remedy quite similar to an appeal, and as such was frequently used under Justinian.[45] This differed greatly from the classical concept of *restitutio in integrum.*[46]

From the brief survey just completed, it will readily be seen that many of the essential features of the appellate procedure in Roman law have since been incorporated by the Church, and that they form a basis for the procedure in its ordinary courts of second instance. The Roman system made every effort to protect the litigating parties in their attempt to rectify an unjust sentence. Careful provision was made for every step in the procedure so as to procure a uniform and orderly sequence in the attempt to secure justice before a higher tribunal of the law.

[42] D. (49.1) 19; C. (1.14) 15.

[43] C. (50.1); (64.1).

[44] D. (4.4) 17.

[45] Cf. Biondi, *Appunti intorno alla Sentenza nel Processo Civile Romano* (Pavia: Successori Fratelli Fusi, 1929), pp. 97-99.

[46] Giustiniano si avvale largamente della *restitutio in integrum,* la quale però resulta assai lontana dall' istituto classico. Mentre per i classici la *restitutio* è un decreto del magistrato che annullando il *iudicium,* consententi agire *ex novo,* ora invece si tratta di un mezzo giuridico con cui giudice, riesaminando la causa, annulà o modificà la precedente sentenza."—Biondi, *ibidem,* p. 97.

The Empire prescribed in its organization of courts the different instances of appeal. An orderly arrangement of tribunals was provided, so that one had to proceed *gradatim* from a lower to an immediately superior court.

The procedural capacity of the parties being demonstrated, the appeal could be made orally after the sentence had been read in court, or it could be made in writing. In the latter event, ten days were allowed in which to make the appeal. The petition of appeal was made to the judge of the court of first instance, who, if he judged that it had been lodged according to legal provisions, forwarded it to the appellate court. Along with this petition were transmitted the acts of the entire proceedings of the lower court. With this transmission the inferior judge terminated his connection with the case. Ordinarily the appeal was *in suspensivo,* i.e., the sentence of the first court was not executed until the appeal had been disposed of. In the appellate court the entire cause was reviewed, and the sentence of the inferior court was confirmed, revised or revoked. Under certain restrictions, new proofs could be introduced in the appellate instance. Against an unjust sentence in the court of second instance a further appeal was permitted, and, if the sentence was invalid, other remedies were provided.

The re-examination of the case was to be completed within one, or, at the most, two years after it had reached the higher court.

The inherent justice of this entire procedure prompted the Church in the centuries to come to adopt it substantially as its own.

CHAPTER TWO

EARLY CANON LAW UP TO THE TIME OF GRATIAN (ca. 1140)

A detailed description of ecclesiastical courts and judicial procedure is notably lacking in the sources up to the twelfth century. Very little is recorded regarding the procedure pertinent to the trials of marriage cases. Sufficient evidence is given, however, throughout these centuries to indicate that the Church was slowly building up a system which would reach its greatest perfection only in modern times. For more than eight centuries the Church's judicial system handled contentious cases almost to the exclusion of those dealing with marriage. Up until that time there were few impediments. In the succeeding ages, however, matrimonial cases so rapidly increased that the Church's ordinary courts were to be found dealing with them almost exclusively.

The historical outline of this period shows clearly the struggle of the Church to maintain its own courts and procedural system against an ever encroaching secular power. Only after ten centuries did the Church succeed in achieving that position in which its lawful rights could be exercised in an exclusive manner.

ARTICLE I. ESTABLISHMENT OF THE ORDINARY COURT OF SECOND INSTANCE

It was clear from the very beginning that the Church was to assert its right to the lawful jurisdiction over marriage cases. That the Christians should maintain their own judicial tribunals was taken for granted by St. Paul.[1]

The legal existence of the Church was not recognized in the early centuries, much less its exclusive competence in the

[1] I Cor., VI: 5. Among the first cases decided were those of which cognizance was taken by St. Paul himself, viz: the case of the incestuous man, and that of the status of marriage contracted in infidelity when the pagan spouse refused to live peacefully with the convert. cf. I Cor., V: 3; VII: 15, 16.

matrimonial causes of Christians. Circumstances of the times could hardly have encouraged those early followers of Christ to submit their cases to the Roman Courts, as that would have been fatal during the period of the persecutions. The laws of the Church were radically different from those of Rome, as the latter did not even consider the question of divorce as a matter for court action.[2] Dissolution of the marriage bond among the Romans always remained a private matter.[3]

Due to the fact that spouses were to submit their marriage plans to the bishop for approval, it is more than a mere conjecture that bishops would also decide on disputes consequent to the marriage, relative to the marriage bond.[4]

The exact date of the introduction of appeals in the Church's judicial system is not known. Devoti (1744-1820) records an appeal from the decision of a bishop to the Pope made in the year 142.[5]

The first introduction of an appellate court system into the general law of the Church occurred in the I Ecumenical Council of Nicaea, held in 325. By its decrees, ecclesiastical provinces were mapped out in such a way as to follow the geographical lines of the civil provinces. Each ecclesiastical province was placed under the supervision of a metropolitan.[6] Two Synods

[2] Corbett, *The Roman Law of Marriage* (Oxford: Clarendon Press, 1930), pp. 226-229; Joyce, *Christian Marriage* (London: Sheed and Ward, 1933), p. 309.

[3] It could be dissolved: (a) by mutual consent of the parties, *divortium ex consensu,* or (b) at the initiative of one of the parties, *repudium.* The latter could be based on such causes as insanity, old age or sterility. Cf. D. (24.1) 60, 61, 62; Nov. (22.4); (117.10); (134.11).

[4] "Decet vero ut sponsi et sponsae de sententia episcopi conjugium faciant. . ."—Ignatius Martyr in *Epist. ad Polycarpum,* 5, 2—Migne, *Patrologiae Cursus Completus, Series Graeca* (161 vols., Parisiis: 1856-1866), V, 723 (hereafter cited *MPG*).

[5] *Institutionum Canonicarum Libri IV* (Venetiis, 1827), Lib. III, tit. XV, *de appellationibus,* Parag. XXVIII, note 2 (hereafter cited *Institutiones Canonicae*). Protestant writers in general deny the authenticity of this appeal. The proof of its historicity was sufficient for Bellarmine, *Opera Omnia* (2. ed., 8 vols., Xisto Riario Sforza, Neapoli, 1872), Vol. I, Lib. II, *De Romano Pontifice,* Ch. XXI, p. 404. It is also recorded by Zaccaria, *Anti-Febbronio* (2. ed., Cesena, 1770), Part. II, Lib. III, Ch. 2, n. 2. This appeal preceded by two hundred years the final proscription of the classical bipartite formulary procedure in Roman law, which had not admitted appeals.

[6] Can. 6—Mansi, *Sacrorum Conciliorum Nova et Amplissima Collectio* (53 vols. in 60, Parisiis, 1901-1927), II, 711 (this work will be henceforth cited as Mansi).

were to be held each year, with all the bishops of the province in attendance to act as an ordinary court of second instance. Its purpose was primarily to review cases of excommunication inflicted by the suffragan bishops, but the general affairs of the province also came under its scope.[7]

Similar legislation calling for a court of second instance comprising an assembly of bishops is found in the centuries immediately following. Noteworthy is the Synod held at Antioch in 341,[8] the Council of Sardica in 343,[9] the IV Council of Carthage (*Statuta Ecclesiae Antiqua*) in 398,[10] the XI Council of Carthage in 407,[11] the I Council of Vaison held in Gaul in 422 [12] and the Council of Chalcedon in 451.[13]

In the sixth century an increase in appeals to the metropolitan himself rather than to the provincial synod is noted. This is evident from the decrees of the V Council of Orleans in 549,[14] of the III Provincial Council of Toledo in 537 [15] and of the Council of Frankfurt in 794.[16] These decrees had only

[7] Can. 5:—". . . in omnes istiusmodi res inquirent, atque etiam in alias, quae coram ipsis in Synodo producuntur: ut negotium ab illis unanimi consensu peragatur."—Mansi, II, 711.

[8] Concilium Antiochenum, Canons 12, 15—*Ecclesiae Occidentalis Monumenta Iuris Antiquissima Canonum et Conciliorum Graecorum Interpretationes Latinae*, edidit Cuthbertus Hamilton Turner (2 vols., Oxonii, 1899-1930), Tom. II, Pars 2 (1913), 269-271; 280-281. Despite the various Latin interpretations of these canons, the fact that an assembly of bishops acted as a court of second instance is clearly demonstrated.

[9] Can. 5—Bruns, *Canones Apostolorum et Conciliorum Saeculorum IV-V-VI-VII* (2 vols., Berolini, 1839), I, 91 (henceforth this work will be referred to as Bruns).

[10] Can. 66—Bruns, I, 147. Van Hove maintains that the *Statuta Ecclesiae Antiqua* (also called *Statuta Ecclesiae Unica, Statuta Ecclesiae Orientis*) have been falsely ascribed to the Fourth Carthaginian Council of 398, or the Synod of Valence held in France in 374, or to a certain unknown Council of Valencia in Spain. He claims that in a more or less systematic order they represent a collection derived from the councils of the Greek Church, from the French councils and from papal decretals.—*Commentarium Lovaniense in Codicem Iuris Canonici*, Vol. I, Tom. I, *Prolegomena* (2. ed., Mechliniae-Romae: Dessain, 1945), n. 149 (hereafter cited *Prolegomena*).

[11] Can. 125—Bruns, I, 193.

[12] Can. 5—Bruns, II, 128.

[13] Can. 9—Mansi, VII, 395.

[14] Concilium Aurelianense, Can. 17—*Monumenta Germaniae Historica, Legum Sect. III, Concilia Aevi Merovingici*, recensuit Friedericus Maassen (Hannoverae, 1893), Tom. I, p. 106 (hereafter cited *MGH*).

[15] Can. 20—Bruns, I, 218.

[16] Concilium Francofurtense, Can. 6—*MGH, Legum Sect. II, Concilia Aevi Karolini*, Tom. II, Pars I, p. 166.

local force for their respective provinces; nevertheless they showed the gradual development to substitute for the decisions of a provincial synod the more simplified one rendered by a metropolitan. In 870, however, a similar provision was incorporated in the canons of the VIII Ecumenical Council, held at Constantinople (869-870).[17]

Although the appeals to the synods and to the metropolitan were concerned mainly with disputes and appeals in penal matters between clerics, or between the latter and their bishops, nevertheless there was being established the judicial system in which marriage cases were to play an ever increasing part.

ARTICLE II. COURT PROCEDURE

Accounts of appellate court procedure from the early days of the Church up to the time of Gratian are very meager. This is especially true in regard to the procedure followed in the ordinary courts of second instance. Marriage causes were rare until the eighth and ninth centuries because of the fewness of impediments before that time.[18]

During the centuries of the persecutions the trials held in the early Christian communities were simple affairs. The principles governing them were drawn mainly from the Scriptures and the natural law.[19]

With the coming of Constantine and the end of the persecutions, the Church was able to come out of the catacombs. The judicial system of the Empire, however, remained substantially what it was before. Roman law still allowed divorce, and was in other respects in conflict with Christian principles regarding the dissolution of the bond.[20]

[17] Can. 26—Hardouin, *Acta Conciliorum et Epistolae Decretales ac Constitutiones Summorum Pontificum* (12 vols., Parisiis, 1714-1715), V, 911.

[18] Wernz, *Ius Decretalium,* Vol. IV, *Ius Matrimoniale* (2. ed., pars prima, Prati, 1911), pp. 676, 677.

[19] Wernz-Vidal, *Ius Canonicum,* Vol. VI, *De Processibus* (Romae: Universitas Gregoriana, 1927-1928), n. 2; Cf. *Didascalia,* II, cc, 45 sq.—*Didascalia et Constitutiones Apostolorum,* ed. F. X Funk (2 vols., Paderbornae, 1905), I, 138-148.

[20] "Aliae sunt leges Caesarum, aliae Christi; aliud Papianus, aliud Paulus noster praecipit."—S. Hieronymus, Epist. LXXXVII, n. 3—*Corpus Scriptorum Ecclesiasticorum Latinorum* (68 vols., Vindobonae, 1866—; *S. Eusebii Hieronymi Opera,* Vol. IV, Sect. I, Pars II, recensuit Isidorus Hilberg, Vindobonae, 1912), LV, 39.

A quasi-judicial authority was given by Constantine to the bishops. The parties to a civil suit could agree to refer the case to the bishop for arbitration and to accept his decision. If this course was adopted, the bishop's verdict was final, and did not admit of an appeal.[21] It seems quite certain that marriage cases were among those submitted to the bishops acting in this capacity.[22]

It is not clear whether the bishops in deciding these cases were bound to follow the provisions of the civil law, or whether they were free to follow the regulations of the Church. There are indications that point to the latter. Under no circumstances, however, could it have fallen to a bishop to pronounce a divorce, as under Roman law the marriage bond was not dissolved by a judge.[23] Although the secular courts could not admit an appeal from an episcopal sentence, the defendant could seek redress before a superior ecclesiastical tribunal.

With the establishment of ordinary courts of second instance by the I General Council of Nicaea (325), fundamental principles of appellate procedure were outlined in subsequent conciliar and synodal legislation, by which an unjust sentence could be taken from an inferior court to a higher tribunal differing in personnel in each instance. Generally the appeal was *in suspensivo*. The first instance of an appeal *in suspensivo* is found in the decrees of the Council of Sardica (343).[24]

For two centuries thereafter there is no record of any detailed procedure along systematic lines. After the time of Justinian there is evidence that the principles of Roman law

[21] Constantine recognized the jurisdiction of the ecclesiastical courts in two Constitutions, one issued in 318, and the other sent to Ablabius in 333. Cf. C. Th. (1.27) 1: *Const. Sirmondiana I—Theodosiani Libri XVI* (ed. Mommsen-Meyer, 3 vols., Berolini, 1905), I, 907 sq. This Constitution is now generally recognized as genuine by most historians. Cf. Wenger, *Institutes of the Roman Law of Civil Procedure*, p. 342, note 11; Vismara, *Episcopalis Audientia*, Pubblicazioni della U. Cattolica del Sacro Cuore, 2. serie, Scienze Giuridiche, n. LIV (Milano: Vita e Pensiero, 1937), p. 21.

[22] Joyce, *Christian Marriage*, p. 215. Cf. letter of Innocent I (402-417) dealing with a marriage case; *Epist. XXXVI* (ad Probum)—Migne, *Patrologiae Cursus Completus, Series Latina* (221 vols., Parisiis, 1844-1864), XX, 602 (hereofter cited as *MPL*).

[23] Joyce, *Christian Marriage*, p. 216.

[24] Can. 4—Bruns, I, 91. Although this had reference to an appeal to the Pope, it demonstrates the acceptance of the principle of appellate procedure.

were incorporated into ecclesiastical procedure, although there is no indication as to what extent. It was only natural that the Church should look to certain provisions of Roman law, which were well suited to its needs, especially in regard to contentious procedure.[25] Pope St. Gregory I (590-604) ordered in 603 that the rules of Roman law procedure should be followed in points which were not regulated by ecclesiastical law.[26] Though this seems to be the first official recognition of Roman law as a subsidiary source of canonical procedure, it was merely a confirmation of a current practice of the ecclesiastical courts.

When the Western Empire gave way under the onslaught of Germanic tribes from the north, the one institution which survived was the Church. The imperial system had come to an end; its powerful officials had disappeared. The Frankish kings assumed judicial as well as legislative control over marriage.[27]

There can be no doubt that in Carolingian times matrimonial causes continued to be heard in the royal courts. This is apparent from Hincmar's *De Nuptiis Stephani,*[28] in which he discussed the matter on doctrinal grounds, expressly stating that what he said had no reference to the civil judgment, as that was no concern of the bishops.[29] There is considerable difference of opinion, however, among authorities about Hinc-

[25] Cicognani, *Canon Law* (Philadelphia: Dolphin Press, 1934, authorized English translation by O'Hara and Brennan), p. 47.

[26] *Registrum Epistolarum,* Ep. XIII, 50—*MGH, Epistolae,* Tom. II, Pars II (ed. Ludovicus M. Hartmann, Berolini apud Weidmannos, 1895), p. 411.

[27] Esmein, *Le Mariage en Droit Canonique* (2. ed., 2 vols., Vol. I, ed. R. Généstal, 1929; Vol. II, ed. R. Généstal-J. Dauvillier, 1935, Paris, Librairie du Recueil Sirey), I, 11; Joyce, *Christian Marriage,* p. 218.

[28] As Archbishop of Rheims (845-882), Hincmar was the most eminent of the Frankish prelates, and wrote a great deal on the Church's doctrine on the formation of the doctrine of marriage. The occasion of this work was the divorce sought by Stephen, an Aquitanian noble, from the daughter of Regimund, another magnate. Hincmar, misinterpreting the writings of St. Augustine and St. Leo, differed widely from the teachings of Pope Nicholas I (851-867). Cf. Joyce, *Christian Marriage,* pp. 56-57.

[29] ". . . in quibus nihil de civili judicio, cujus cognitores non debemus esse episcopi, ponere, sed, quae ecclesiasticae definitioni noscuntur competere, quantum occurrit memoriae, breviter studui adnotare."—*MGH, Epistolae,* Tom. VIII, *Karolini Aevi,* Fasc. I, *Hincmari Archiepiscopi Remensis epistolarum pars prima* (Berolini apud Weidmannos, 1939), 136, 90.

mar's views as to the precise limits of the secular and ecclesiastical jurisdiction in regard to marriage.[30]

By the beginning of the tenth century the ever increasing power of the bishops over marriage cases is evident from the *De Sponsalibus Causis* of Regino of Prüm (+915). This work was compiled in the year 906 to provide Archbishop Radbod of Treves (833-915) with practical guidance in the exercise of his jurisdiction when on his episcopal visitation.[31]

Esmein (+1913) gave it as his opinion that the process by which the Church was given more and more of her rightful jurisdiction over marriage cases was complete by the end of the tenth century.[32] Certainly by that date the episcopal courts were widely recognized as the competent authority.

It is unlikely that the procedural norms in the centuries in which the Church was so restricted by secular control were based to any great extent upon Roman law. After the German invasions there was only a limited knowledge of the latter in the West. The *Digest* had been forgotten, and only abstracts of the Justinian Code and Novels were known. Most of these were known only in the form given by the Visigoths in the Lex Romana.[33]

About the year 1070 Justinian's *Digest* was rediscovered in a manuscript at Pisa.[34] Its importance was seized upon by Irnerius (1050?-1130?), a teacher in the University of Bologna, and he began to expound it in his classes.[35] The new

[30] Cf. Hefele-Leclerq, *Histoire des Conciles* (10 vols. in 19, Paris: Letouzey et Ané, 1907-1938), IV, Part I, 244-247, note 1.

[31] *De Ecclesiasticis Disciplinis,* Lib. II, nn. 15-23: "Deinde interrogandum de adulteriis et fornicationibus,"—*MPL,* CXXXII, 282, 283. This collection is listed among the sources used by Burchard, Bishop of Worms (1002-1025). Cf. Van Hove, *Prolegomena,* nn. 313-315.

[32] *Le Mariage en Droit Canonique,* I, 27. Joyce believes it lasted on into the eleventh century.—*Christian Marriage,* p. 224.

[33] This body of law, also known as the Breviary of Alaric, was promulgated by Alaric II in 506 for the use of the Roman citizens in Visigothic Spain, and eventually became known in other parts of Europe. Cf. Haenel, *Lex Romana Visigothorum* (Leipzig, 1849), p. VI; Laurin, *Introductio in Corpus Iuris Canonici* (Friburgi Brisgoviae et Vindobonae, 1889), p. 266.

[34] It was the only extant copy of the sixth century text.

[35] He is considered as the founder of the medieval school of jurisprudence of Bologna. In the first half of the twelfth century he introduced a new method of explaining Roman law by means of glosses, inaugurating an era of Glossators which was destined to last for 150 years.

impetus given to the study of Roman law which took place at this time was very opportune in the history of ecclesiastical judicial procedure. As a result of the breakdown of royal authority, the Church gained exclusive possession of competence in marriage cases. Being freed from secular control, the Church was enabled to develop its own procedural system.

Bologna had become famous as the mother of Studies and the most ancient storehouse of law, comprising both the human and the divine. It was in this city and under these happy circumstances that John Gratian flourished. "The glory that Irnerius brought to Bologna by his study of Roman law was enhanced to the highest degree by Gratian with his study of Canon law."[86]

Thus it was that Gratian in the early part of the twelfth century (c. 1140) was able to set forth a complete system of appellate procedure, based almost exclusively upon the Justinian compilations. His *Decretum* became the most widely-known canonical collection prior to the decretals of Gregory IX (1227-1241). It was not an authentic collection, hence it had only that force which was contained in its separate and individual component parts. Nevertheless it had great influence on subsequent legislation and jurisprudence, and was incorporated in the *Corpus Iuris Canonici.* It was not a collection of new laws, but rather a compilation of old ones. This was especially true in its treatment of appellate procedure. Most of it is contained in c. 41, C. II, q. 6, of his *Decretum;* this in turn simply furnished a summary of the appellate procedure as presented in Justinian's *Code.* Due to the fact that these principles of Roman law are referred to in the Decretals, and are there adapted still more suitably to ecclesiastical procedure, they will be surveyed under the light of the Decretal law in the following chapter.

86 Cicognani, *Canon Law,* p. 272. Kuttner calls the renaisance of Roman law one of the most momentous events in the history of the medieval mind.—"The Father of the Science of Canon Law"—*The Jurist* (Washington, D. C.: The Catholic University of America, 1941—), I (1941), 12.

CHAPTER THREE

FROM THE DECRETALS (1234) TO THE COUNCIL OF TRENT (1545-1563)

With the appearance of the Decretals of Gregory IX (1227-1241) in 1234, the Church was in the possession of an authentic collection that had the force of universal law.[1] Every law contained in it, even those which previously had been regarded as particular, had become universal.[2] The second book of this collection contains an extensive body of regulations governing appeals and contentious trials in general. There is no section devoted especially to the matrimonial procedure of the court of second instance. This is due to the fact that matrimonial trials followed the general pattern of other contentious trials, and even though there were a number of special rules for trials concerning the validity of the bond, they were to a great extent disregarded. This fact was recognized and deplored by Innocent III (1198-1216).[3] The lack of legal compulsion requiring diocesan authority to appeal matrimonial cases tended to lessen the prominence, if not the importance, of the appellate tribunal in regard to such trials.

Two other collections, the *Liber Sextus* of Boniface VIII (1294-1303) and the Constitutions of Clement V (1305-1314), comprise, together with the Decretals of Gregory IX, the most important sources of matrimonial procedure in the period up to the Council of Trent.[4]

ARTICLE I. ORGANIZATION OF THE ORDINARY COURT OF SECOND INSTANCE

1. Proper Court

From the twelfth century to the Council of Trent a unified and orderly system of ecclesiastical courts was lacking. The increasingly important position of archdeacons, long standing

[1] Van Hove, *Prolegomena,* n. 364.

[2] Cicognani, *Canon Law,* p. 303.

[3] C. 1, X, *ut lite non contestata non procedatur ad testium receptionem vel ad sententiam diffinitivam,* II, 6.

[4] Cf. Van Hove, *Prolegomena,* nn. 364-372.

customs and the jurisdictional encroachments of metropolitans on their suffragans, all tended to create no little confusion for the general rule that appeals were to be made *gradatim,* and not *per saltum.*[5]

Archdeacons had either delegated or ordinary power to try marriage cases in the court of first instance,[6] and appeals from these tribunals went to the court of the bishop. The metropolitan's court was the appellate instance for cases originating in the bishop's court.[7] Appeals from the archdeacon directly to the metropolitan became quite general, but special limitations were decreed so as to bring more cases before the tribunal of the bishop.

Honorius III (1216-1227), in a Decretal written in 1221, stated that in the future no appeals could be made from the court of the archdeacon to the metropolitan if one of the parties entered an exception against it. If an appeal took place in disregard of such an exception, it was thereby rendered invalid.[8]

Innocent IV (1243-1254) placed a further limitation against such appeals. In a Decretal addressed to the Archbishop of Rheims he declared that it was absolutely forbidden to appeal *per saltum* from an archdeacon's court to the metropolitan, unless this procedure was tolerated by custom.[9]

5 Wernz, *Ius Decretalium,* Vol. V, *De Iudiciis Ecclesiasticis* (3. ed., Prati, 1914), n. 695.

6 Cc. 7, 9, 10, X, *de officio archdiaconi,* I, 23.

7 Durantis, *Speculum Iuris* (3 vols., Venetiis, 1577), lib. II, Partic. III, *de appellationibus,* Parag. 4, n. 1.

8 C. 66, X, *de appellationibus, recusationibus et relationibus,* II, 28; Potthast, *Regesta Pontificum Romanorum inde ab anno post Christum natum 1198 ad annum 1304* (2 vols., Berolini: R. De Becker, 1874-1875), n. 7776 (hereafter cited as Potthast); cf. Schmalzgrueber, *Jus Ecclesiasticum Universum* (5 vols. in 12, Romae, 1843-1845), Lib. II, tit. 28, nn. 50-52 (hereafter cited Schmalzgrueber); Reiffenstuel, *Jus Canonicum Universum* (6 vols., Romae, 1831-1835), lib. II, tit. 28, n. 7 (hereafter cited Reiffenstuel).

9 ". . . nisi aliud Remensi ecclesiae de consuetudine competat in hac parte."—C. 3, *de appellationibus,* II, 15, in VI°. There was no appeal from the official of an archdeacon to the latter, nor from an official of the bishop to the bishop himself, as it was not considered as proceeding from a lower to a higher court. Cf. *Glossa Ordinaria* in c. 66, X, *de appellationibus, recusationibus et relationibus,* II, 28, ad v. *post huiusmodi appellationem.*

A suffragan bishop who decided a case in the first instance and later became a metropolitan could decide the same case in the court of second instance.[10]

The privilege of appealing to the Holy See was always permitted without the necessity of going through the intermediate courts.[11]

2. Court Personnel

There was no uniform rule governing the number of judges necessary in the court of second instance, but the more common practice evidently favored the court consisting of a single judge as found in Roman law. While the judge was frequently surrounded by *assessores, conciliarii* or *canonici,* it was he alone who had the deciding voice.[12]

In the matrimonial trials during this period there was no official whose duties corresponded to the present-day *defensor vinculi.*[13] It sometimes happened, however, that if the parties were both in agreement on the nullity of the marriage, or for some reason did not want to appear in court, the accusation was published so that some friend or even stranger might defend the bond.[14]

[10] Durantis, *Speculum Iuris,* Lib. II, Partic. III, *de appellationibus,* Parag. 4, n. 21. Cf. Wernz, *Ius Decretalium,* V. n. 695, note 56.

[11] C. 66, X, *de appellationibus, recusationibus et relationibus,* II, 28, ad v. *post huiusmodi appellationem* in the *Glossa;* c.l, *de electione et electi potestate,* I, 6, in VI°; Durantis, *Speculum Iuris,* Lib. II, Partic. III, *de appellationibus,* Parag. 4, n. 1; Hostiensis, *Commentaria in Quinque Libros Decretalium* (5 vols., Venetiis, 1581), Lib. II, tit. *de appellationibus,* c. 7, n. 1 (hereafter cited *Commentaria*); Reiffenstuel, Lib. II, tit. 28, n. 6. If an appeal was to be made to the Holy See instead of the court of second instance, it was to be done before the citations were sent out by the latter court. Cf. c. 9, X, *de appellationibus, recusationibus, et relationibus,* II, 28.

[12] Cf. c. 4, *de sententia et re iudicata,* II, 14, in VI°.

[13] The office of *defensor vinculi* was not created until 1741 by Benedict XIV in his constitution *"Dei miseratione."—Codicis Iuris Canonici Fontes,* cura Emi Petri Card. Gasparri editi (Vols. I-VI, Romae [postea Civitatis Vaticanae], 1922-1932); cura Emi Justiniani Card. Seredi editi (Vols. VII-IX, Romae, 1935-1939), n. 381 (hereafter cited *Fontes*). Cf. Dolan, *The Defensor Vinculi, His Rights and Duties,* The Catholic University of America Canon Law Studies, n. 85 (Washington, D. C.: The Catholic University of America, 1934), p. 4 (hereafter cited *The Defensor Vinculi*).

[14] "Si vere hi nolunt venire vel defendere... accusatio est in ecclesia publicanda, ut, si quis cognatus vel amicus vel... quilibet extraneus velit defendere matrimonium, admittitur..."—Durantis, *Speculum Iuris,* Lib. IV, Parag. 2, n. 3.

Pope Innocent III approved a law passed by the IV General Council of the Lateran (1215), which required the presence of a notary at ecclesiastical trials. It was his duty to commit all the formalities of the trial to writing.[15] That marriage trials were not excepted from these formalities in the thirteenth century is evident from the fact that Durantis (1238-1296), writing in the same century of the Decretals of Gregory IX, did not include them in the list which specified the cases in which the summary or speedy process of Justinian law could be used.[16]

ARTICLE II. PROCEDURE IN THE ORDINARY COURT OF SECOND INSTANCE

Although the Decretals did not present a systematic order of formal procedure which was to apply exclusively to marriage cases, nevertheless it is evident that special norms were to be applied as exceptions from the general procedure governing contentious cases. The failure to apply these special norms prompted Innocent III (1198) to state that, while the rules of procedure were followed in contentious cases in general, such was not true in regard to matrimonial cases.[17]

The revival of Roman law studies in the twelfth century did not bring with it an immediate and general acceptance of

15 "...qui fideliter universa iudicii acta conscribant, videlicet, citationes, dilationes, recusationes, exceptiones, petitiones et responsiones, interrogationes et confessiones, testium depositiones et instrumentorum productiones, interlocutiones et appellationes, renuntiationes, conclusiones et cetera quae occurrerint..."—C. 11, X, *de probationibus,* II, 19.

16 Durantis, *Speculum Iuris,* Lib. I, Partic. I, *de officio judicum,* Parag. 8, n. 3.

17 "...licet ordo iudiciarius in aliis controversiis sit servandus, et in matrimonialibus causis non usquequaque servetur..."—c. 1, X, *ut lite non contestata non procedatur ad testium receptionem vel ad sententiam diffinitivam,* II, 6. An indication of the precise procedural norms peculiar to marriage trials which were not very carefully observed is given in the *Gloss* to the same Decretal ad v. *servetur*:" Nota quod plura sunt specialia in causis matrimonialibus: quia ubi agitur de foedere matrimoniali, potest agi contra contumacem lite non contestata ad definitivam sententiam... minor potest esse in causa etiam per procuratorem... confessio contra matrimonium non praeiudicat... pater et mater possunt testificari tam in coniungendo quam in disiungendo matrimonio... sententia lata contra matrimonium ad separationem eorum qui iam coniuncti erant, non transit in rem iudicatam... nec transactio sive compositio potest in matrimonio intervenire... nec arbitrium... nec poena locum habet... licet in aliis causis possit remitti iuramentum testibus, non tamen in causa matrimoniali."

formal Roman law procedure in the ecclesiastical trials of matrimonial cases. It was adopted here and there, but did not become universal, despite the fact that popes of the time wished that the formal procedure of Roman law should be the rule for such trials. Because of unnecessary delays and great expense, procedural norms tending toward a swifter trial began to be introduced.[18]

Finally, in 1312 Pope Clement V in his Decretal *"Dispendiosam"* sanctioned the use of a shortened or summary process for the whole Church for certain contentious cases, including those concerned with marriage.[19] It was clear from the beginning, however, that this summary trial was not obligatory.[20] At times one party wished the full, formal trial, which was not desired by the second party. In such an event the judge was to clear the way through an interlocutory sentence to favor the summary process, inasmuch as it had been established as a special remedy by law.[21] The following survey of procedure is concerned with that which prevailed in formal trials under Decretal law. The arrangement follows, as far as possible, the order of the judicial trial.

1. Introductory Stage of the Trial

Decretal law accepted the provisions of Roman law in that the appeal had to be filed within the space of ten days after the sentence was pronounced.[22] It had to be evident that the

[18] Persons who had appealed to Rome were aften obliged to go there in person or to send procurators, and to pay all the expenses consequent on the trip, residence and trial. "... secundum locorum distantiam personarum et negotii qualitatem tempore prosecutionis indulto, si voluerit appellatus et petierit, principales personae per se vel per procuratores... accedant ad sedem apostolicam."—c. 1, *de appellationibus,* II, 15, in VI°. These cumbersome formalities gave lawyers and procurators opportunities to prolong the trial so as to obtain greater stipends.

[19] C. 2, *de iudiciis,* II, 1, in Clem.; c. 2, *de verborum significatione,* V, 11, in Clem. Cf. Kennedy, *The Special Matrimonial Process in Cases of Evident Nullity,* The Catholic University of America Canon Law Studies, n. 93 (Washington, D. C.: The Catholic University of America, 1935), p. 20.

[20] "... non dicit debeat: per quod patet quia iudex potest etiam contradicentibus partibus servare iudiciarium ordinem in causis praedictis."—*Glossa* ad v. *valeat,* c. 2, *de iudiciis,* II, 1, in Clem. Cf. Lega, *Praelectiones de Iudiciis Ecclesiasticis* (4 vols., Romae, 1896-1901), I, n. 598.

[21] "... iudex potest procedere summarie, vel etiam, si velit, potest observare ordinem iudiciarium."—*Glossa* ad c. 2, *de verborum significatione,* V, 11, in Clem.

[22] Nov. (23.1) 28; c. 28, C. II, q. 6.

party having the right to appeal had an opportunity of knowing the sentence, before the ten day period could begin. It was absolutely peremptory and could neither be abbreviated nor prolonged by the judge.[23]

Again, following the Roman law, the appeal could be made immediately after the pronouncement of the sentence, *stante pede et viva voce,* after which it was to be inserted in the acts; if not done then, the appeal was to be made through an appellatory petition, made out in conformity with the prescriptions of the law.[24] Boniface VIII (1294-1303) decreed that an appeal made in writing did not have to be read to the judge *a quo.* The fact that it was put in writing and sent to him was sufficient.[25]

If the ten day period had elapsed, could a case involving the marriage bond be reintroduced without the accompaniment of new arguments and documents? The Decretals themselves made no exception from the general rule that appeals were not to be heard after the period allowed for their interposition. The *Glossae* seem to labor under considerable uncertainty in attempting to give a clear interpretation.[26]

In the opinion of the classical Decretalists, however, a sentence which had not been appealed within the ten day limit had the same force as a sentence that had been twice confirmed. A further hearing was denied in either case, unless new evi-

[23] C. 15, X, *de sententia et re iudicata,* II, 27; c. 8, *de appellationibus,* II, 15, in VI°; Durantis, *Speculum Iuris,* Lib. II, Partic. III, *de appellationibus,* Parag. 5, nn. 1, 2; Bouix, *Tractatus de Judiciis Ecclesiasticis* (2. ed., 2 vols., Parisiis, 1866), I, Pars, 2, p. 282 (hereafter cited *De Judiciis*).

[24] C. 11, X, *de probationibus,* II, 19, and *Glossa* ad v. *appellationes;* Durantis, *Speculum Iuris,* Lib. II, Partic. III, *de appellationibus,* Parag. 6, n. 1; Wahrmund, *Quellen zur Geschichte des römisch-kanonischen Processes im Mittelalter,* Band III (Innsbruck: Verlag der Wagner' schen Universitäts-Buchhandlung, 1916), *Ordo Judiciarius,* Heft I, C. LXXII, *de appellationibus,* p. 128.

[25] C. 11, *de appellationibus,* II, 15, in VI°.

[26] Cf. *Glossa* ad v. *suspendatur* and *fuisse* of c. 8, X, *de officio iudicis ordinarii,* I, 31; *permanere* in *glossa* of c. 7, X, *de sententia et re iudicata,* II, 27; *per errorem* in *glossa* of c. 6, X, *de frigidis et maleficiatis et impotentia coeundi,* IV, 15. Cf. Bernardus Papiensis, *Summa de Matrimonio* printed as an appendix to his *Summa Decretalium* (Ratisbonae, 1860), p. 360: "Si infra decem dies post latam de matrimoniis sententiam appellatum non fuerit, potest tamen adhuc sententia revocari, propterea quia ibi periculum animae vertitur." With such general terms, however Papiensis did not specifically touch the question at issue.

dence warranted its reintroduction. The application of such a norm to marriage cases is clearly seen from the conclusions drawn by Panormitanus (1386-1453).[27]

An appeal from an interlocutory sentence had to be made in writing with the cause indicated.[28] The appeal in which the aggrieved party asked legal redress was to be filed with the judge of the court in which the decision was rendered. Clement V declared that an appeal from a tribunal in which several judges rendered the decision could be made from a majority of them, or even separately; such an appeal would be just as valid as if it were made in the presence of all of them. The opposing party had to be properly notified of such an appeal.[29]

If this ordinary method of lodging an appeal was not available, other methods were prescribed by law. For instance, if one were to make a journey to a superior judge, the appeal was considered to have been made in fact, if not in word.[30] It was also possible to make the appeal before the judge *ad quem,* if the judge *a quo* could not be found in his accustomed place, or if one was hindered through fear from approaching the latter.[31] If other means were not available, the appeal could even be made before a notary and two witnesses, the fact being properly drawn up in a written instrument. Whenever the

[27] "Et circa hujusmodi sententias, quae non transeunt in rem iudicatam, cape aliquas limitationes notabiles. Primo enim scias, quod post decendium non potest appellari... Secundo non potest in talibus causibus appellari tertio, sicut nec in aliis causis... Tales sententiae non transeunt in rem iudicatam, quominus possint docto de errore retractari; tamen pro eis praesumitur tam pro justitia quam pro processu, donec contrarium probetur, quod intellige post lapsum decem dierum... Quin imo in tantum praesumitur... quod licet sententia in causa matrimonii non transeat in rem iudicatam, non tamen debet post decem dies quis indifferenter admitti ad probandum contrarium, sed oportet quod allegetur aliqua iusta et verisimillis causa iniustitiae, quae habeat movere iudicem ad credendum illam iniustam." —Nicholaus de Tudeschis (Abbas Panormitanus), *Commentaria in Quinque Libros Decretalium* (8 vols., Venetiis, 1588), Tom. IV, c. 7, *de sententia et re iudicata,* nn. 10-11 (hereafter cited *Commentaria*).

[28] C. 59, X, *de appellationibus, recusationibus et relationibus,* II, 28; cc. 1, 3, *de appellatione,* II, 15, in VI°; c. 5, *de appellationibus,* II, 12, in Clem.

[29] C. 59, X, *de appellationibus, recusationibus et relationibus,* II, 28; c. 1, *de appellationibus,* II, 12, in Clem.

[30] "Cum plus sit ad Sedem Apostolicam facto provocare quam verbo."—c. 52, X, *de appellationibus, recusationibus et relationibus,* II, 28. "Et si non verbo, facto tamen intelligitur provocasse, arrepto itinere ad Sedem Apostolicam."— c. 7, X, *de dolo et contumacia,* II, 41.

[31] C. 1, *de appellationibus,* II, 12, in Clem.

invoked appeal was made not directly to the judge *a quo,* he was to be subsequently informed that such an action had been taken.

If the appeal was made in the absence of the opposing party, the latter was to be informed by the appellant; it was also permissible, however, to have this information transmitted by the judge. If the latter course was selected, it had to be so expressed in the appellatory petition.[32]

The written petition was to be followed by a request for the *apostoli.* The use of the latter had been adopted from Roman law,[33] and adapted to use in ecclesiastical procedure. They were so called because they consisted of certain documents sent from the lower court to the appellate tribunal in which the case was to be retried.[34] There were five kinds of *apostoli,* known as (a) *dimissorii,* (b) *reverentiales,* (c) *refutatorii,* (d) *conventionales* and (e) *testimoniales.*[35]

The *apostoli dimissorii* were those documents, sent from the judge of the lower court to the higher tribunal, in which he testified that the appeal had been duly made and admitted. In sending such *apostoli,* the judge *a quo* certified that he was giving up all his power and jurisdiction over the case.

Apostoli reverentiales were those in which the judge *a quo* admitted the appeal, not because of the justice of the cause, but because of the reverence for the judge of the appellate court. These documents were employed especially when there was a doubt about the truth or justice of the appeal, as, for instance, when a diversity of opinions existed among the doctors of the law.[36]

Apostoli refutatorii were those in which the judge *a quo* denied the appeal. In that case he had to give the cause of his refusal, otherwise he was subject to penalties, including dis-

[32] C. 1, *de appellationibus,* II, 12, in Clem.; c. 3, *de electione et electi potestate,* I, 3, in Clem.

[33] Wenger, *Institutes of the Roman Law of Civil Procedure,* p. 307.

[34] Cf. Wahrmund, *Quellen zur Geschichte des römisch-kanonischen Processes im Mittelalter,* Band III, Heft, I, C. LXXXIII, p. 145.

[35] C. 1, *de appellationibus,* II, 15, in VI°, and the *Glossa* of this decretal ad v. *Casus.*

[36] C. 1, *de appellationibus,* II, 15, in VI°, and the *Glossa* ad v. *delatum.*

missal from office.[37] Despite this refusal on the part of the judge *a quo,* the *apostoli* were sent to the judge *ad quem,* who then decided whether the judge of the lower court was justified in refusing the appeal. If it was found that there was no legitimate cause for the appeal, the case was to be remanded to the judge *a quo.* And, of course, if the judge in the court of first instance was correct in refusing the appeal, the case was ended.

There was a great difference between this type of *apostoli* and those called *dimissorii* and *reverentiales.* In the latter kind, the judge *a quo* gave up completely his jurisdiction over the case. Even if the appeal was only from an interlocutory sentence when such *apostoli* were given, then the judge *ad quem* assumed entire jurisdiction over the case, including the principal cause. This was true even if he found that there was no legitimate cause for the appeal, or if it was interposed from frivolous or frustratory motives. He was not, however, compelled to assume operative jurisdiction.[38]

Apostoli conventionales were those in which both the loser and the victor agreed to appeal. The possibility of this was given even though the judge *a quo* was unwilling to grant the appeal.

Apostoli testimoniales were those which were given by a notary or some other reputable men when the judge *a quo* was not available. They testified that an appeal had been duly made to them, and then sent a notification of it to the judge *a quo.*[39]

Boniface VIII, in 1303, insisted upon the ancient rule that the *apostoli* were to be sought within thirty days after the making of the appeal, and within the same time were to be shown to the judge *ad quem.* Otherwise it was presumed that the appeal was deserted. The appeal was also considered deserted if the *apostoli* were not sought at all during this period.[40]

37 C. 1, *de appellationibus,* II, 15, in VI°.

38 C. 5, *de appellationibus,* II, 15, in VI°.

39 Reiffenstuel, Lib. II, tit. 28, nn. 132, 133.

40 C. 6, *de appellationibus,* II, 15, in VI°; Scaccia, *Tractatus de appellationibus* (3. ed., Coloniae, 1717), q. XIII, n. 56; Reiffenstuel, Lib. II, tit. 28, n. 134.

They were to be sought in a proper place and at a suitable time, and were to be asked for "*instanter et saepius.*" In other words, it was not sufficient to ask for them merely once; they had to be sought a number of times—this was because of the honor and reverence due to the judge. Furthermore, the repeated seeking of the *apostoli* could well have as a potential effect the judge's revocation of his interlocutory sentence.

Clement V (1305-1314) introduced a more convenient way of seeking the *apostoli,* whereby the appellant could still remain within the letter of the law. One could approach the judge and say: "Domine Judex, appello, et peto apostolos, et quidem instanter, eosque iterum atque iterum postulo."[41] This could be done *viva voce,* although it was recommended that the plea be put in writing so as to afford better judicial proof that it had been invoked.[42]

Clement V, while insisting that the *apostoli* were necessary for the validity of the trial in the appellate court, declared that if the judge did not give them, when all other prescriptions of law concerning them had been fulfilled, the appellant, out of natural equity, was allowed to proceed to the appellate court without them.[43]

It was insisted upon in the Decretals that while the appeal was pending all the acts of the judge of first instance, if they were performed for the purpose of changing or otherwise altering the cause in which the appeal was made, or if they proved prejudicial to the legal rights of the appellant, were to be revoked by the judge of the superior tribunal in accordance with the principle, *lite pendente, nihil innovetur.*[44]

Durantis (1238-1296) indicated an exception to this rule in marriage cases. He stated that the judge *a quo* could inter-

41 C. 2, *de appellationibus,* II, 12, in Clem.

42 Cf. Pirhing, *Ius Canonicum in V Libros Decretalium* (5 vols., Dilingae, 1674), Lib. II, tit. 28, n. 142 (hereafter cited Pirhing).

43 C. 2, *de appellationibus,* II, 12, in Clem.

44 C. 19, X, *de iudiciis,* II, 1; c. 10, X, *de exceptionibus,* II, 25, Potthast, n. 9612; c. 49, X, *de appellationibus, recusationibus et relationibus,* II, 28; c. 7, *de appellationibus,* II, 15, in VI°.

vene, whenever necessary, in the face of a *periculum animarum,* and also when the intervention proved *in favorem matrimonii.*[45]

Such appeals were always *in suspensivo.*[46]

2. Probatory Stage of the Trial

Before proceeding further in the trial, the judge *ad quem* had the duty of determining whether or not the legal formalities required in the interposition of the appeal had been suitably fulfilled. Unless the *libellus appellatorius* was made out according to the proper form, the resultant proceedings were invalid.

If the appeal had been made from a definitive sentence, no specific cause was necessary other than to say *"Apello."* If the appeal proceeded from an interlocutory sentence, however, an indication of the cause was necessary. Its sufficiency was to be determined by the appellate judge.[47]

The right of the parties to make the appeal was to be investigated. For the sake of bringing some cases to a speedier termination, this right of appeal was sometimes denied, as is evident from the phrase *appellatione remota* in particular papal responses.[48]

Alexander III (1159-1181) gave several answers in which he set forth general principles prohibiting appeals in cases wherein the crime or impediment was quite evident. Thus, in a Decretal to the Archbishop of Toledo, he insisted that the decision in the court of first instance was to be considered as final when it was manifest and notorious that a man was living with another's wife.[49] To the Archbishop of Rheims he de-

[45] *Speculum Iuris,* Lib. II, Partic. III, *de appellationibus,* Parag. II, n. 2.

[46] C. 19, X, *de iureiurando,* II, 24, Potthast, n. 1178; c. 28, X, *de officio et potestate iudicis delegati,* I, 29, Potthast, n. 2350; cc. 16, 55, X, *de appellationibus, recusationibus et relationibus,* II, 28.

[47] C. 59, X, *de appellationibus, recusationibus et relationibus,* II, 28; c. 15, X, *de sententia et re iudicata,* II, 27, and the accompanying *glossa* ad v. *causam non exprimens.*

[48] C. 36, 41, 43, X, *de appellationibus, recusationibus et relationibus,* II, 28; cf. *glossa* ad v. *ante sententiam;* cf. also c. 59, X, *de appellationibus, recusationibus et relationibus,* II, 28.

[49] "... aliquando aliqui quos manifestum sit et notorium uxorem alterius detinere... appellaverint, eorum appellationi non est aliquatenus deferendum ..."—c. 14, X, *de appellationibus, recusationibus et relationibus,* II, 28.

clared that there was to be no appeal when the crime of *raptus* was most evident.[50] In a Decretal to the Archbishop of Canterbury he declared that the same prohibition was to be in force when an appeal had been lodged by a party to allow a continuance in his notoriously sinful relationship.[51]

A *citatio* to the parties to appear in court was necessary in the second as well as in the first instance.[52] If contumacy was evident on the part of the defendant, then the trial could proceed without a *litis contestatio,* even to the final sentence. If for any number of reasons the cited party refused to appear, then the discussion and the decision regarding the disputed marriage was nevertheless to be undertaken. From a reply of Innocent III in 1198 it can be indirectly deduced that this exception was taken for granted. A woman had sought a separation from her husband because of his adultery. Despite the latter's refusal to appear and answer, the court had heard the witnesses, but then felt uncertain whether it should pass sentence. The Pope replied that "since there was no question of a marriage bond, but only of separation, the judge could not proceed to the sentence in consequence of the lack of the *litis contestatio.*" Through his denial of the possible granting of a separation from a contumacious and adulterous spouse, apart from a previous *litis contestatio,* the Pope implicitly admitted that in other matrimonial questions a trial could be valid even without the *litis contestatio.*[53] This became clearer from a general reply of Innocent III in 1209. Having firmly insisted on the necessity of the *litis contestatio* ordinarily, the Pontiff admitted exceptions, e.g., when one of the parties proved contumacious.[54]

If additional evidence was desired in the court of second instance, it was permitted to call in witnesses who had been

[50] C. 5, X, *de appellationibus, recusationibus et relationibus,* II, 28.

[51] C. 13, X, *de appellationibus, recusationibus et relationibus,* II, 28.

[52] Cc. 7, 58, X, *de appellationibus, recusationibus et relationibus,* II, 28. Cf. Wahrmund, *Quellen zur Geschichte des römisch-kanonischen Processes im Mittelalter,* Band III, Heft I, C. LXXVII, p. 138.

[53] C. 1, X, *ut lite non contestata non procedatur ad testium receptionem vel ad sententiam diffinitivam,* II, 6.

[54] C. 5, X, *ut lite non contestata non procedatur ad testium receptionem vel ad sententiam diffinitivam,* II, 6. Cf. Durantis, *Speculum Iuris,* Lib. IV, Partic. IV, *qui matrimonium accusare possunt,* Parag. 2, n. 5.

already heard in the lower court. New witnesses could likewise be heard. It was insisted upon that all danger of subornation and perjury be excluded.[55] The taking of the oath, which could be omitted with the consent of the parties in other contentious cases, was necessary in matrimonial causes.[56]

New documents could likewise be introduced in the appellate trial. It was essential, however, that in the introduction of new evidence, whether documentary or personal, it should pertain to the same cause which was tried in the first instance.[57]

It was different, however, when an appeal was made from an interlocutory sentence. In that case, only such proofs as had been brought forward in the lower court could be produced in the appellate tribunal.[58]

3. Concluding Stage of the Trial

A. The Sentence

The distinct obligation of the court of second instance was to judge the case on its own merits, independently of the decision of the court of first instance. The sentence, therefore, in the appellate tribunal was to result from a consideration of the case *denuo et ex integro*—a distinct canonical sentence, and not merely a revision, emendation, approval or disapproval of a previous judgment.

The general rule under Decretal law was that, when a number of judges decided a case, the decision rested with the majority.[59]

[55] C. 14, 15, X, *de probationibus,* II, 19; cc. 17, 46, X, *de testibus et attestationibus,* II, 20. Cf. Panormitanus, *Commentaria,* IV, *de testibus et attestationibus,* c. 17, nn. 3, 4.

[56] ". . . licet in aliis causis possit remitti iuramentum testibus. . . non autem in causa matrimoniali."—Cf. *glossa* ad v. *servetur* of c. 1, X, *ut lite non contestata non procedatur ad testium receptionem vel ad sententiam diffinitivam,* II, 6.

[57] C. 17, X, *de testibus et attestationibus,* II, 20; Durantis, *Speculum Iuris,* Lib. II, Partic. III, *de appellationibus,* Parag. 10, n. 2; Reiffenstuel, Lib. II, tit. 28, n. 15.

[58] "Appellanti ab interlocutoria vel a gravamine iudicis, non licet alias causas prosequi, quam in appellatione sua nominatim dumtaxat expressas, nec processus primi iudicis ex novis aut de novo probandis iustificari potest, vel etiam impugnari, sed tantum ex illis quae acta fuerunt, vel exhibita coram ipso."—C. 5, *de appellationibus,* II, 12, in Clem.

[59] C. 26, X, *de sententia et re iudicata,* II, 27, and the *glossa* of this decretal ad v. *diversas sententias proferentibus.*

Panormitanus favored an exception to this rule in marriage cases. He taught that if a Doctor held for the validity of the marriage, it was to be considered as decisive, even though a majority held otherwise. That rule was inapplicable, however, if it was clearly evident that the Doctor was subscribing to a false opinion. The same held true also when his opinion could be countered with reasons and arguments of probable value and force, for then there is question of favoring the marriage with an individual's opinion as against the rules of the law.[60]

If in a tribunal of two judges opposite opinions were rendered, then that which favored the marriage bond was to prevail.[61]

Boniface VIII (1294-1303) ordered that the sentence was to be written and then read by the judge to the parties. If the case was judged by the bishop himself, he could delegate another to read it for him. The sentence was considered as invalid unless it was written, read to the parties, and pronounced by the judge when seated. In the application of these rules to marriage cases, however, it was disputed among the authors whether, for its validity, a sentence in a matrimonial trial had to be written, or whether it could be pronounced orally, a copy of it being put into the record. Durantis seemed to voice the more common opinion when he maintained that the sentence could be pronounced orally without first being committed to writing.[62] If the appeal was deserted before the final sentence, the judge could nevertheless continue the case *ex officio,* if such action on his part was demanded by the public good.[63]

60 "... si una reperitur Doctorum opinio pro matrimonio, illa sequenda est, licet multi teneant contra matrimonium... nisi illa opinio esset evidenter falsa... Idem, si potest convinci probabilibus rationibus, hic enim in favorem matrimonii praevalet sententia unius contra iuris regulas."—*Commentaria,* II, *de sententia et re iudicata,* c. 26, n. 3. In the writings of Panormitanus, as well as in other sources of that time, the term "Doctor" referred to those who were experienced in the law and who were consulted by the judges in giving their decisions.

61 Cf. *glossa* ad v. *diversas sententias proferentibus* of c. 26, X, *de sententia et re iudicata,* II, 27. If two judges were acting with delegated power only, the decision in such a case would rest with the *delegans.*

62 *Speculum Iuris,* Lib. II, Partic. III, *de sententia et re iudicata,* Parag. 8, n. 12.

63 C. 45, X, *de appellationibus, recusationibus et relationibus,* II, 28.

B. *Expenses of the Trial*

It was the general rule that the loser was to pay the expenses of the trial.[64] However, if from the balance of proofs the fact was evident that both parties had a just cause for entering the proceedings, then the expenses were divided.[65]

If the defeated party failed to justify his entry upon the proceedings, it was presumed that he had acted rashly or maliciously, and he was ordered to pay the costs, and also to indemnify the adversary. If the victor did not request indemnification, the judge was not bound to command it.[66] If the losing party in the court of first instance lost also in the appellate court, he was to pay the expenses of the trial under the presumption that he had prosecuted his case without a just cause and in bad faith.[67] Durantis believed that the appellant should be made to pay the expenses when it was evident that he had appealed from deceitful motives or *temerarie aut frustratorie*; otherwise, however, if it could be shown that he appealed with an attendant just or probable reason.[68]

The problem arose whether the party who won in the court of first instance, but lost to the appellant in the superior court, would thereby be condemned to pay the expenses. According to the Decretalists, the solution rested upon a necessary distinction. Such a party would have to pay the expenses if the decision in the second instance was based upon the very same proofs as in the first. It was thus presumed that he did not have a just cause in the first trial, and had no right to enter the proceedings.[69]

He would not have to pay the expenses, however, if the appellant won the case because of new proofs produced in the

64 "Victus victori in expensis sit condemnatus."—Reiffenstuel, Lib. II, tit. 28, n. 209.

65 Cf. *Glossa ordinaria* ad v. *expensas* of c. 5, X, *de dolo et contumacia*, II, 14.

66 Reiffenstuel, Lib. II, tit. 27, n. 192; Schmalzgrueber, Lib. II, tit. 27, n. 126.

67 Panormitanus, *Commentaria*, III, c. 5, *de dolo et contumacia*, n. 24.

68 *Speculum Iuris*, Lib. II, Partic. III, *de expensis*, Parag. 8, nn. 2, 3; Panormitanus, *Commentaria*, III, *de dolo et contumacia*, c. 5, n. 26.

69 Panormitanus, *Commentaria*, III, *de dolo et contumacia*, c. 5, n. 25.

second instance. The reason for the distinction was this: the party against whom the appeal was lodged labored under an *ignorantia facti* (in view of the fact that he could not foresee the new proofs), and thus could be excused for that reason. The presumption that he had a just cause for taking part in the proceedings was still valid. In the previous case, however, there was the element of an *ignorantia iuris,* and thus the Decretalists applied the rule of law: "Ignorantia facti, non iuris, excusat."[70]

If the appellant abandoned the trial before the final sentence, he was obliged to pay the expenses incurred.[71]

C. *Legal Redress against the Sentence*

After the sentence in the appellate court had been pronounced, a further appeal was permitted, according to the rule that in any matrimonial cause two appeals were allowed, except in the cases wherein this option was denied by law.[72]

It should be noted that under the Decretal law, just as there was no obligation on the part of the parties or of any official of the court to appeal from the sentence of the court of first instance, so also there was no similar obligation to make a further appeal from the sentence of the second tribunal. This was true even if the appellate court gave a sentence which was opposed to that of the court of first instance. Thus, if the first sentence stood for the validity of the marriage, and the appellate court declared for its nullity, the latter was presumed in law to be the just sentence, unless it was changed upon a further appeal or through some other form of legal redress. It was not until 1741 that an obligation to appeal a decision declaring for the nullity of a marriage was imposed.[73]

70 Panormitanus, *Commentaria,* III, *de dolo et contumacia,* c. 5, n. 25; Reg. 13, R.J., in VI°.

71 C. 70, X, *de appellationibus, recusationibus et relationibus,* II, 28.

72 Cc. 39, 65, X, *de appellationibus, recusationibus et relationibus,* II, 28; c. 1, *de sententia et re iudicata,* II, 11, in Clem.

73 Benedictus XIV, const. *"Dei miseratione,"* 3 nov. 1741—*Fontes,* n. 318.

According to Durantis, each party had the right to two appeals.[74]

From the metropolitan's court a further appeal could be directed to the Pope, who usually delegated judges to try the case for him,[75] and the same procedure was to be followed in lodging the appellate petition as was done in transferring it from the first to the second instance. Although three conformable decisions closed the way to further appeals, a marriage case could, inasmuch as it never became a *res iudicata,* be reopened if sufficient evidence warranted it.[76]

If the sentence was alleged to be null, it could be attacked by means of a judicial action for the declaration of its nullity. Ordinarily this took place before the same judge who had rendered the sentence.[77] While noting the opinion that such an action was to be tried in this fashion, Durantis[78] nevertheless declared that an action of nullity could be included in the appellate petition in a cumulative manner.[79]

It was frequently doubtful whether the sentence was actually null. The sources of nullity were so numerous, the reasons so subtle, and other factors so disputed (as can be seen from the text of Durantis), that one was not certain whether or

[74] "Bis posse appellari tantum a sententia, vel a quolibet gravamine, intellige verum ab eadem parte, nam altera pars poterit etiam super eodem capitulo, vel sententia, appellare. Si enim appellavero a sententia pro te contra me lata, et iudex appellationis sententiam confirmat, possum secundo appellare a confirmatione sententiae. Sed si haec confirmatio confirmatur, non possum amplius appellare, quia non licet tertio provocare. Si autem confirmatio infirmetur, tu poteris ab illa sententia appellare, quia hoc non est tertia appellatio, sed prima quo ad te; et si judex appellationis infirmationem sententiae infirmet, poteris secundo appellare, ultra a tibi non licet." —*Speculum Iuris,* Lib. II, Partic. III, *de appellationibus,* Parag. 8, n. 1.

[75] C. 46, X, *de testibus et attestationibus,* II, 20; c. 4, X, *de in integrum restitutione,* I, 41; Cf. Pirhing, Lib. II, tit. 28, n. 90; Reiffenstuel, Lib. II, tit. 28, n. 58.

[76] Cf. *glossa ordinaria* of c. 7, X, *de sententia et re iudicata,* II, 27, ad v. *permanere.*

[77] Cf. *glossa* of c. 1, *de sententia et re iudicata,* II, 11, in Clem., ad v. *agendum de nullitate;* Durantis, *Speculum Iuris,* Lib. II, Partic. III, *de sententia et re iudicata,* Parag. 8, n. 27.

[78] "Causa nullitatis debet tractari coram eo qui de principali cognovit... causa vero appellationis apud superiorem... Quidam tenent hoc..."—*Speculum Iuris,* Lib. II, Partic. III, *de sententia et re iudicata,* Parag. 8, n. 27.

[79] *Speculum Iuris,* Lib. II, Partic. III, *de sententia et re iudicata,* Parag. 8, n. 27.

not a sentence could be declared null. In that event, a cumulative petition was permitted. The *libellus* could ask for all remedies—the plaint of nullity, the lodging of an appeal and the *restitutio in integrum.* Such cumulative petitions are found mentioned in the Decretals themselves.[80]

Durantis, after noting the arguments to the contrary, stated that the Roman Curia observed the practice of admitting such petitions and that he himself, at the mandate of Clement IV (1265-1268), had frequently received them and passed upon them.[81] Durantis recounted a long list of deficiencies which rendered a sentence invalid, and arranged them under headings: deficiencies in the judge, in his jurisdiction, in the litigants, in the factors of time and of place, in the cause itself, in the quality or mode, and in the circumstances attending the pronouncement of the sentence. Under each generic cause he listed explicit examples drawn from the Decretals, or from the *Decretum,* or even from the Roman law.[82]

Occasionally, when the way for a further appeal was closed, a remedy known as a *supplicatio* was used. It was a *remedium extraordinarium* which was not to be employed as long as the ordinary remedies were available.[83] It was a petition made only to the Pope. [84] In this petition it was asked that he gratuitously allow the case to be retried. In a *supplicatio* to Pope Innocent III (1198-1216), the party who sought redress included mention also of an appeal inasmuch as he was not completely certain that the latter remedy was no longer available.[85]

Another extraordinary remedy that could be employed was the *restitutio in integrum.* It differed, however, from the *supplicatio,* in that it was not granted unless a just cause warranted

80 C. 8, X, *de in integrum restitutione,* I, 41; c. 14, X, *de privilegiis,* V. 33.

81 *Speculum Iuris,* Lib. II, Partic. III, *de sententia et re iudicata,* Parag. 8, n. 27.

82 *Speculum Iuris,* Lib. II, Partic. III, *de sententia et re iudicata,* Parag. 8, nn. 1 sq.

83 Reiffenstuel, Lib. II, tit. 28, n. 18.

84 This resembled somewhat the *supplicatio* directed to the Emperor from the sentence of a Praetorian Prefect. There was no appeal from the latter, since he was the immediate representative of the Emperor. Cf. Wenger, *Institutes of the Roman Law of Civil Procedure,* p. 308.

85 C. 4, X, *de in integrum restitutione,* I, 41.

it.[86] A just cause, for instance, could be the fraud on the part of the opponent, or the negligence on the part of one's procurator.[87] A Decretal of Innocent III referred to the granting of a *restitutio in integrum* in a marriage case. In this case one of the consorts claimed that a sentence had been rendered while she was declared to be contumaciously absent. In her petition she swore that she was ignorant of the fact that the trial was taking place in consequence of the fraudulent action on the part of a third party.[88] Panormitanus, while speaking of the remedy of the *restitutio in integrum,* referred also to the *querela* as an action through which an acknowledgment of the nullity of a sentence was sought before the judge who had pronounced it.[89] Writers after Panormitanus spoke of the *querela* rather than the *restitutio in integrum* in connection with the effort at a rehearing of a case, especially in trials which concerned the *status personarum.*

86 "Sententia transit in rem iudicatam post decendium, quoad instantiam causae, nisi quis audiatur per viam restitutionis in integrum adversus sententiam ex iusta causa."—Panormitanus, *Commentaria,* II, *de sententia et re iudicata,* c. 7, n. 12.

87 C. 1, X, *de in integrum restitutione,* I, 41, and the accompanying *glossa.*

88 C. 4, X, *de in integrum in restituione,* I, 41.

89 *Commentaria,* II, *de sententia et re iudicata,* c. 7, n. 12.

CHAPTER FOUR

FROM THE COUNCIL OF TRENT (1545-1563) TO THE CODE OF CANON LAW (1918)

Although the Council of Trent brought important reforms regarding appellate procedure, they were far from sufficient to remedy the defects in those trials in which the matrimonial bond was brought into question. The Council was concerned chiefly with insisting that matrimonial causes belonged to ecclesiastical judges[1] and that a reorganization of the various grades of tribunals be effected.[2]

During the two centuries following the Council of Trent, the procedural laws regarding marriage trials were widely neglected and this with the "connivance of the bishops."[3] Pleas of nullity were alleged with the utmost ease; and it was not unknown that parties would pledge themselves under the penalty of a fine to make no appeal, if at some time or other the marriage should be adjudged null at the instance of one of the parties. Scandalous conditions were especially prevalent in Poland. Catholic as that country was, the marriage tie, at least in certain classes of society, was no firmer there than in the neighboring lands which had been overrun by Protestantism. In an attempt to remedy the abuses existing in Poland, Pope Benedict XIV (1740-1758) addressed two encyclical letters, couched in the strongest terms, to the bishops of that nation.[4] In one of them[5] he threatened the bishops that, if things did not improve, he would reserve all Polish matrimonial cases, even those in the court of first instance, for examination before the Roman tribunals.

Although conditions in Poland were especially deplorable, it must be said that there was a general need for legislation

[1] "Si quis dixerit, causas matrimoniales non spectare ad iudices ecclesiasticos: A.S."—Sess. XXIV, *de matrimonio,* can. 12.

[2] Sess. XXIV, *de ref.,* c. 20.

[3] Joyce, *Christian Marriage,* p. 399.

[4] Ep. encycl. *"Matrimonii,"* 11 apr. 1741—*Fontes,* n. 307; ep. encycl. *"Nimiam licentiam"* 18 maii 1743—*Fontes,* n. 337.

[5] Ep. encycl. *"Nimiam licentiam,"* 18 maii 1743, n. 17—*Fontes,* n. 377.

which would afford greater protection for the preservation of the nuptial bond. On November 3, 1741, that legislation was proclaimed to the whole world in the celebrated Constitution "*Dei miseratione*" of Benedict XIV.[6] Through that Constitution the judicial procedure in matrimonial causes became stabilized, so that there resulted from it the basis of the present day judicial system for the hearing of matrimonial causes in the ordinary courts of second instance.

The necessity for the new legislation and the extent of the conditions then prevailing are evident in the preamble. Benedict XIV deplored the facility and haste with which marriages were being pronounced invalid in some of the ecclesiastical courts, and deeply grieved over the resultant scandal. Among the causes of this abuse he adverted to the following:[7] (a) certain ecclesiastical judges were pronouncing marriages invalid after only a slight or, at times, even no investigation; (b) frequently only the one party who sought a declaration of nullity appeared at the trial, the other party failing to appear for a defense of the marriage bond; thus it happened that the party who desired a declaration of nullity easily obtained a sentence of nullity and was enabled to remarry; (c) even when both parties appeared for the trial, it frequently happened that, if the sentence declared the marriage invalid, neither of them appealed to the higher court. They neglected to invoke this appeal either because they were in collusion with each other for the purpose of having their marriage declared invalid, or because, even when they had acted in good faith, the defendant or the party who had sustained the validity of the marriage regarded all appeal as futile or unavailable, once the sentence of invalidity had been rendered. The latter course was frequently followed when he or she was destitute of the money or other means necessary for the prosecution of the appeal, or else when he or she had undergone a change of mind on the subject.[8]

The Constitution "*Dei miseratione*" set the norm for all subsequent legislation until the time of the Code, with reference

6 *Fontes*, n. 318; cf. Bouix, *De Judiciis*, II, 434.

7 Benedictus XIV, const. "*Dei miseratione*" 3 nov. 1741, nn. 1-3—*Fontes*, n. 318.

8 Cf. Smith, *Elements of Ecclesiastical Law*, Vol. II, *Ecclesiastical Trials* (5. ed., New York, 1892), p. 391.

to the judicial procedure in matrimonial trials. The Sacred Congregation of the Council, under the date of August 22, 1840, issued an Instruction which was concerned chiefly with a further elucidation of the proper procedure in the courts of first instance;[9] on June 22, 1883, the Sacred Congregation of the Holy Office sent to the Oriental bishops an Instruction which contained a more detailed description of the proceedings necessary for marriage trials in courts of second instance.[10] In the same year this Instruction, with the introduction of but minor changes, was dispatched by the Sacred Congregation for the Propagation of the Faith to the bishops of the United States.[11] It was incorporated, along with the Constitution "*Dei miseratione,*" in the Acts of the III Plenary Council of Baltimore in 1884.[12]

The same Council recommended to the bishops of America that they might make advantageous use of the Austrian Instruction of 1855[13] in regard to matrimonial causes.[14]

This Instruction, drawn up and promulgated for his archdiocese by Joseph Cardinal Rauscher (1797-1875), Prince-Archbishop of Vienna, was approved by the Holy See in "*forma ordinaria*" for all of Austria, and subsequently exercised a great influence on the particular legislation of other countries as well as on the universal legislation of the church.[15]

In the survey of the post-Tridentine organization of the courts of second instance and of the procedural norms em-

[9] *Fontes,* n. 4069.

[10] S.C.S. Off., instr. (ad Ep. Rituum Orient.) a. 1883—*Fontes,* n. 1076.

[11] S.C. de Prop. Fide, instr., "*Causae matrimoniales,*" a. 1883—Fontes, n. 4091.

[12] "In agendis hisce causis pro rei gravitate exacte servetur tum Constitutio Benedicti XIV, "*Dei miseratione,*" 3 Nov., 1741, tum Instructio a S. Cong. de Prop. Fide Nobis communicata quae incipit "*Causae Matrimoniales. . .*"—*Acta et Decreta Concilii Plenarii Baltimorensis Tertii, A.D. MDCCCLXXIV* (Baltimore: John Murphy and Co., 1886), n. 304.

[13] *Instructio Austriaca Josephi Cardinalis Rauscher,* 4 maii, 1855—*Analecta Juris Pontificii* (Romae: 1855-1869; Paris: 1872-1891), II (1857), 2546-2565 (henceforth referred to as the Austrian Instruction).

[14] ". . . utiliter etiam consuli poterit Instructio pro judiciis ecclesiasticis Imperii Austriaci in causis matrimonialibus, a 1855 a gravibus theologis et canonistis Romanis, licet solo privato suo judicio, commendata."—*Acta et Decreta Concilii Plenarii Baltimorensis Terti, A.D. MDCCCLXXIV,* n. 304.

[15] Cf. Doheny, *Canonical Procedure in Matrimonial Cases, Formal Judicial Procedure* (Milwaukee: Bruce Publishing Co., 1938), pp. 213, 221.

ployed by them in the hearing of marriage cases affecting the bond, a systematic rather than a chronological order will be followed. Emphasis will primarily be given to the changes that came into being since the Council of Trent, especial note being taken regarding those procedural regulations which applied to the courts of second instance. Reference will be made to previous legislation, and also to the procedure which obtained in the courts of first instance, but only whenever a unified treatment or a clarified explanation may call for such reference.

ARTICLE 1. ORGANIZATION OF THE ORDINARY COURT OF SECOND INSTANCE

1. Proper Court

By the decrees of the Council of Trent, matrimonial causes, when heard in the court of first instance, were no longer to be left to the judgment of a dean, of an archdeacon,[16] or of other inferiors, but were to be reserved to the exclusive examination and jurisdiction of the bishop.

Regarding the procedure to be followed in the appellate court, the Council declared that the form and tenor of the Sacred Constitutions was to be followed, "particularly that of Innocent IV, which begins *"Romana."*[17] This meant that appeals were to be made to the immediately superior tribunal, usually that of the metropolitan, as the ordinary court of second instance. It also meant that the court of second instance for cases tried in the metropolitan courts was a court of the Holy

[16] The prohibition placed upon archdeacons in the matter of taking judicial cognizance of matrimonial cases in the court of first instance was not immediately put into practice in France. "Licet Concilium Tridentinum potestatem archdiaconi valde limitaverit et causas matrimoniales eius competentiae subtraxerit, tamen archidiaconi Parisienses(ob receptionem Concilii Tridentini in Gallia—iuxta Gallicanorum doctrinam—non factam) praxim traditionalem continuasse videntur."—Léon Pommeray, *L 'Officialite archdiaconale de Paris aux XVe-XVIe siécle* (Paris: Recueil Sirey, 1933), as reviewed by B. Kurtscheid, O.F.M., in *Apollinaris* (Romae, 1928—), IX (1936), 332. Cf. Conc. Trident., sess. XXIX, *de ref.*, c. 20.

[17] Sess. XXII, *de ref.*, c. 7; c. 3, *de appellationibus,* II, 15, in VI°.

See. In the centuries that followed, this particular rule was relaxed for particular cases and for particular regions.[18]

In 1883 the Sacred Congregation for the Propagation of the Faith granted to the bishops of the United States special permission whereby appeals from the metropolitan court, when it had acted as the court of first instance, were to be heard in the nearest neighboring metropolitan court.[19] The distance was measured according to the nearness of the Cathedral churches.[20]

2. Personnel of the Court

In the legislation of this period, beginning with the promulgation of the Constitution *"Dei miseratione,"* special insistence was placed upon the necessity of three officials in the courts of second instances—the judge, a secretary and a new official called the *defensor matrimonii.*[21]

The judge could be either the bishop in person, or someone authorized through delegation to act for him in his name. There was no restriction as to the number of judges that might be employed, and neither was there any rule requiring that the same number of judges act in the court of second instance as had acted in the lower tribunal.[22]

18 The Bishop of Sonora, Mexico, was authorized by a special rescript from the Sacred Congregation of the Council in 1848 to place the appeal in marriage cases in some neighboring curia instead of in a distant metropolitan tribunal, or even to accept the case in second instance himself, as long as a different set of priests assisted him in the hearing of the case.—S.C.C. *in Sonora,* 28 aug. 1848—*Thesaurus Resolutionum Sacrae Congregationis Concilii* (167 vols., Romae, 1718-1908), CVIII (1848), 362-367 (hereafter cited *Thesaurus Resolutionum* S.C.C.); cf. Feije, *De Impedimentis et Dispensationibus Matrimonialibus* (3. ed., Lovanii, 1885), p. 485.

19 S.C. de Prop. Fide, instr. a. 1883—*Fontes,* n. 4901; cf. Bassibey, *Le Mariage devant les Tribunaux Ecclesiastiques, Procedure Matrimoniale Generale* (Paris: Librairie Religieuse H. Oudin, 1899), p. 416.

20 Gasparri, *Tractatus Canonicus De Matrimonio* (3. ed., 2 vols., Parisiis, 1904), II, 386, 387 (hereafter cited *Tractatus De Matrimonio*).

21 Cf. De Smet, *De Sponsalibus et Matrimonio* (Brugis, 1909), p. 424.

22 There could be no appeal from a delegated judge to the bishop, as that would have been an *appellatio tamquam ab eodem ad seipsum.* The delegated judge was to act as an official of the bishop; consequently any appeal from him would have to go to the metropolitan. The bishop could delegate his jurisdiction, however, in such a way that the decision would always remain with him. This custom was frequently followed. Cf. Mansella, *De Impedimentis ac de Processu Iudiciali in Causis Matrimonialibus* (Romae, 1881), pp. 216, 217; Pirhing, Lib. I, tit. 29, n. 107.

The use of a collegiate tribunal in criminal trials, as well as the employment of a collegiate judiciary in the tribunals of the Congregations in Rome, strongly influenced diocesan courts to employ more than one judge in the deciding of matrimonial cases. Lega (1860-1935), writing in 1898, stated that such a usage obtained not only in Italy, but in other countries as well. The number of judges varied, but four was the usual number associated with the presiding judge.[23]

In all judicial proceedings it was required that there be present a secretary, whose duty it was to keep a careful and correct record of each stage of the process.[24]

The third necessary official was the *defensor matrimonii.* It is commonly held that his position or office was created by Benedict XIV.[25] The importance of this official's part in the proceedings in the court of second instance, and in the light of the legislation of this period, will be seen in the treatment on procedure in this chapter.

All the afore-mentioned officials were to make the profession of faith according to the formulary as established by Pius IV[26] and as later amended by Pius IX on January 20, 1877. They were likewise to take the oath. The *defensor matrimonii* was to furnish an oath not only in connection with his appointment to office, but also at the beginning of every matrimonial trial at which he assisted in his official capacity.

Other officials were added to these according to the customs and practices of particular courts. As under the Decretal law, *assessores* could be assigned to assist the judge, along with other officials, such as substitutes, who could take the place of one of the three necessary members of the court, or two consultors, one of them a theologian and the other a canonist.[27]

23 "Hodie enim tum in Italia tum extra Italium apud curias dioecesanas causae disciplinares et matrimoniales ab Episcopo demandantur iudicandae cuidam iudicum ad hoc delegatorum collegio... Praeter praesidem constitui solent quatuor iudices aut saltem duo, sed non facile ultra sex."—Lega, *Praelectiones de Iudiciis Ecclesiasticis* (4 vols., Romae, 1896-1901), II, 400.

24 S.C. de Prop. Fide, instr. a. 1883, n. 6—*Fontes,* n. 4901.

25 For a historical synopsis concerning the possible origins of this official, cf. Dolan, *The Defensor Vinculi,* pp. 5-13.

26 Conc. Trident., sess. XXV, *de ref.,* c. 2.

27 Cf. De Smet, *De Sponsalibus et Matrimonio,* p. 424.

ARTICLE II. PROCEDURE IN THE ORDINARY COURT OF SECOND INSTANCE

1. Introductory Stage of the Trial

A. Obligation to Lodge an Appeal

The Council of Trent had made no change in regard to the obligation to lodge an appeal from a sentence of nullity in the court of first instance. According to Decretal law the parties were free to marry after but a single sentence which declared the nullity of their marriage. This privilege was to remain in force inasmuch as the Council of Trent had declared that the provisions concerning appeals as found in the chapter entitled *"Romana"* in *Sexto* were to continue.[28]

In 1741 the Constitution *"Dei miseratione"* demanded that the sentence of nullity pronounced in the court of first sentence was to be necessarily appealed.[29] Some doubt arose, however, whether this rule applied even in cases wherein the nullity was clearly evident from the hearing in the court of first instance. The argument for this was based upon the wording of the Constitution: "Cum igitur coram Ordinario, ad quem causae huiusmodi cognoscere pertinet, controversia aliqua proponetur, in qua de Matrimonii validitate *dubitabitur. . .*"[30] The conclusion drawn from this was that only those cases should be appealed in which there was some *doubt* which favored the validity of the marriage.

In 1848 the Bishop of Sonora, Mexico, in a petition to the Sacred Congregation of the Council, sought a relaxation from the obligation requiring a second confirmatory sentence of nullity in all clear and evident cases *"in qua aperta et notoria sit matrimonii nullitas."* He maintained that appeals in such cases were useless, and that the consequent delays were filled with spiritual hazards. The Sacred Congregation of the Council, however, replied that the appeal was to be made even in such cases, declaring that such was the evident meaning of the wording in the Constitution *"Dei miseratione."*[31]

28 Sess. XXII, *de ref.*, c. 7; c. 3, *de appellationibus,* II, 15, in VI°.

29 N. 8 in this Constitution—*Fontes,* n. 318.

30 *Loc. cit.*

31 S.C.C. *in Sonora,* 28 aug., 1848—*Thesaurus Resolutionum S.C.C.,* CVIII (1848), 362-367.

If the sentence in the court of first instance stood against the validity of the marriage, the *defensor matrimonii* was to appeal within the time prescribed.[32] If he failed to do so within ten days, he was not thereby estopped from making an appeal later. In the event that he neglected his duty, he could be compelled to invoke the appeal either by his own bishop or by the judge of the tribunal before which the appeal was to be lodged.[33] If the sentence had been pronounced for the validity of the marriage, and neither of the parties appealed against the sentence, then also, the *defensor matrimonii* would forego invoking any appeal.[34]

If after such a sentence the parties did not appeal within the ten days, the sentence became a *quasi res iudicata,* in the sense that the cause could not be introduced again unless the presence of new evidence warranted its introduction. In such an event the rehearing of the cause followed not upon an appeal, but in consequence of the use of some other remedy made available in law, ordinarily the *querela* addressed to the judge whose sentence had supported the validity of the bond.[35]

B. Appeal from an Interlocutory Sentence

Under Decretal law there were very few restrictions regarding an appeal from an interlocutory sentence. This followed from the principle that one had the right to appeal from any sentence, unless a special exception was indicated in the law.[36]

The Council of Trent enacted a needed reform when it restricted appeals from interlocutory sentences to those only which had a definitive force and in causes in which the re-

[32] Benedictus XIV, const. *"Dei miseratione"* 3 nov., 1741, n. 8—*Fontes,* n. 318.

[33] S.C. de Prop. Fide, instr. a. 1883, n. 25—*Fontes,* n. 4901.

[34] S. C. de Prop. Fide, instr. a. 1883, n. 25: "Iudex, si pro validitate matrimonii sententiam dixerit, et nemo ex coniugibus contra eam appellaverit, neque defensor matrimonii appellabit, et causa finita censeatur."—*Fontes,* n. 4901; Benedictus XIV, const. *"Dei miseratione"* 3 nov. 1741, n. 25—*Fontes,* n. 318.

[35] Cf. Reiffenstuel, Lib. II, tit. 27, n. 136.

[36] A popular way of expressing this was: "Appellationis remedium nec diabolo denegandum foret si esset in iudicio."—Lega, *Praelectiones de Iudiciis Civilibus* (2. ed., Romae, 1905), 536, note 2.

sultant injury could not be remedied by means of a definitive sentence.[37]

Reiffenstuel (1642-1703), in setting forth a norm by which one could determine whether an interlocutory sentence had a definitive force, stated that it was the type of sentence so decisive that it would put an end to the cause in question as far as the final result was concerned.[38]

C. Interposition of the Appeal

The custom of asking for *apostoli,* which usage had been accepted in Decretal law from the Justinian compilations, began to fall into disuse in many places after the Council of Trent, and especially after the promulgation of the Constitution "*Dei miseratione.*" The latter seemed to indicate that the judge himself send all the necessary documents and records from the lower to the appellate court. A clearer indication of this was contained in the Instruction of 1883.[39]

After the appeal was properly filed by the appellant, it was to be prosecuted in the court of second instance within one month from the time it had been invoked in the lower court. The latter tribunal, however, could extend this time.[40]

Benedict XIV forbade the consorts to enter into a second marriage while their case was pending in the court of second instance. It was likely for such a marriage to be attempted, especially after the sentence in the first instance had been passed in favor of the nullity of the marriage. Severe penalties were decreed for the violation of this regulation.[41]

37 Sess. XXIV, *de ref.*, c. 20.

38 Lib. II, tit. 27, n. 18; cf. Ferraris, *Prompta Biblioteca, Canonica, Iuridica, Moralis, Theologica, nec non Ascetica, Polemica, Rubricistica, Historica* (ed. Migne, 9 vols., Romae, 1885-1899), s. v. "*Appellatio,*" Art. IX, n. 18.

39 S. C. de Prop. Fide, instr. a 1883, n. 27—*Fontes,* n. 4901; cf. Devoti, *Institutiones Canonicae,* Lib. III, tit. XV, n. 11.

40 Cf. Austrian Instruction, § 102—*Analecta Juris Pontificii,* II (1857), 2527.

41 Const. "*Dei miseratione,*" 3 nov. 1741, n. 9: "Appellatione a prima sententia pendente... si ambo vel unus ex coniugibus novas nuptias celebrare ausus fuerit... volumus et decernimus ut non solum serventur quae adversus eos, qui matrimonium contra interdictum Ecclesiae contrahunt, statuta sunt... sed ulterius ut contrahens, vel contrahentes matrimonium huiusmodi, omnibus poenis contra poligamos constitutis, omnino... subiaceant ..."—*Fontes,* n. 318; Cf. S. C. de Prop. Fide, instr. a. 1883, n. 25—*Fontes,* n. 4901.

D. Time Allowed for the Appeal

In the Decretal law there was allowed a whole year in which to try the case in the court of second instance. This rule remained unchanged during the period after the Council of Trent. It is here to be remembered, too, that a lapse of the *fatalia legis* in matrimonial cases did not imply that the issue at court had become a *res iudicata.* For a just cause the time could be extended another year; Pirhing (1606-1679) wrote that even this amount of time could be lengthened if a legitimate cause were present.

It was usually the judge *a quo* who determined the time in which the case was to be prosecuted in the appellate court,[42] but the judge *ad quem* could likewise extend the time if a *periculum animarum* was present.[43] The computation of the lapse of time was to begin with the interposition of the appeal.[44]

2. Probatory Stage of the Trial

The primary duty of the court of second instance was not merely the revising or the amending of the sentence of the lower court, but rather the instituting of a new and independent trial of the case. Its distinct obligation was to judge the case on its own merits, independently of the decision of the court of first instance.[45]

After the proper documents, including the sentence, the appeal and the acts of the trial presented in the court of first

42 Bouix, *De Judiciis,* II, 285.

43 Schmalzgrueber, Lib. II, tit. 28, nn. 87, 88.

44 Bouix, *De Judiciis,* II, 284; Pellegrini, *Praxis Vicariorum* (Venetiis, 1696), Pars III, Sect. III, nn. 2-4.

45 It was disputed among the authors whether the Constitution *"Dei miseratione"* of Benedict XIV did away with the summary marriage trial as instituted by Clement V in 1312 in his decretal *"Dispendiosam"* (c. 2, *de iudiciis,* II, 1, in Clem). Many authors writing before 1889 maintained that even matrimonial cases of nullity could be tried summarily, inasfar as such a summary procedure was compatible with the formalities decreed in the Constitution *"Dei miseratione."* Cf. *Smith, Elements of Ecclesiastical Law,* II, *Ecclesiastical Trials,* p. 379; Feije, *De Impedimentis et Dispensationibus Matrimonialibus,* n. 593; Lega, *Praelectiones De Iudiciis Ecclesiasticis,* II, n. 361. According to Bouix, it was considered more prudent and safe to observe the full solemnities of the formal trial.—*De Judiciis,* II, 306. Official recognition of a summary trial came after the year 1889. Cf. S.C.S. Off., decr. 5 iun. 1889—*Fontes,* n. 1118.

instance, had been sent to the appellate tribunal, they were to be examined by the latter court for the purpose of determining whether the prescriptions of the law had been fulfilled according to requirements.[46]

If the court of second instance decided to receive the appeal, then it could proceed in one of two ways. Either a new process was instituted, in which case all the prescriptions pertaining to the court of first instance were to be followed; or, if there were no valid reasons for beginning the trial all over again, the *acta* of the court of first instance could be used as the basis for arriving at a new sentence. Even in the latter case, however, if at any time further investigations were deemed necessary, they were to be carried out. In the event that any new evidence was brought in, this was always to be in the presence of the *defensor matrimonii,* or a least the notice and content of it was to be communicated to him so that he might have the opportunity of studying it and forming any resultant conclusions.[47]

The legislation of the time followed Decretal law in permitting new documents to be introduced as well as new witnesses. Also, witnesses heard in the court of first instance could testify again in the court of second instance. The only change in this regard was the regulation that they be introduced in the presence of the *defensor matrimonii.* The right to bring in new proofs was permitted both to the parties and to the *defensor matrimonii.*[48]

The judge was to fix the time for the production of new evidence, and after the lapse of this time he was to inquire of the *defensor matrimonii* if he had anything further to add. Thus the *defensor matrimonii* was the last one to take part in the probatory period, after all the others had completed their testimony.[49]

46 S.C. de Prop. Fide, instr. a. 1883, n. 28—*Fontes,* n. 4901; Benedictus XIV, const. *"Dei miseratione,"* 3 nov. 1741, n. 10—*Fontes,* n. 318.

47 S. C. de Prop. Fide, instr. a. 1883, n. 28—*Fontes,* n. 4901. The Rota had similar regulations for the introduction of new proofs. Cf. *Regulae servandae in iudiciis apud S. R. Rotae Tribunal,* 4 aug. 1910, Parag. 230, n. 2—*Fontes,* n. 6461.

48 Cf. Austrian Instruction, § 186—*Analecta Juris Pontificii,* II (1857), 2537.

49 S.C. de Prop. Fide, instr. a. 1883, n. 29—*Fontes,* n. 4901.

3. Concluding Stage of the Trial

A. The Sentence

Whenever possible, the judge, before pronouncing sentence, was to submit the *integra causa* to two or three consultants experienced in the law. These men were to examine the testimony in the case and the points of law involved, and then to present their opinions to the judge.[50] Their vote was to be consultative rather than decisive.[51]

The sentence was to be signed by the judge and the secretary, and stamped with the seal of the episcopal curia. A copy of it was to be sent by means of a messenger to the parties concerned, and the fulfillment of that delivery was to be duly recorded in writing.[52]

Pre-Code authors were not in agreement as to the exact procedure to be followed in regard to an appeal from an interlocutory sentence. The controverted question was whether or not the judge of the court of second instance, in receiving an appeal from an interlocutory sentence with definitive force, also assumed jurisdiction over the principal issue.[53] The more common opinion was that the appellate court had no authority to judge the principal cause along with the interlocutory appeal. Pirhing, in writing on this point, taught that the appellate judge could pass sentence only upon what had actually been appealed. But, inasmuch as the judge in the court of first instance had not yet given a sentence on the principal issue, the judge in the appellate tribunal had no authority to render a decision on it.[54] The same view was held by Reiffenstuel.[55]

Some tribunals, however, followed a contrary practice, and hence insisted upon judging the principal issue along with the

[50] S.C. de Prop. Fide, instr. a. 1883, n. 24: "...integra causa duobus aut tribus viris peritis, si haberi possint, examinanda subiiciatur, et nonnisi audito eorum voto sententia profertur."—*Fontes,* n. 4901.

[51] Cf. Bassibey, *Le Mariage devant les Tribunaux Ecclésiastiques,* pp. 392, 393.

[52] S.C. de Prop. Fide, instr. a. 1883, n. 24—*Fontes,* n. 4901.

[53] Cf. Santi, *Praelectiones Iuris Canonici* (4. ed., 3 vols., cura M. Leitner, Ratisbonae, 1903-1905), Lib. I, tit. 28, n. 45.

[54] Lib. II, tit. 25, n. 42.

[55] Lib. II, tit. 28, n. 87.

interlocutory appeal. The custom followed in the Rota influenced this practice.[56]

Some authors made a distinction in accordance with whether the interlocutory sentence was confirmed or disavowed in the court of second instance. If it was confirmed, then the principal cause was to be judged in the court of first sentence;[57] if the sentence was disavowed in the appellate tribunal, then the principal cause was to be tried there also.[58] But even when the sentence was confirmed in the second instance, the judge of the court of first instance could renounce his rights and thereupon the whole cause pertained to the superior tribunal.

B. *Expenses of the Trial*

The Council of Trent decreed that the appellant was to pay the costs for the transfer of the acts of the court of first instance to the appellate tribunal. If the appellee wished to use these acts also, he was bound to bear a proportionate amount of the expenses of such a transfer. If it was the local custom, however, that the entire cost was to be borne by the appellant, then such a custom was permitted to prevail.

Upon receipt of a suitable fee, the notary of the court of first instance was bound to furnish the appellant within a month's time with a copy of the proceedings.[59]

The Council also declared that if a party in a matrimonial cause furnished proof of his poverty in the presence of the bishop, he was not to be compelled to litigate his case in the second instance outside the province, unless the other party was prepared to provide for his maintenance and bore the expenses of the trial.[60] Outside of this exception, the general rule of the Decretal law was observed, namely, that during the

[56] Santi, *Praelectiones Iuris Canonicis,* Lib. II, tit. 28, n. 45.

[57] Santi, *loc. cit.*

[58] Cf. Lega, *Praelectiones De Iudiciis Ecclesiasticis,* I, 544. Roberti, in his historical reference to this practice, gives as the reason: "quia iudex inferior censebatur habere animum nimis praeoccupatum ob reformationem sententiae interlocutoriae."— *De Processibus* (2 vols., Romae, 1926), II, 210.

[59] Sess. XXIV, *de ref.,* c. 20

[60] *Loc. cit.*

course of the trial the judicial expenses were shared by the litigants.[61]

At the conclusion of the trial the sentence of the appellate court was to state who was required to pay the cost of the proceedings. In general practice the losing party was to be condemned in this sentence to pay the entire costs of the trial, namely, not only the costs incurred by himself, but also the expenses of his opponent and of the court. It was presumed that a litigant who failed to establish and win his case had entered upon the proceedings carelessly and without due regard for the rights of his opponent.[62]

This was in line with the custom as practiced by the Rota. De Luca (1614-1683), however, stated that the practice of condemning the losing party to pay all the expenses was a corruption of law, and hence was not to be maintained as a reasonable custom.[63]

There were exceptions to the rule that the defeated party had to pay all the expenses. A party could ask for a *patrocinium gratuitum*. The appellate judge was to consider such a plea according to the evidence produced by the judge of the court of first instance. Recourse to the pastor was one of the recommended ways of investigating the truth of the plea.[64] Those were considered poor who had earned merely the ordinary wages of a laborer, and had no other income.[65] In 1908 the norms regulating court expenses relative to cases introduced with the Rota gave consideration to those who were not paupers, but who at the same time enjoyed only limited financial means. For them the payment of the expenses of a trial would have resulted in a considerable hardship. Consequently they were permitted to seek a reduction; for obtaining it there was

61 C. 11, *de rescriptis*, 1, 3, in VI°; c. 11, *de accusationibus, inquisitionibus et denunciationibus*, V, 1, in VI°. Cf. Smith, *The Matrimonial Process in the United States* (New York, 1895), n. 892 (hereafter cited *Matrimonial Process*).

62 Smith, *Matrimonial Process*, n. 890.

63 *Theatrum Veritatis et Justitiae* (16 vols., Coloniae Agrippinae, 1706) Tom. VII, Disc. XXXIX, nn. 7, 10, 12.

64 Gasparri, *Tractatus De Matrimonio*, II, 423.

65 Smith, *Matrimonial Process*, n. 895.

required, along with certain documents attesting to their financial condition, a libellatory petition seeking such a favor.[66]

Another cause for exemption from paying all the expenses obtained when the defeated party had a just reason or probable right for entering upon the proceedings, and therefore had acted in good faith. In that case the judge was to oblige each party to pay his own expenses, and was to assess the costs of the court equally for both litigants.

Also when the marriage was impugned *ex officio,* no costs were to be levied on those whose marriage was called into question, and who were therefore the defendants, even in the event that they lost.[67]

To insure the payment of expenses, at least partially, the judge could demand that a sum of money be deposited by the parties with the tribunal before the trial began.[68]

Although matrimonial causes never became a *res iudicata,* yet the allocation of expenses was not for that reason a matter that could be left in abeyance. The failure to observe the ten day limit for making the appeal resulted in the same issue as if the cause had become, as far as the meeting of court expenses was concerned, a *res iudicata.*[69]

C. Legal Redress against the Sentence

a. Further Appeal.

When the sentence of the appellate tribunal conformed to that in the court of first instance for the validity of the marriage bond, the party opposing the marriage could lodge a further appeal within ten days to the Holy See.[70]

The Austrian Instruction, however, did not allow a further appeal after two sentences had conformably confirmed the validity of the bond.[71]

66 Lex Propria Sacrae Romanae Rotae et Signaturae Apostolicae, Appendix, Cap. IV, nn. 3, 4.—*AAS,* I (1909), 34-35.

67 Smith, *Matrimonial Process,* n. 895.

68 Gasparri, *Tractatus De Matrimonio,* II, 423.

69 Mansella, *De Impedimentis ac de Processu Iudiciali in Causis Matrimonialibus,* p. 213.

70 S. C. de Prop. Fide, instr. a. 1883, n. 30—*Fontes,* n. 4901.

71 § 180: "Quodsi validitas in secunda instantia confirmatur, nulla amplius provocatio locum habet."—*Analecta Juris Pontificii,* II (1857), 2536. Cf. Gasparri, *De Matrimonio,* II, 421.

After two conformable sentences for the nullity of the marriage, the parties likewise had the right to appeal to the Holy See. However, if the parties did not appeal, there was no obligation upon the *defensor matrimonii* to do so, unless he felt in conscience that it was necessary.[72]

b. Use of the *Querela* and *Restitutio in Integrum*

Except in those cases in which the *defensor matrimonii* was not under any obligation to govern his action in accord with the constituted *fatalia legis,* any failure to appeal within the time limit set by the law resulted in a sentence that was a *quasi res iudicata.* The cause was not to be considered again unless there had become available such proofs as convinced the judge that the sentence might have been erroneous. This view, subscribed to under the Decretal law, was approved and given legal force by Benedict XIV.[73]

Between the time of Benedict XIV and the promulgation of the Code of Canon Law, the remedy resorted to in such a case underwent a change. The *supplicatio* of which Hostiensis (+1271) had spoken[74] became a *querela* in the time of Reiffenstuel (1642-1703). The difference was in this: whereas the *supplicatio* was addressed to the Pope, the *querela* was brought before the judge who had rendered the sentence. Scaccia, writing in the early part of the eighteenth century, pointed out that the *supplicatio* was founded on an error committed by the judge, whereas the *querela* was based upon an error of the party himself or on the fraud of the other litigant party. He also stated, however, that considerable confusion existed because of the promiscuous use of these terms. At times they were used in the same sense as *recursus, reclamatio* and *revisio.*[75]

According to Reiffenstuel, the judge, upon receiving the *querela,* had to grant a *restitutio in integrum,* if the hearing of

[72] S.C. de Prop. Fide, instr. a. 1883, n. 30—*Fontes,* n. 4901. Cf. Lega, *Praelectiones De Iudiciis Ecclesiasticis,* IV, 510.

[73] Const. *"Dei miseratione,"* 3 nov. 1741, n. 11—*Fontes,* n. 318.

[74] *Commentaria,* I, *de sententia et re iudicata,* c. 4, n. 13. Cf. Feeney, *Restitutio in Integrum,* The Catholic University of America Canon Law Studies, n. 129 (Washington, D. C.: The Catholic University of America Press, 1941), p. 42.

[75] *Tractatus de Appellationibus,* q. XVIII, n. 30.

the case was to be made possible.[76] Pirhing held that the *querela* in itself was sufficient in order that a retrial of the case take place.[77]

Before admitting a *querela,* the judge before whom the sentence had been rendered was to make a preliminary investigation of the alleged injustice in order to determine whether the party was entitled to another hearing.[78]

The practice of the Sacred Congregation of the Council regarding this procedure is not easily discernible during the centuries. Apparently not until the past century did the Congregation mention the *restitutio in integrum* whenever it allowed new hearings of marriage cases to be undertaken.

After the restoration of the Rota in 1908, the first case which bears on this point was brought into that tribunal in 1911. Two sentences had been pronounced in favor of the nullity of the marriage. The Rota, quoting Reiffenstuel, stated that a rehearing of the case became available solely *per viam querelae.* It omitted all mention of the *restitutio in integrum.*[79]

The latter remedy became useless for the reintroduction of a marriage case with the advent of the Code of Canon Law. In deciding a case soon after the publication of the Code, the Supreme Tribunal of the Signatura declared that there was no place for the *restitutio in integrum* in marriage cases, in view simply of the fact that they never became irrevocably adjudged. The *restitutio in integrum,* as a legal remedy for redress, was thenceforth to be used in the face of judicial sentences which implied that a cause had become a *res iudicata.*[80]

76 Lib. II, tit. 27, n. 138.

77 Lib. II, tit. 27, nn. 51, 52.

78 Cf. Mansella, *De Impedimentis ac de Processu Iudiciali in Causis Matrimonialibus,* p. 213.

79 Baltimoren., *Nullitatis Matrimonii,* 29 nov. 1811 dec. XLIII, n 2—*S. Romanae Rotae Decisiones seu Sententiae,* III (1911), 502 (henceforth cited as *Decisiones*).

80 Paderbornen., *Nullitatis Matrimonii,* 31 nov. 1919—*AAS,* XI (1919). 295, 297. Cf. can. 1905.

PART II

CANONICAL COMMENTARY

CHAPTER FIVE

NATURE AND ORGANIZATION OF ORDINARY COURT OF SECOND INSTANCE

ARTICLE I: DETERMINATION OF THE PROPER COURT

The Code of Canon Law enumerates a threefold hierarchy of tribunals in the Church's judicial system. The general division comprises the ordinary courts of first instance, the ordinary courts of second instance and the tribunals of the Holy See.[1]

In this classification the three tribunals are differentiated on the basis of superiority of jurisdiction which one has over the other; the ordinary court of first instance is under that of the second instance, and these two tribunals in turn are subject to the tribunals of the Holy See. Ascendency in grade from a lower to a higher court is an essential aspect in arriving at a proper concept of the Church's hierarchical system of different grades of tribunals.[2]

[1] Roberti, *De Processibus,* I (2. ed., Romae: Apud Custodiam Librariam Pontifici Instituti Utriusque Iuris, 1941), n. 82, p. 224; Wernz-Vidal, *Ius Canonicum,* V, *Ius Matrimoniale* (3. ed., a P. Philippo Aguirre recognita, Romae: Apud Aedes Universitatis Gregorianae, 1946), n. 688, p. 895; Vermeersch-Creusen, *Epitome Iuris Canonici* (6 ed., 3 vols. Mechliniae-Romae: Dessain, 1937-1946), III (1946), nn. 25, 26, p. 16 (hereafter this work will be referred to as *Epitome*); Noval, *Commentarium Codicis Iuris Canonici, Lib. IV, De Processibus,* Pars I, *De Iudiciis* (Augustae Taurinorum-Romae, 1920), n. 99, p. 52 (hereafter referred to as *De Iudiciis*); Coronata, *Institutiones Iuris Canonici* (5 vols., Taurini-Romae: Marietti), III, *De Processibus* (2. ed., 1941), n. 1110, pp. 20, 21; Blat, *Commentarium Textus Codicis Iuris Canonici,* Lib. IV, *De Processibus* (Romae, 1927), nn. 24-27, pp. 30-36 (hereafter referred to as *Commentarium*); Cocchi, *Commentarium in Codicem Iuris Canonici,* VII (3. ed., Taurini: Marietti, 1940) n. 15, pp. 39, 40 (hereafter referred to as *Commentarium*).

[2] Coronata, *Institutiones Iuris Canonici,* III, n. 1110, p. 20.

That there should be a twofold grade of jurisdiction is evident *ex iure divino* because of the powers accorded to the Supreme Pontiff and those enjoyed, under him, by the bishops. The addition of a third intermediate grade, however, is *ex iure humano.*[3]

The term "instance" is commonly used in referring to tribunals of different rank or grade, but *gradus tribunalium* and *gradus instantiarum* do not necessarily mean the same thing. For example, in the Sacred Roman Rota an appeal from one *turnus* to another is a change of instance, but the grade of the tribunal remains the same.[4]

Considered strictly, therefore, an instance refers to the judicial trial of an action[5] rather than to a superiority of one grade of tribunal over another.[6] Thus, when it is said that a matrimonial cause has been tried in the second instance, it means that it has been subject for the second time to a judicial examination and decision. It is not infrequent that a cause is tried in three instances in the tribunal of the Rota.[7]

As indicated in the Code, the ordinary courts of first and second instance are constituted as different grades of tribunals as well as courts of successive instances,[8] and proceed in virtue of ordinary power.[9]

By what norms is the ordinary court of second instance determined? Provision is made for the establishment of such tribunals by canon 1594, which reads as follows:

§ 1. *A tribunali Episcopi Suffraganei appellatur ad Metropolitam.*

§ 2. *A causis in prima instantia pertractis coram metropolita, fit appellatio ad loci Ordinarium, quem ipse Metropolita, probante Sede Apostolica, semel pro semper designaverit.*

[3] Noval, *De Iudiciis,* n. 95, p. 51.

[4] Vermeersch-Creusen, *Epitome,* III, n. 25, p. 16.

[5] "Instantia iudicialis dicitur quilibet gradus examinis et decisionis iudicialis."—Roberti, *De Processibus,* I, n. 87, p. 239.

[6] Cf. Coronata, *Institutiones Iuris Canonici,* III, n. 1110, p. 21.

[7] Cf. Wernz-Vidal, *Ius Canonicum,* VI, n. 67, p. 71.

[8] Cf. canons 1572; 1594-1596.

[9] Roberti, *De Processibus,* I, n. 106, pp. 280, 281.

§ 3. *Pro causis primum agitatis coram Archiepiscopo qui caret Suffraganeis vel coram loci Ordinario immediate Sedi Apostolicae subiecto, fit appellatio ad Metropolitam, de quo in can. 285.*

Thus, the appeal from the court of a suffragan bishop goes to the metropolitan of that particular province.[10]

When a delegated diocesan tribunal has given the first sentence in a matrimonial cause, the appeal must not be directed to the one who delegated the tribunal, but to the court of second instance. The bishop who delegated the tribunal is to be con-

[10] Special provisions have been made for some countries. For example, on December 20, 1940, the Sacred Congregation of the Sacraments, acting upon the request of the Ordinaries of the Philippine Islands, reorganized the ecclesiastical tribunals of those islands. All cases regarding the nullity of marriage in the first instance are to be considered in one of three tribunals. Those tribunals are: (1) Manila, for its entire province with the exception of the diocese of Lipa; (2) Cebu, for its entire province; and (3) Lipa. Appeals are to be made from Manila to Lipa, from Lipa to Cebu, and from Cebu to Manila. The officers of the courts of Manila and Cebu are selected by those Ordinaries who must send their cases to these tribunals.—*AAS*, XXXIII (1941), pp. 363-368.

In a letter from the Sacred Congregation of the Sacraments, July 1, 1932, directed to the "Most Excellent Archbishops, and Ordinaries of Places, Regarding the Handling of Matrimonial Cases," the following provisions were made in Sections III and IV:

"III. If in view of the smallness of his diocese and especially its scarcity of priests, any of the Most Excellent Bishops or Ordinaries of Places is unable to constitute an ecclesiastical tribunal which can perform its functions in the manner required by the special importance of the matrimonial cases and the respect due to so great a sacrament, let him not hesitate, after having well considered the importance of the matter, to ease his conscience by informing this Sacred Congregation of the aforementioned circumstances, so that it may at least temporarily relieve the situation by transferring the jurisdiction of the tribunal to the curia of some other ecclesiastical province or district, which may be better fitted, by reason of its more learned officials and other officers, to bear the burden.

"IV. The same provision to meet similar circumstances may also be resorted to in the case of those suffragan and metropolitan curiae which have been designated as appellate tribunals with the approval of the Holy See, according to canon 1594, § 3, if the circumstances there are such that in addition to the cases of first instance they are unable to handle also appellate cases. In this event, let them designate for appeals some special curia, which should if possible, be a metropolitan one; and this curia, if it is found to be endowed with the necessary qualifications, will be approved by the Holy See, always, however, without prejudice to the right of appeal to the Sacred Roman Rota according to the provisions of canon 1599."—*AAS*, XXIV (1932), 272-274. Cf. Bouscaren, *The Canon Law Digest* (2 vols., Milwaukee: Bruce, 1934-1943), I (1934), 802, 803 (hereafter cited *Digest*).

sidered as having seen the cause through the delegates. Wherefore he cannot see the cause in the higher grade.[11]

The appellate court for causes tried in the tribunal of the metropolitan see is that court which the metropolitan, with the approval of the Holy See, *semel pro semper,* designates.[12]

It is not necessary, therefore, that he choose the tribunal of another metropolitan, but he may select any tribunal of another ecclesiastical province as the court of appeal.[13] He may also choose the court of one of his own suffragans. Vermeersch-Creusen seem to imply that the metropolitan is obliged to select one of the suffragan bishops as the judge of appeals.[14] Canon 1594, § 3, does not allow for such a restricted interpretation. Coronata has likewise interpreted the provisions of this canon incorrectly. He states that for causes tried in the metropolitan court, acting as a tribunal of first instance, the appeal goes to the "tribunal dioecesis vicinioris semel pro semper electae."[15]

Causes tried in the first instance in the court of an archbishop who has no suffragan sees, or in the court of a local ordinary who stands under the immediate jurisdiction of the Apostolic See, are appealed to that metropolitan who is to be selected according to the norms of canon 285. By the provisions of that canon, bishops who are not subject to a metropolitan, and archbishops without suffragans, if they have not

11 Cf. canon 1571; Art. 218, S. C. Sacr. *Instructio Servanda a Tribunalibus Dioecesanis in Pertractandis Causis de Nullitate Matrimoniorum,* 15 aug., 1936—*AAS,* XXVIII (1936), 313-361 (hereafter this Instruction will be referred to as *Instructio*). Cf. Kay, *Competence in Matrimonial Procedure,* The Catholic University of America Canon Law Studies, n. 53 (Washington, D. C.: The Catholic University of America, 1929), p. 103; Cabreros, "Apelación contra la sentencia del juez delgado"— *Revista Española de Derecho Canonico* (Salamanca: San Pablo, 1946—), I (1946), 115, 116.

12 Canon 1594, § 2. Cf. Roberti, *De Processibus,* I, n. 84, p. 225; Gasparri, *Tractatus Canonicus de Matrimonio,* ed. nova ad mentem Codicis Iuris Canonici, II (Romae: Typis Polyglotis Vaticanis, 1932), n. 1241, p. 283 (hereafter referred to as *De Matrimonio*); Wernz-Vidal, *Ius Canonicum,* VI, n. 125, p. 108. Because the metropolitan court tries cases in both first and second instance, the same set of judges may comprise both tribunals.

13 Cf., e.g., *AAS,* XVIII (1926), 311, 345; *AAS,* XIX (1927), 56, 414; *AAS,* XXII (1930), 393.

14 "Iudex secundae instantiae est... suffranganeus semel pro semper electus, probante Sede Apostolica, pro Metropolita."—*Epitome,* III, n. 45, p. 25.

15 *Institutiones Iuris Canonici,* III, n. 1481, p. 420.

done so already, should once and for all, and with the approbation of the Holy See, choose one of the neighboring metropolitans.[16]

After the choice has been approved, no change is permitted.

ARTICLE II: COMPETENCY OF THE COURT

1. Competency Ratione Gradus

The competency of the ordinary court of second instance differs greatly from that of the lower tribunal. The general rule for judicial competence in the court of first instance is based upon territorial limits. The competent judge is the judge of the place in which the marriage took place or in which the *pars conventa* maintains a domicile or quasi-domicile. In the event that one of the parties is a non-Catholic, the competent tribunal is the diocesan court of the domicile or quasi-domicile of the Catholic party.[17]

The competency of the court of second instance, however, is based neither on the *forum contractus* nor on the *forum domicilii.* It is competent *ratione gradus.* Due to the fact that the court of second instance is the legally established appellate tribunal for a particular court of first instance, it thereby possesses the necessary jurisdiction to hear causes properly appealed from that court. This type of competency is not explicitly stated in the Code, but it is implied in a number of canons.[18]

The competency as enumerated under the title *"De foro competenti"* in canons 1560-1568 speaks only of that competency which is determined according to the elements of the cause itself, or according to territorial limits. Its purpose is to distribute and apportion the trial of specific actions among various judges, and not to define the activities of diverse tribunals in regard to their jurisdiction in respect to one and the

16 Vermeersch-Creusen, *Epitome,* III, n. 45, p. 25. Cf. Augustine, *A Commentary on the New Code of Canon Law* (8 vols., St. Louis: B. Herder and Co.), II (4. ed., 1923), p. 301 (hereafter cited *A Commentary on Canon Law*); Wernz-Vidal, *Ius Canonicum,* VI, n. 125, pp. 109, 110.

17 Canon 1964; *Instructio,* Art. 3, § 1.

18 Cf., for example, canons 1571; 1572, § 1; 1594; 1599, § 1, 1°; 1879-1891, § 1.

same cause. It is this latter type of jurisdiction which is not systematically treated in the Code, and the norms relating to it must therefore be taken from various canons in the fourth book.[19]

Roberti refers to such competency as *"competentia functionalis,"* having for its object the extent and the limitation of the jurisdiction exercised by diverse tribunals over one and the same cause. This functional competency has special application to various grades of jurisdiction and to the remedies of law against a sentence.[20]

Competency *ratione gradus* is absolute, and as a result a cause once heard in the court of first instance cannot be heard again in that grade of tribunal, but only in a superior court after an appeal has been properly filed. That this is the proper interpretation of canon 1989[21] is clear from the negative response given to the following question put to the Pontifical Commission for the Authentic Interpretation of the Code: *"An vi canonis 1989 eadem causa matrimonialis, ab uno tribunali iudicata, ab alio tribunali eiusdem gradus iterum iudicari possit."*[22]

This response was later incorporated in the *Matrimonial Instruction* of 1936.[23]

19 Cf. Roberti, *De Processibus,* I, n. 62, pp. 182, 183.

20 *De Processibus,* I, n. 62, p. 179:" De competentia... functionali, quem doctores moderni in Germania et Italia recentiore tempore introduxerunt ut eadem comprehenderent nedum varias instantias iudiciales, sed omnes activitates circa eandem causam a deiversis tribunalibus exercendas, usque adhuc loqui canonistae praetermiserunt. Quin immo ipsa Codicis schemata haud magnam lucem afferunt huic quaestioni, cum tantum initio loquantur de competentia ratione gradus et postea videantur, specie saltem, hanc ipsam praetermisissae. Codex ipse de hoc competentiae capite sub titulo de foro competenti minime loquitur.

Existentia competentiae functionalis nihilominus in Codice ferit oculos. Eadem comprehendit praesertim gradus iurisdictionis, remedia iuris contra sententiam et sententiae executionem nec non aliquot alios casus."

21 "Cum sententiae in causis matrimonialibus unquam transeant in rem iudicatam, causae ipsae, si nova argumenta praesto sint, retractari semper poterunt firmo praescripto can. 1903."

22 Resp. 16, iun. 1931—*AAS,* XXIII (1931), 353.

23 Art. 218, § 1: Causa matrimonialis ab uno tribunali iudicata, ab alio tribunali eiusdem gradus iterum iudicari nunquam potest, etiamsi praesto sint nova argumenta vel documenta, sed de ea videre potest iterum *tantummodo* tribunal superioris instantiae, praevia appellatione.

This regulation applies only when the appeal refers to the *same matrimonial cause* as that tried in the court of first instance. Art. 218, § 2, defines the same matrimonial cause as that which is concerned with the same marriage, between the same persons and tried on the same grounds of nullity.[24]

Thus, if the lower tribunal tried a cause on the basis of force and fear, the appellate court could not try the same marriage cause on the grounds of impotency. The ordinary court of second instance, competent *ratione gradus,* has appellate and not original jurisdiction.[25]

2. Prorogation of Competency

Prorogation is the extension of the competency or jurisdiction of a judge beyond its limits to persons or causes not otherwise falling under his competency or jurisdiction. The result is the transfer of competency to one judge which ordinarily belongs to another.[26]

Absolute competency[72] cannot be prorogued, and in the event that such were attempted the resulting sentence would be vitiated with irremediable nullity.[28]

Although voluntary prorogation of relative competency was permitted in pre-Code legislation, the Code of Canon Law has abolished it.[29] Nevertheless, the effect of this type of proroga-

24 "... ita intelligitur ut locum habeat si agatur revera de *eadem causa*, hoc est, propter idem matrimonium et ob idem nullitatis caput."

25 Cf. Roberti, *De Processibus,* I, n. 62, pp. 181, 182.

26 Cf. Burke, *Competence in Ecclesiastical Tribunals,* The Catholic University of America Canon Law Studies, n. 14 (Washington, D. C.: The Catholic University of America, 1922), p. 25; Roberti, *De Processibus,* I, n. 60, p. 174: "Prorogatio iurisdictionis habetur cum competentia quae ex lege propria esset alicuius iudicis in alium iudicem transfertur."

27 Absolute incompetency may arise: (1) from the dignity of the parties involved in the case; (2) from the nature of the cause in the trial; (3) from the grade of the tribunal; (4) because of the transfer of the cause to the Holy See. Cf. Burke, *Competence in Ecclesiastical Tribunals,* p. 14; Wernz-Vidal, *Ius Canonicum,* VI, n. 47, pp. 52, 53.

28 Cf. canon 1892, 1°; Vermeersch-Creusen, *Epitome,* I, n. 10, p. 9; Coronata, *Institutiones Iuris Canonici,* III, n. 1094, p. 10.

29 Canon 1559, § 1: Nemo in prima instantia conveniri potest, nisi coram iudice ecclesiastico qui competens sit ob unum ex titulis qui in can. 1560-1568 determinantur. Cf. Eichman, *Das Prozessrecht des Codex Iuris Canonici* (Paderborn: Schöningh, 1921), 48.

tion can be accomplished in a number of ways. For example, if neither the judge adverts to the fact that he is relatively incompetent, nor the parties make an exception to such incompetency, there results a prorogation of competency, and the ensuing process and sentence are valid.[30]

Notwithstanding the fact that the Code has abolished the voluntary prorogation of relative competency, the *Instruction* of 1936, in permitting a new cause to be introduced in the appellate instance, permits prorogation under certain conditions.

Article 219, § 1, in referring to the court of first instance, states that "if another basis for nullity is presented while the trial is pending, the decision must be made whether this new phase ought to be admitted according to the ordinary norms of competency. If it is admitted, the other regulations for the drawing up of the case must be observed."[31]

In § 2 of the same Article it is stated: "Si novum hoc nullitatis caput afferatur in gradu appellationis, illudque, nemine contradicente, a collegio admittatur, de eo iudicandum tamquam in prima instantia."

Thus, a new basis of nullity may by chance appear only during the course of the appellate proceedings. If it is admitted by the tribunal without objections from anyone, the decision on this point should be pronounced by the court acting as a tribunal of first instance. From a comparison of the provisions of § 2 with those contained in § 1, it seems clear that the new basis of nullity cannot be proposed in the court of second instance until after the case begins to pend.[32] This stage of the trial takes place only after the legitimate serving of the summons.[33]

[30] Roberti, *De Processibus,* I, n. 61, p. 178: "... concludere licet liberam fori prorogationem fuisse a Codice abolitam, sed effectus prorogationis adhuc multipliciter haberi posse, quandoque etiam cum antiquo iure non habebatur."

[31] "Si, lite pendente, aliud nullitatis caput offeratur, decernendum est utrum illud admitti debeat iuxta ordinarias normas competentiae; eoque admisso, serventur reliquae regulae pro causae instructione."

[32] Art. 219, § 1: Si, lite pendente, aliud nullitatis caput afferatur...

[33] Canon 1725, 5°. Cf. Lega-Bartoccetti, *Commentarius in Iudicia Ecclesiastica iuxta Codicem Iuris Canonici* (3 vols., Romae: Anonima Libraria Cattolica Italiana, 1938-1941), II (1939), n. 1, pp. 537, 538 (hereafter this work will be referred to as *Commentarius*).

If the new ground of nullity was proposed before that, for example, in the *libellus appellatorius,* the appellate court would have to remand it to the court of first instance.

The new basis of nullity may be admitted in the court of second instance under two conditions: (1) that there be no objections from anyone, and (2) that the cause be judged by the court acting as a tribunal of first instance. Thus, if neither the parties, the *defensor vinculi,* the *promoter iustitiae* (if he is engaged in the case), or the tribunal object, the new cause may be admitted. As regards the tribunal, it seems that a majority vote is sufficient,[34] and therefore the opposition of one judge would not be such as to reject the new basis of nullity.

If valid objections are brought forward and sustained by the court, the new cause would have to be remanded to the court of first instance.[35]

If it is decided to admit the new cause, the court would have to proceed as as a court of first instance, beginning with a properly formulated *libellus.*[36]

The necessity of acting as a court of first instance is demanded so as to obviate the impediment of absolute incompetency that would arise if the new cause were tried by the appellate tribunal acting as a court of second instance.[37]

Regatillo believes that the new basis of nullity should be treated separately from the cause that was appealed, due to the fact that it is a cause distinct from the latter. Being acted upon as in the court of first instance, the new cause can thus be appealed from the metropolitan court to the latter's court of second instance. The original cause which was tried both in

[34] Canon 1577, § 1.

[35] Cf. Doheny, *Canonical Procedure in Matrimonial Cases,* p. 368.

[36] Bernardini, in commenting on the *Instruction* of 1936, states: "Censemus tribunal appellationis novum caput admittere debere si omnia concurrunt quae in Art. 61-67 requiruntur."—*Apollinaris,* IX (1936), 579, note on art. 219, § 2.

[37] Cf. canon 1891, § 1. Roberti explains that the underlying reason for such a prorogation is that of the connection of one cause with the other. "Ratione connexionis competentia prorogatur, nisi obstet incompetentia absoluta. Hac ratione explicatur cur, nemine contradicente, nova causa pentendi in causis matrimonialibus admittatur etiam in secunda instantia, quia tribunalia ordinaria appellationis eadem sunt ac primae instantiae..."— *De Processibus,* I, n. 235, p. 645.

the first and second instance would of course have to go to the Rota or to the Holy Office, if a further appeal were filed.[38]

Doheny claims, however, that "if an appeal were filed against the sentence of the appellate court, the entire case with both bases of nullity would go either to the S.R. Rota or the tribunal of the Holy Office even though the sentence were pronounced as in first instance on one point."[39]

The procedure as set forth by Regatillo seems preferable. In passing sentence on the new grounds of nullity as a separate cause, the appellate court would be acting only as a court of first instance, and consequently its decision could be appealed either to that particular court's tribunal of second instance, or to Rome. The latter's courts would not enjoy such exclusive competency over it that it would have to be appealed there directly. By trying the causes separately there would be the possibility that the case would not have to be sent to Rome at all, in the event that two concordant sentences were reached and no further appeal lodged.

If the metropolitan's court of second instance were the very suffragan tribunal in which the cause first originated, the latter court could still act as the appellate tribunal for the trial in second instance on the new basis of nullity. This follows from the fact that the new cause of nullity was not first heard in its tribunal, and thus it can act upon it in the appellate instance. In these circumstances, however, a party may petition that the personnel of the court be changed, or file an exception of suspicion against the tribunal, if he feels that the judges may be prejudiced in any way.[40]

The cause which was first tried in the suffragan tribunal and later in that of the metropolitan cannot be further appealed to that same suffragan tribunal, but only to the Rota, or in the event that one of the parties is a non-Catholic, to the Holy Office.[41]

38 *Ius Sacramentarium* (2 vols., Santander: Sal Terrae, 1945-1946), II, Appendix, pp. 427, 428.

39 *Canonical Procedure in Matrimonial Cases,* p. 368.

40 Cf. canons 1613-1615; Regatillo, *Ius Sacramentarium,* II, 428.

41 Canon 1571; *Instructio,* Art. 218, § 1. Cf. Pontificia Commissio Interpretationis Codicis, resp. 16 iun. 1931—*AAS,* XXIII (1931), 353 (hereafter reference will be made to this Commission with the letters P.C.I.).

3. Disputed Competency

A. Disputed Competency between Tribunals

Article 10 of the *Instruction* states that in the event that there is a controversy between two or more tribunals as to which is competent, the rulings of canon 1612[42] are to be observed.

Consequently, if a controversy arises between two or more judges as to which is competent in a certain matter, the question is to be decided by the tribunal immediately higher. However, if the judges between whom the controversy exists are subject to different higher tribunals, the dispute is to be settled by the immediately higher tribunal of that judge before whom the action was first instituted. If this judge has no higher tribunal, the matter is to be settled by the Legate of the Holy See, if there is one, or by the Signatura Apostolica.

An illustration of the cases in which the norms of canon 1612 may be applied are the following:

(a) If a controversy involving their competency should arise between two suffragan courts of the same ecclesiastical province, the matter would be settled by the court of the metropolitan see.[43]

(b) If the dispute is between two suffragan courts of different provinces, the decision rests with the metropolitan court of that suffragan see before which the action was first presented.[44]

(c) If it is a question of disputed competency between two metropolitan sees, or between a metropolitan see and a suffragan see, or between sees subject to the Holy See, the conflict is to be settled by the Legate of the Holy See, if there is one, or by the Signatura Apostolica.

[42] § 1. Si inter duos pluresve iudices controversia oriatur quisnam eorum ad aliquod negotium competens sit, res definienda est a tribunali immediate superiore.

§ 2. Quod si iudices, inter quos existit competentiae conflictus, subsint distinctis tribunalibus superioribus, controversiae definitio reservatur tribunali superiori illius iudicis, coram quo actio primo promota est; si non habent tribunal superius, conflictus dirimitur vel a Legato Sanctae Sedis, si adsit, vel ab Apostolica Signatura.

[43] Roberti, *De Processibus,* I, n. 150, p. 437; Wernz-Vidal, *Ius Canonicum,* VI, n. 145, p. 125.

[44] Roberti, *De Processibus,* I, n. 150, p. 438.

In regard to this class, however, Wernz-Vidal believe that in the event of disputed competency, the question is to be settled by the appellate tribunal established according to the norms of canon 1594, § § 2, 3, and that it is only when such an appellate tribunal is lacking that the Legate of the Holy See or the Signatura Apostolica is to be the judge of the dispute.[45]

The more common view, however, among the authors, is that expressed by Roberti. According to the latter, the appellate tribunals of canon 1594, § § 2, 3, are excluded in controversies between courts mentioned in (c), so that the decision is to be made exclusively by the Legate or the Signatura Apostolica.[46]

This opinion seems preferable for two main reasons: (a) inasmuch as all courts have their designated tribunals of appeal, it seems that if one followed the opinion of Wernz-Vidal the conflicts envisioned by canon 1612, § 2, would never be brought before the Legate of the Holy See or the Signatura Apostolica; (b) impossible cases would otherwise result. For example, if a conflict arose between a metropolitan court and a suffragan court (the latter also being the court of second instance for the metropolitan), so that each is the appellate tribunal of the other, which one would decide the question of disputed competency? No matter which one decided it, it would be a case of *"iudex in causa propria."*[47]

It seems, therefore, that the Code has in mind the settlement of such disputes by the invocation of the hierarchical order of administrative power, rather than by relying upon the different ranks of tribunals.

The Legate of the Holy See to which canon 1612, § 2, refers can be the Papal Nuncio or Inter-Nuncio or the Apostolic

[45] *Ius Canonicum,* VI, n. 145, pp. 125, 126: "Cum tribunal appellationis sit tribunal gradus superioris, ideoque verum tribunal superius, censerem canonem [1612, § 2] esse hoc sensu intelligendum ut nomine tribunalis immediate superioris intelligatur tribunal appellationis quod infra Romanum Pontificem ex iure Codicis pro omnibus debet esse stabiliter constitutum."

[46] *De Processibus,* I. n. 150, p. 438, 439. Cf. also Noval, *De Iudiciis,* n. 195, p. 118; Blat, *Commentarium,* IV, n. 81, p. 96; Lega-Bartoccetti, *Commentarius,* I, 215; Benedetti, *Ordo Iudicialis Processus Canonici Super Nullitate Matrimonii Instruendi* (2. ed., Taurini: Marietti, 1938), pp. 16, 17, note 1 and 2 (hereafter this work will be referred to as *Ordo Iudicialis*).

[47] Roberti, *De Processibus,* I, n. 150, p. 439.

Delegate, who would exercise administrative power in deciding such conflicts.[48]

It appears, however, that both tribunals affected by the controverted competency would have to be under the authority of the Papal Legate before he could give a decision in such cases.[49] Otherwise the case would necessarily go to the Signatura Apostolica. The same would be true in the event that a country was without a Legate of the Holy See.[50]

An appeal or recourse from the decision of the higher court in those cases in which the latter tribunal is the proper judge of competency is not explicitly denied in the *Instruction*. Therefore, an appeal or recourse is possible in exceptional cases unless the decision had been made by the Signatura Apostolica.[51]

Doheny[52] does not exclude the services of the Rota for the settling of cases of disputed competency. While admitting that this course seems ruled out by the wording of canon 1612, he argues from those decisions in which the Rota has declared that it is concurrently competent with the lower tribunals.[53] In virtue of this concurrent jurisdiction, so he states, the Rota enjoys the authority necessary to settle controversies over disputed competency which are referred to it.

He proposes a second argument based on the fact that there is no definite ruling in the *Lex Propria* or the *Normae* of the S.R. Rota prohibiting this.

As a further support for his opinion, Doheny points to the terminology of Art. 31, § 2, and Art. 32, § 3, of the *Instruction* of 1936, in which the words *iudici appellationis* and *iudex ap-*

48 Cf. canon 267.

49 Cf. Roberti, *De Processibus,* I, n. 150, pp. 439, 440: "Ut Legatus possit conflictum dirimere, censemus utrumque tribunal debere eidem subici sive ob principium generale subiectionis, sive ob politicam opportunitatem."

50 Benedetti, *Ordo Iudicialis,* p. 17.

51 Doheny, *Canonical Procedure in Matrimonial Cases,* p. 29. Cf. canon 1880, 1°.

52 *Op. cit.,* pp. 29, 30.

53 Cf. *AAS,* XXV (1933), 94. Other authors make no allowance for such a procedure. Cf. Roberti, *De Processibus,* I, n. 150, pp. 437, 438; Wernz-Vidal, *Ius Canonicum,* VI, n. 145, pp. 125, 126; Coronata, *Institutiones Iuris Canonici,* III, n. 1145, p. 53; Noval, *De Iudiciis,* n. 195, p. 118; Vermeersch-Creusen, *Epitome,* III, n. 60, p. 32.

pellationis are used respectively.[54] He maintains that the addition of these very significant words to the canons,[55] which mentioned only *iudici immediate superiori,* was done precisely to permit disputed cases to be referred to the Rota for settlement.[56] On the basis of these arguments it would seem that cases of disputed competency could be settled by the Rota, at least in regard to matrimonial causes.

Because of the fact that the diocesan tribunal of second instance may be passed over and the appeal made directly to the Rota or the tribunal of the Holy Office, there could arise a question as to the respective competence of these courts in the event that an appeal is directed to both the court of second instance and a Roman tribunal. In that case which is the competent tribunal?

By the rulings of Article 216 of the *Instruction,* any conflict of jurisdiction in this regard is averted,[57] whether the appeal is filed by the *defensor vinculi* or the parties. The authority of the diocesan tribunal is superseded by that of the Rota or the Holy Office. Consequently, even though a party or the *defensor vinculi* has appealed to the ordinary court of second instance, the possibility of an appeal to the Holy See is still available. However, if the court of second instance has already sent out the citations according to the prescriptions

[54] Art. 31, § 2: Si ipsemet Ordinarius sit iudex et contra ipsum exceptio suspicionis opponantur, vel abstineat a iudicando vel quaestionem suspicionis definiendam committat iudici immediate superiori (canon 1614, § 2), seu iudici appellationis.

Art. 32, § 3: Quod si ipsemet Ordinarius declaratus fuerit suspectus idem peragat iudex immediate superior (canon 1615, § 3), seu iudex appellationis.

[55] 1614, § 2; 1615, § 3.

[56] *Canonical Procedure in Matrimonial Cases,* p. 71.

[57] §1. Tum defensor vinculi tum partes possunt, omisso medio, si id expedire iudicent in causis praesertim magni momenti, ad S. R. Rotam, vel in casu de quo in art. 12, ad tribunal S. Officii appellare.

§ 2. Si appellantium alteruter ad praefata tribunalia Sanctae Sedis provocet, coram tribunalibus istis appellatio exclusive prosequenda est.

§ 3. Ita pariter parti, quae ad tribunal appellationis dioecesanum tempore utili provocavit, ius est petendi ut de sua appellatione videat S. R. Rota, vel, in casu art. 12, tribunal S. Officii, nisi tamen a tribunali appellationis dioecesano citationes iam legitime factae fuerint (cf. art. 85). Itidem dicendum de vinculi defensore.

of law,[58] it thereby assumes exclusive jurisdiction over the cause, in the sense that an appeal to the Holy See is no longer possible until the sentence has been given by the court of second instance.

After the summons has been legally served, the case is no longer a *res integra,* and the jurisdiction of the competent court issuing the summons becomes permanently established against other competent tribunals. Before the official serving of the summons the parties and the *defensor vinculi* were free to choose between the tribunals of the Holy See and the ordinary diocesan court of second instance, but with the issuing of the citations by the latter the parties concerned are confined to its jurisdiction.

B. Exception of Competency against Tribunal

The preceding discussion was concerned with the question of the competency of one tribunal in relation to another. Sometimes the parties in a matrimonial case, without reference to any other tribunal, may question the competency of a certain tribunal itself to judge the case. The exception of competency thus pleaded will now be considered mainly in its relation to the possibility of an appeal from the decisions of the court involved regarding its own competency.

It is a general rule that the tribunal is bound to examine the question of its competency before accepting a cause for judicial examination and decision.[59]

If an exception of incompetency is lodged against a tribunal, it should be presented and reviewed before the *litis contestatio.*[60] Thus, the Code in permitting the parties to raise exceptions against a tribunal insists nevertheless that this be done before the trial gets under way. With the *litis contestatio* the nature and scope of the cause is clearly defined and the instance of the trial formally begins.[61] However, the exception of absolute

58 Cf. canon 1725, 1°, 2°, 5°; *Instructio,* Art. 85.

59 Canon 1609, § § 1, 2.

60 Cf. canon 1726; *Instructio,* Art. 87 sq.

61 Canons 1726; 1732.

incompetency of the tribunal can be entered at any stage of the trial or instance of the case.[62]

If an exception of relative incompetency is brought against a tribunal and the court declares itself competent, there is no appeal from such a ruling.[63] If, however, the tribunal should declare itself relatively incompetent, the party who considers himself aggrieved may appeal to the higher tribunal within a period of ten days.[64]

This period of ten days is equitable time,[65] and should be computed from the date of the receipt of the notification of the court's decision on this matter by the party. It is not obligatory that the appeal in such a case from the court of first instance be directed to the ordinary court of second instance, as there is no restriction placed as to the tribunal. Consequently, it may be made also to the tribunal of the Rota, if the party so desires. An appeal from the court of second instance, however, would necessarily go to the Holy See.

In cases of absolute incompetency the appeal should be made within ten days to the higher tribunal against the decision of the lower court for the confirmation or rejection of the objection on the grounds of such incompetency.[66] The period of time permitted for the lodging of an appeal in cases of absolute incompetency is also ten days, equitable time.[67] This period does not begin until the date the parties become cognizant of their right to appeal or from the time that they are enabled to appeal.

When a court of first instance declares itself absolutely incompetent, the appeal may be lodged from the lower tribunal to the ordinary court of second instance or to the Rota. From a court of second instance such an appeal would have to go to the Rota.

62 Canon 1628, § 2.

63 Canon 1610, § 2; *Instructio,* Art. 28. Cf. Roberti, *De Processibus,* I, n. 149, pp. 435, 436.

64 Canon 1610, § 3; *Instructio,* Art. 28, § 2.

65 Cf. canon 35.

66 *Instructio,* Art. 29.

67 Cf. canon 35.

ARTICLE III: PERSONNEL OF THE COURT

1. The Collegiate Tribunal

The appellate tribunal is to be constituted in the same manner as the court of first instance.[68]

Canon 1596 states that if the cause in the court of first instance was heard before a collegiate tribunal, it must also be heard before a collegiate tribunal in the appellate instance. The latter court must comprise a number of judges not fewer than the number employed in the lower court.[69]

Now, according to canon 1576, § 1, 1°, the collegiate tribunal before which marriage causes *de vinculo* must be tried is to consist of three judges. In Art. 13 the *Instruction* states that *at least* three judges are required for the trial of such causes.[70] In the light of this article in the *Instruction* it appears that, although only three judges are essential, the Ordinary may commit a cause to a tribunal of five judges, if he so desires. This conclusion can also be drawn from canon 1565, § 2.[71]

If a tribunal of less than three judges tries a matrimonial cause in which the nullity of the bond is brought into question, the resulting sentence is vitiated by irremediable nullity.[72]

68 Canon 1595; *Instructio,* Art. 213. Cf. Noval, *De Iudiciis,* n. 158, pp. 88, 89; Coronata, *Institutiones Iuris Canonici,* III, n. 1131, p. 42; Wernz-Vidal, *Ius Canonicum,* VI, n. 126, p. 110.

69 Canon 1596: "...nec a minore iudicum numero definiri debet."

70 "...causae de vinculo matrimonii tribunali collegiali trium saltem iudicum reservantur."

71 "Loci Ordinarius tribunali collegiali trium vel quinque iudicum cognitionem committere potest etiam aliarum causarum, idque praesertim faciat quando de causis agitur quae, attentis temporis, loci et personarum adiunctis et materia iudicii, difficiliores et maioris momenti videantur." Cf. Labouré-Byrnes, *Procedure in the Diocesan Matrimonial Courts of First Instance* (New York: Benziger Bros., 1928), n. 38, p. 11 (henceforth this work will be referred to as *Procedure*).

72 Canon 1892, 1°. Examples of causes appealed to the S. R. Rota that had been tried by only one judge, and thus were in need of sanation, may be found in various decisions of the Rota. Cf. e.g., *Nullitatis Matrimonii,* 12 nov. 1924, dec. XLIII—*Decisiones,* XVI (1934), 383, 391; *Nullitatis Matrimonii,* 2 dec. 1924, dec. XLVII—*Decisiones,* XVI (1934), 416; *Nullitatis Matrimonii,* 31 jul. 1928, dec. XXXVII—*Decisiones,* XX (1936), 342, 346. In missionary countries matrimonial causes may be decided according to special instructions or indults issued by the competent Congregations. Cf. *Instructio,* Art. 13, § 2. These special instructions or indults frequently permit marriage cases of nullity to be tried by only one judge. Cf. Payen, *De Matrimonio in Missionibus ac Potissimum in Sinis Tractatus Practicus et Casus* (2. ed., 3 vols., Zi- ka-wei; Typographia T'ou-sè-wè, 1935-1936), III (1936), n. 7, p. 507 (hereafter this work will be cited as *De Matrimonio*).

Does this provision apply with equal force to both the court of first instance and also the court of the second instance? Kay,[73] in writing on this question, admits that the court of appeal should be composed of judges in no lesser number than that employed in the lower tribunal, but that this "is not required, however, under pain of invalidity of the sentence. Canon 1576, § 1, 1°, legislates for the ordinary tribunal of first instance. Canon 1596, which treats of the ordinary tribunal of second grade does not require any definite number of judges under pain of invalidity." He refers to Roberti[74] and Vermeersch-Creusen[75] in support of his opinion, but these authors, it must be pointed out, were referring to the acts of the process, exclusive of the sentence.

It is difficult to see how the opinion mentioned above can be sustained. It is true that canon 1576, § 1, 1°, which provides for a collegiate tribunal of three judges, is found under the chapter heading *"De Tribunali Ordinario Primae Instantiae,"*[76] and that canon 1892, 1°, specifically refers to the necessity of that provision in canon 1576, § 1, 1°, under the pain of nullity of the sentence. In the light of other canons and the *Instruction* of 1936, however, it appears that the same provisions apply to the ordinary courts of second instance also.

Canon 1596 states that the court of appeal must be established in the same manner as the court of first instance, and that the same rules, adapted to the procedure of appeals, are to be followed as in the lower tribunal. In order to comply with this provision, it seems that, if the collegiate tribunal of three judges is demanded under pain of nullity of the sentence in the court of first instance, the same rule should apply in the court of second instance. Otherwise there would be a radical difference between the two tribunals which are instructed to proceed in the "same method and manner."[77]

Article 13 of the *Instruction* seems to confirm this opinion, inasmuch as it requires a collegiate tribunal of at least three

[73] *Competence in Matrimonial Procedure,* p. 105.

[74] *De Processibus* (Romae, 1926), I, n. 108, p. 178.

[75] *Epitome,* III, n. 45, p. 25.

[76] Canons 1572-1593.

[77] Cf. *Instructio,* Art. 213.

judges for matrimonial causes *de vinculo,* without distinguishing between the courts of first and second instance, and then adds the phrase: *"sententia autem forte prolata contra huiusmodi praescriptum vitio insanabilis nullitatis laborat."*[78]

The purpose of the stringency of this ruling is just as evident in the court of second instance as in the lower tribunal. Questions involving the bond of marriage are too sacred and important to be entrusted to the decision of one judge.

In general, this specific question is not treated by writers on the subject of matrimonial procedure. Doheny, in referring to the organization of the matrimonial tribunal of second instance, cites canons 1576, § 1, 1°; 1892, 1°; and art. 13 of the *Instruction.* It can be concluded from these references to the Code and to the *Instruction,* that he subscribes to the opinion that a sentence given by the court of second instance by less than three judges would be vitiated by irremediable nullity.[79]

Conclusions drawn from a Rota decision in 1930 give further support to this opinion.[80] In a case involving property rights, the tribunal which decided it in first instance was composed of three judges, but only one judge rendered the decision in the court of second instance. The Rota affirmed that the decision in the latter court, although illicit because of canon 1596, was nevertheless valid. It also declared that canon 1576, § 1, 1°, referred to only a specific kind of causes, and that, by analogy it could not be applied to other causes. From this it could be concluded that in causes *de vinculo* which are mentioned in canon 1576, § 1, 1°, a sentence given by an appellate tribunal of less than three judges would not only be illicit but irremediably null as well. A similar conclusion is reached by Coronata, who, in referring to the above mentioned decision of the Rota regarding the validity of the sentence in the appellate tribunal, states: "Id tamen valet solum pro casu quo non agatur de causis in can. 1576, § 1, 1°."[81]

78 *Instructio,* Art. 13, § 1.

79 *Canonical Procedure in Matrimonial Cases,* p. 356.

80 *Proprietatis,* 11 aug. 1930, dec. LII—*Decisiones,* XXII (1938), 587, 590.

81 *Interpretatio Authentica Codicis Iuris Canonici et circa Ipsum Sanctae Sedis Iurisprudentia, 1916-1940* (Taurini-Romae: Marietti, 1940), p. 364, can. 1596 (hereafter cited *Interpretatio Authentica*).

If, in violation of canon 1576, § 1, 1°, a sentence of irremediable nullity should result, does it also follow that the acts of the process are in the same way null and void? Cappello[82] states that both the process and the sentence result in invalidity.

In virtue of canon 1892, 1°, however, only the *sentence* becomes null and void when the required number of judges is lacking according to the norms of canon 1576, § 1, 1°. No invalidating effect is mentioned in regard to the acts of the process itself. Roberti likewise holds this view,[83] and, in stating that the individual acts of the process are not affected, refers to canon 1680, § 1, by whose provisions an act is null and void only when either the essential constituents of the act are wanting, or when there are lacking some formalities or conditions which are demanded under pain of nullity by the canons.

No argument can be gained from canon 1596,[84] inasmuch as it mentions no invalidating effect in the event that its regulation is violated.[85]

Would the sentence also be null and void if a tribunal of five judges decided the cause in the court of first instance, and only three judges acted in the appellate tribunal? From what has already been said, it can easily be seen that it would be illicit, [86] but not invalid. Only three judges are necessary for matrimonial causes *de vinculo*.[87] Any additional judges are ap-

82 *Tractatus Canonicus de Sacramentis,* III, Pars II, *De Matrimonio* (4. ed., Romae: Apud Aedes Universitatis Gregorianae, 1939), n. 873, 416 (hereafter cited *De Sacramentis*).

83 *De Processibus,* I (1941), n. 111, pp. 289, 290: "...deficiente statuto numero iudicum, sententia sive definitiva sive interlocutoria semper nullitate laborat (canon 1892, 1°), quia reprobatur quaelibet contraria consuetudo et revocatur quodlibet contrarium privilegium (canon 1576, § 1, 1°) ante Codicem concessum (art. 13, § 1); singuli vero actus processuales non item, cum pro iisdem non urgeatur sanctio nullitatis."

84 "Si collegialiter causa in prima instantia cognita fuerit, etiam in gradu appellationis collegialiter nec a minore iudicum numero definiri debet."

85 Vermeersch-Creusen, *Epitome,* III, n. 45, p. 25: "Hoc tamen praescriptum validitatem actorum non afficit." The same opinion is expressed by Roberti, *De Processibus,* I (1941), n. 111, p. 290, and Vlaming, *Praelectiones Iuris Matrimonii* (3. ed., 2 vols., Bussum in Hollandia, 1919-1921), II (1921), n. 790, p. 375, note (1).

86 Canon 1596.

87 Canon 1576, § 1, 1°.

pointed at the will of the Ordinary, and not in fulfillment of the requirements of the law. Canon 1892, 1°, indicates that a sentence is incurably null only when less than three judges decide a case. Consequently, the same invalidity could not result if five judges pronounced sentence in the court of first instance and only the lawfully required three in the appellate tribunal.

On the other hand, if there were only three judges in the court of first instance, it is permitted to have three or five in the second instance.[88] Labouré-Byrnes have evidently interpreted the phrase, *"nec a minore iudicum numero definiri debet"* of canon 1596, as meaning the same as "an equal number of judges."[89] The canon, however, does not allow for such an unwarranted restriction.

2. Change of Judges in Different Tribunals

One who has judged a cause in one grade of tribunal cannot also be a judge of the same cause in another grade.[90] The same group of judges may decide the same case only once. One of the purposes of an appeal court is to have different persons examine the same cause.

According to Wernz-Vidal,[91] if a bishop from whose sentence an appeal has been taken were in the meantime promoted to the metropolitan see, he could judge the cause again in the appellate instance since *"quasi alius homo videtur."* Connolly,[92] following this opinion, goes on to say that such a person "would be occupying another office; he would be the same person but clothed with a new dignity." These authors recommend, however, that in the interests of justice the metropolitan should designate another to hear the cause, or simply leave the matter to his *officialis* who would be a *persona diversa.*

It is difficult to find canonical support for the foregoing opinion. It is expressly stated in canon 1571: "Qui causam

88 Cf. Noval, *De Iudiciis,* n. 159, p. 89.

89 *Procedure,* n. 236, p. 108: "Canon 1596 provides that both tribunals shall be composed of the same number of judges. When the lower court has been composed of three judges, the appellate tribunal must also be composed of three judges."

90 Canon 1571.

91 *Ius Canonicum,* VI, pp. 556, 557, note (52).

92 *Appeals,* The Catholic University of American Canon Law Studies, n. 79 (Washington, D.C.: The Catholic University of America, 1932), p. 141.

vidit in uno iudici gradu, nequit eandem causam in alio iudicare." Noval,[93] in his commentary on this canon, seems justified in pointing out that *"qui"* refers either to the tribunal or to the individual judge, and that in either case a judge is incompetent to try the same case in the appellate instance if he had previously passed judgment on it in the court of first instance. If such were done, he continues, the trial would be null and void.

Roberti is also of this opinion.[94] He notes that the Code is not in agreement with the opinion of pre-Code authors who considered the judge of the first instance "tamquam alium hominem" after he was made an archbishop and as such became competent to judge a cause again in the appellate instance.[95]

3. Other Officials of the Court

Besides the collegiate tribunal, other essential officials in the court of second instance are a *defensor vinculi,*[96] a notary,[97] and, when the cause demands it, a *promotor iustitiae.*[98]

The presiding judge of the collegiate tribunal should designate one of the associate judges as *ponens* or referee. With the consent of the tribunal the presiding judge can fulfill the office of *ponens* himself.[99]

Other officers, although not necessary, may be appointed to expedite the process.[100] Such officers are: an auditor,[101] court messengers and apparitors.[102]

The manner of appointing these officials is the same as in court of first instance. If not previously taken, the oaths are to be administered to the judges and all members of the court.[103]

[93] *De Iudiciis,* n. 105, p. 56.

[94] *De Processibus,* I, (1941), n. 87, p. 240: "... iudex qui causam iudicavit in primo gradu nequit eandem rursus examinare, e.g., ut membrum tribunalis metropolitani."

[95] *Op. cit.,* n. 87, p. 240, note (2): "Ante Codicem... poterat accidere ut eadem persona bis causam examinaret, e.g., si iudex primae instantiae interea factus esset archiepiscopus: eamdem personam sub nova dignitate tamquam alium hominem doctores considerabant." Cf. Coronata, *Institutiones Iuris Canonici,* III, n. 1114, p. 23.

[96] Canons 1586; 1967; *Instructio,* Art. 15, § 1.

[97] Canon 1585; *Instructio,* Art. 17.

[98] Canons 1586; 1971; *Instructio,* Art. 16.

[99] Canon 1584; *Instructio,* Art. 22.

[100] Cf. Roberti, *De Processibus,* I, (1941), n. 92, p. 249.

[101] Canon 1580; *Instructio,* Art. 23.

[102] Canon 1591-1593; *Instructio,* Art. 18.

[103] Canon 1621; *Instructio,* Art. 20.

CHAPTER SIX

THE RIGHT TO APPEAL

According to canon 1879, a party who feels himself aggrieved by a sentence has the right to appeal, that is, to refer a cause to a higher court from the tribunal that has rendered the sentence.

This legal redress called appeal is derived *quoad substantiam,* i.e., in so far as it constitutes a means of defense, from the principle of the natural law which forbids the denial of the right of defense; however, *quoad formam,* i.e., inasmuch as it is a determined species of defense, it is derived from and subject to the rules of positive law. While safeguarding the right of defense, the natural law does not prescribe that the right must be actualized through any one particular kind of defense, as in this case, by having a new examination of the cause before a higher tribunal.[1]

Thus it is that the Church, through its Code of Canon Law, has considered it as properly within its province to set up restrictions in regard to the particular persons who shall enjoy the right to appeal to a higher court. Having ever in mind the common good and the salvation of individual souls, it has been extremely careful to avoid any injustice in its provisions relating to the right of appeal.

Three classes of individuals are permitted the right to appeal: (1) the consorts, and their procurators and advocates; (2) the *defensor vinculi;* (3) the *promotor iustitiae.*[2]

The first three articles of this chapter will investigate the conditions under which each of these persons may enjoy the right to appeal to a higher tribunal, and the fourth article will

[1] Cf. Noval, *De Iudiciis,* n. 639, p. 419; Coronata, *Institutiones Iuris Canonici,* III, n. 1408, p. 319; Lega-Bartoccetti, *Commentarius,* II, n. 2, pp. 974, 975; Roberti, *De Processibus,* II, n. 467, p. 197; Król, *The Defendant in Contentious Trials,* The Catholic University of America Canon Law Series, n. 146 (Washington, D. C.: The Catholic University of America Press, 1942), pp. 166, 167.

[2] Cf. canon 1879; *Instructio,* Art. 212, § 1.

treat of the possibility of an appeal after the death of one or both of the consorts.

ARTICLE I.

THE CONSORTS, AND THEIR PROCURATORS AND ADVOCATES

Consorts who have been legally permitted to impugn the validity of their marriage[3] in the court of first instance, have the right to appeal to a higher court when an adverse sentence is pronounced against them.[4] If they merely had the right to denounce the nullity of their marriage, either through themselves[5] or through others, in the lower tribunal,[6] they are lacking in the procedural capacity later to lodge an appeal. Canon 1971 clearly shows the distinction between the attack upon a marriage and its denunciation. To attack a marriage, *accusare matrimonium,* is a strictly judicial act whereby the party takes legal action before a competent ecclesiastical court. Denunciation, on the other hand, is only a formal notification to the Ordinary or the *promotor iustitiae* of certain facts and information whereby a marriage may be rightfully attacked or impugned by the *promotor iustitiae.*[7]

Whenever the first sentence is in favor of the nullity of the marriage, the *defensor vinculi* has a strict obligation in law to file an appeal.[8] If it should happen that one party may uphold the validity of the marriage while the other party attacks it, it is evident that the appeal of the *defensor vinculi* can accidentally benefit the party who defends the validity of the marriage. This does not mean, however, that such a party is prevented thereby from filing a separate appeal. It is thus

3 Canon 1971, § 1, 1°; *Instructio,* Art. 35, § 1, 1°; 37.

4 Canon 1879; *Instructio,* Art. 212, § 1. Cf. Coronata, *Institutiones Iuris Canonici,* III, n. 1498, p. 436; Wernz-Vidal, *Ius Canonicum,* V, n. 703, p. 914; Cappello, *De Sacramentis,* III, n. 886, p. 433.

5 *Instructio,* Art. 37, § 4; canon 1971, § 2. P.C.I., resp. 12 mart. 1929—*AAS,* XXI (1929), 171; P.C.I., resp. 17 febr., 1930—*AAS,* XXII (1930), 196; P.C.I., resp. 17 iul. 1933, ad I, II, III—*AAS,* XXV (1933), 345. Cf. Toso, "De matrimonio accusando vel denunciando"—*Ius Pontificium* (Romae, 1921—), XVII (1937), 5-12.

6 Canon 1971, § 2; *Instructio,* Art. 35, § 2.

7 Cf. Toso, "De munere promotoris iustitiae matrimonium accusantis"—*Ius Pontificium,* XVIII (1938), 4. Cf. Art. III of this chapter, p. 83 sq.

8 Canon 1986; *Instructio,* Art. 212, § 2.

possible that two appeals may be filed against the one sentence: one by the *defensor vinculi,* and the other by the party defending the validity of the marriage.[9]

Do procurators and advocates of the consorts also enjoy the right to appeal? By the provisions of canon 1664, § 2, it is clear that at least the procurator has this right. In fact he has not only the right but also the duty to file an appeal. It is presumed, however, that the party has not expressly withheld this right from him.[10]

According to the provisions of article 52, § 2, of the *Instruction,* it would seem that the advocate also has the right and the duty to appeal. After treating, in the first paragraph of this article, of the conditions under which both procurators and advocates may be removed from their office, the *Instruction,* in the second paragraph of the same article states: "Mandatum expirat causa per sententiam definitivam decisa, salvo iure et officio interponendae appellationis inter decendium, nisi mandans renuat."

It will be observed that there is a significant difference in terminology employed in canon 1664, § 2, as compared with article 52, § 2, of the *Instruction.* The specific mention in canon 1664, § 2, of only the procurator as having the right and duty to appeal, is omitted in article 52, § 2. In the latter, it can be logically concluded that the reference is to the same persons mentioned in the preceding paragraph in which both the procurator and the advocate are mentioned. Taking article 52, therefore, as a unit, it would seem that, at least in marriage cases, the advocate, like the procurator has the right and the duty to appeal, unless the party has expressly refused to permit it.[11] In the event that the procurator files an appeal, the advocate has no obligation to file a second one.

Ordinarily, the mandate of appointment of a procurator and of an advocate is valid for the trial in only one instance. Due to the fact, however, that a marriage cause *de vinculo*

[9] Cf. *Instructio,* Art. 212, § 3.

[10] Canon 1664, § 2: "Lata definitiva sententia, ius et officium appellandi, si mandans non renuat, procuratori manet."

[11] Doheny, *Canonical Procedure in Matrimonial Cases,* p. 118.

must be tried in at least two instances, the authorization[12] of attorney and advocate is generally given in specific terms for both instances of the trial. It is nevertheless necessary that new approval of the attorney and advocate be obtained in the appellate instance.[13] Unless the mandate specifically states that the authorization of these legal assistants is for both instances, the presumption as well as the law would be in favor of authorization for only one instance. A mandate to represent a party in court is extremely important, due to the fact that a sentence is vitiated by irremediable nullity if a person acted in the name of another without a legitimate mandate.[14]

The parties are free, if they so desire, to select new attorneys and advocates for the second instance. This will frequently be found to be a more convenient practice.

Owing to the rôle of the *defensor vinculi,* the procurator or advocate of a client upholding the validity of the marriage bond is not compelled to file an appeal against a declaration of nullity. The appeal of the defender of the bond would suffice, although the legal assistant may likewise lodge an appeal if he wishes to do so.[15]

An appeal cannot be filed before the sentence has been formally published.[16] The question may arise whether the parties, and in particular their legal assistants, must await that publication in order to receive the information relative to the sentence rendered. Publication of the sentence, it will be noted, may occur a month after the actual decision has been given.[17]

The question assumes a practical aspect, especially when the client and agent are separated by a great distance, inasmuch as only ten days are permitted for the filing of an appeal. Following the practice of the Rota,[18] the *Instruction* of 1936 helps to

12 Canon 1987.

13 Cf. Coronata, *Institutiones Iuris Canonici,* III, p. 95, note 4.

14 Canon 1892, 3°.

15 Cf. canons 1887, § 1; 1986; *Instructio,* Art. 212, § 3. Cf. also Hogan, *Judicial Advocates and Procurators,* The Catholic University of America Canon Law Studies, n. 133 (Washington, D. C.: The Catholic University of America Press, 1941), p. 166.

16 *Instructio,* Art. 196.

17 *Instructio,* Art. 200. Cf. Hogan, *op. cit.,* p. 167.

18 *Regulae servandae in iudiciis apud S. R. Rotae Tribunal,* 4 aug., 1910, § 179—*AAS,* II (1910), 835.

remedy such a situation. Provided that the tribunal has not ordained secrecy, the court's decision may be made known orally, and even in writing, upon request. Such a communication of the decision has no bearing on the time limit set for the interposing of the appeal.[19]

If during the trial the indication is that the decision may be placed under secrecy, the legal assistant may consider proposing a timely request with a view toward obtaining the decision himself under oath of secrecy for specific reasons.[20]

When a marriage is attacked by the *promotor iustitiae* in accordance with articles 35, § 1, n. 2; 38 and 39 of the *Instruction,* the consort who lacks the right to impugn the marriage may appoint an advocate.[21] In the event that there is an appeal, only the *promotor iustitiae* could file it. The advocate has the right to appeal only when the consort whom he represents has legitimately impugned the marriage.

ARTICLE II. THE DEFENSOR VINCULI

The *defensor vinculi* has not only the right[22] but also the obligation to appeal, within the time prescribed by law, to a higher tribunal from the first instance in which a marriage was declared null and void. If he neglects to do so, he can be compelled by the presiding judge of the lower court to lodge the appeal.[23]

19 *Instructio,* Art. 199.

20 *Regulae servandae in iudiciis apud S. R. Rotae Tribunal,* 4 aug., 1910, § 179, n. 2—*AAS,* II (1910), 835; Hogan, *Judicial Advocates and Procurators,* p. 168.

21 *Instructio,* Art. 46.

22 Canon 1879; *Instructio,* Art. 212, § 1. Cf. Haring, "Gelten die Notfristen auch für den *defensor vinculi* im Eheprozess?"—*Theologisch-praktische Quartalschrift* (Linz-1832—), LXXXIII (1930), 597, 598.

23 Canon 1936; *Instructio,* Art. 212, § 2. Cf. Noval, *De Iudiciis,* n. 868, p. 578; Cappello, *De Sacramentis,* III, n. 886, p. 433; Muñiz, *Procédimientos Eclesiásticos* (2. ed., 3 vols., Sevilla, 1925), III, n. 466 pp. 396-397; Wernz-Vidal, *Ius Canonicum,* V, n. 704, p. 914; Lega-Bartoccetti, *Commentarius,* II, n. 1, p. 977; Coronata, *Institutiones Iuris Canonici,* III, n. 1498, p. 436; Dolan, *The Defensor Vinculi,* p. 101; Augustine, *A Commentary on Canon Law,* V (1919), 432; Cappello, *Praxis Processualis,* Taurini-Romae: Marietti, 1940), n. 123, p. 107.

The judge of the court of second instance has no authority to command that this appeal be lodged, for he has as yet no legal cognizance of the cause.[24]

The appeal on the part of the *defensor vinculi* from a sentence of nullity does not necessarily indicate that it is based on his disagreement with the sentence in the lower court. He appeals primarily for the reason that the law commands it, and he does so with a view to the greater security in the judgment obtained from the consideration of the same cause by more than one tribunal.[25]

If the sentence in the court of first instance stood for the validity of the marriage, the *defensor vinculi* is unable to lodge an appeal against the sentence, and in the event that the parties fail to do so, the case is ended.[26] The right of the *defensor vinculi* to appeal is based on his office, and hence his rights cannot extend beyond the scope of his duties as defender of the marriage bond. Certainly it is not his duty as *defensor vinculi* to appeal from a sentence which declares a marriage valid; on the contrary, he would be acting in contradiction to his official obligations in so doing. Not being a party personally concerned in this action, but an official,[27] he may appeal only when he is commissioned by law to do so. "Not being so authorized, he not only should not appeal, but he cannot appeal from the first definitive sentence for validity."[28]

An appeal filed by the *defensor vinculi* can benefit the party who upheld the validity of the marriage, without impeding in any way the party's own personal right to appeal. It should be noted, however, that the appeal filed by a party does not exempt the *defensor vinculi* from the obligation of filing a separate appeal. This is explicitly stated in article 212, § 3, of the *Instruction* of 1936.[29]

[24] Cf. Roberti, "De appellatione defensoris vinculi in causis matrimonialibus."—*Apollinaris,* II (1929), 517, 518.

[25] Wernz-Vidal, *Ius Canonicum,* V, p. 903, note 37.

[26] Coronata, *Institutiones Iuris Canonici,* III, n. 1498, p. 436.

[27] Cf. Cappello, *De Sacramentis,* III, n. 880, p. 423.

[28] Dolan, *The Defensor Vinculi,* p. 101; cf. Wernz-Vidal, *Ius Canonicum,* V, n. 703, p. 914.

[29] "Appellatio a vinculi defensore interposita prodest et parti quae pro matrimonii validitate stat, salvo illi iure proprio appellandi; appellatio e contra a parte interposita vinculi defensorem non relevat ab obligatione appellandi."

In the light of this clear declaration of the *Instruction,* therefore, the opinion of Vlaming can no longer be held.[30] According to him, the *defensor vinculi* must appeal only when the defendant whose marriage has been declared null and void refuses to appeal; if the defendant appeals, the *defensor vinculi* is thereby freed from his obligation of appealing.[31]

Even before the appearance of the *Instruction* of 1936, no support can be found in the Code for such an opinion.[32]

ARTICLE III. THE PROMOTOR IUSTITIAE

Thanks to the *Instruction* of 1936, the office and the duties of the *promotor iustitiae* are now outlined more clearly and more fully than ever before. In some tribunals the *promotor iustitiae* was looked upon as a supernumerary official of the court,[33] perhaps due to the lack of knowledge of his duties and responsibilities, and to a misunderstanding as to his proper place in matrimonial procedure.[34]

The *Instruction* gives clear and practical norms that are a great aid in setting forth the proper procedure in cases that were previously somewhat involved.

At the outset, it may prove helpful to state the general principle that the right of the *promotor iustitiae* to appeal from an adverse sentence flows from his right to impugn a marriage in the lower tribunal. Article 35, § 1, 2°, of the *Instruction* declares that he may attack the validity of a marriage: (1) In his own right and without any precious denunciation, in impedi-

30 *Praelectiones Iuris Matrimonii,* II, n. 802, p. 383.

31 The opinion of Connolly in this regard is not clear. Although he states that the *defensor vinculi* must appeal whether the party against whom the sentence has been pronounced has or has not been appealed, nevertheless he seems to agree with the opinion of Vlaming as an "obvious qualification."—*Appeals,* p. 65.

32 Cf. Labouré-Byrnes, *Procedure,* n. 227, p. 104; Dolan, *The Defensor Vinculi,* p. 104.

33 Doheny, *Canonical Procedure in Matrimonial Cases,* p. 75.

34 In Spain the *promotor iustitiae* is not only an important official in trials, but also in various administrative matters of the diocese. Cf. Muñiz, *Procédimientos Eclesiáticos,* I, n. 134, p. 118: "En las curias españolas se le da al Fiscal por costumbre intervención en todos pleitos y aún en muchos asuntos gubernativos, algunos de ellos por prescripción de la ley, como los arreglos parraquiales, y hasta en los expedientes de dispensas matrimoniales en algunas diócesis."

ments that are public by their very nature;[35] (2) in other impediments, after a previous denunciation, if the denunciator lacks the right to institute legal action to obtain a declaration of nullity of his marriage, under the proper safeguard, however, of the regulations of articles 38 and 39 of the *Instruction*.

Article 38 states that in cases of denunciation of the nullity of a marriage by one or both consorts inasmuch as either or both (1) excluded the marriage itself by a positive act of the will, or every right to the marital act or to any essential property of the marriage, or (2) placed a condition contrary to the substance of marriage, the *promotor iustitiae* should not impugn the marriage, but should exhort the parties, to the best of his ability, to consider the matter in conscience and to remove the cause, if possible, of the impediment; for example, by the renewal of the consent.[36] Under four conditions, however, he may intervene to impugn the validity of such a marriage. These conditions are: (1) the reputed nullity of the marriage must be public; (2) the existence of scandal; (3) the evidence of amendment on the part of the petitioner in the judgment of the Ordinary; (4) the probable nullity of the union.

[35] On this point, as Doheny points out, there is an endless discussion and varied opinion, leading to the practical conclusion that there is a real *dubium iuris*, so that any well-substantiated opinion may be followed until the matter is settled authoritatively by the Holy See.—*Canonical Procedure in Matrimonial Cases*, pp. 77, 78. According to some authors, "public by its nature" refers to those impediments which are founded on facts which are of themselves public, such as facts that are recorded in public documents. The distinction, then, would be between impediments public by their nature, and those occult by their nature. For this view, cf. Cappello, *De Sacramentis*, III, n. 878, p. 422; Coronata, *Institutiones*, III, n. 1486, pp. 426, 427; De Smet *Tractatus Theologico-Canonicus De Sponsalibus et Matrimonio* (4. ed., Brugis: Car. Beyaert, 1927), n. 703, p. 183; Gasparri, *De Matrimonio*, II, n. 1260, p. 292. Noval (*De Iudiciis*, n. 850, p. 569), while agreeing that the nature of the fact is the determining note in this regard, considers the possibility of an occult fact becoming public and causing scandal and prejudice to the public good. In such a case he would allow the *promotor iustitiae* to impugn the marriage, since the nature of the matter then demands such action. Wernz-Vidal (*Ius Canoncium*, V, n. 147, p. 181) contend that the interpretation of an impediment public by its nature is to be understood in the light of the pre-Code division of impediments into those that are *iuris publici* as distinct from those that are *iuris privati*. The latter are those which are established principally, although not exclusively, for the private good, while the former are those which are established for the common good, the public welfare and the safeguarding of the sanctity of marriage. This also seems to have become the accepted interpretation of the Sacred Roman Rota—cf. *Nullitatis Matrimonii*, 11 aug. 1928, coram R. P. D. Wynen, dec. XL, nn. 6-8—*Decisiones*, XX (1936), 405-407.

[36] *Instructo*, Art. 38, § 1.

When the afore-mentioned factors are present the *promotor iustitiae* has both the right and the duty to attack the validity of the marriage.[37]

If these factors are either non-existent or not verified, the *promotor iustitiae* acts illicitly, but validly in the act of impugning the validity of the marriage.[38]

Due exception being made for the cases mentioned in article 38, article 39 of the *Instruction* states that, if the nullity of a marriage is denounced by one or both consorts who have been the culpable cause of the impediment or of the nullity, the *promotor iustitiae* may not attack the marriage unless the following three factors exist concomitantly: (1) the impediment must be one which has become public, and its presence in the case is supported with arguments so certainly and strongly established both in fact and in law that there can be no serious doubt about the existence or force of the impediment; (2) the public good, namely, the removal of scandal, must demand the accusation, in the judgment of the Ordinary; and (3) even upon the cessation of the impediment, the circumstances of the case must be such that the marriage could not be properly contracted in accordance with the demands of the law.[39]

Apart from the consorts, all other persons, even blood relations, have not the right to attack the marriage, but only to denounce the nullity of the marriage to the Ordinary or to the *promotor iustitiae*.[40]

After the presentation of this brief summary of the principles regarding the right of the *promotor iustitiae* to attack a marriage in the court of first instance, his right to appeal to a higher court may now be appropriately considered.

37 *Instructio,* Art. 38, § 2.

38 Roberti, "De nullitate sententiae ob defectum habilitatis ad accusandum matrimonium"—*Apollinaris,* XII (1939), 416.

39 If the *promotor iustitiae* impugns the validity of a marriage without observing these norms, he would be acting validly but illicitly. Cf. Roberti, *art. cit., Apollinaris,* XII (1939), 416; Doheny, *Canonical Procedure in Matrimonial Cases,* p. 96.

40 Canon 1971, § 2; *Instructio,* Art. 35, § 2. Even if the denunciation of the nullity of the marriage is made to him, the Ordinary never institutes the action whereby the validity is impugned, but refers the matter to the *promotor iustitiae* of his tribunal. Cf. *Instructio,* Art. 40.

First of all, what is his right to appeal in those circumstances regarding impediments which have been established principally for the common good, that is, with reference to the impediments that are *natura sua publica?*[41] Here the *promotor iustitiae* is acting in virtue of his office, and on his own initiative, regardless of whether the consorts have or have not been the culpable cause of the impediment. If they were not the culpable cause, then the *promotor iustitiae* cumulatively with the consorts, can attack the marriage, and thus both he and the consorts have the right to appeal. In this case, if the *promotor iustitiae* fails to appeal, the consorts may still enjoy the right to do so according to the norms of canons 1971, § 1, 1°, and 1879.

If, however, the consorts were the culpable cause of the impediment, they are estopped from making the appeal, due to the fact that they are disqualified from attacking the marriage.[42]

This method of procedure was verified by a response of the Pontifical Commission for the Authentic Interpretation of the Code:[43]

> D. "*An coniugi, inhabili ad accusandum matrimonium ad norman can. 1971, § 1, 1°, competat ius appellandi vel recurrendi adversus sententiam in fovorem matrimonii latam.*
>
> R. *Negative, salvis extraiudicialibus recursibus.*"

By the phrase "*extraiudicialibus recursibus*" is meant that the culpable consorts may avail themselves of extrajudicial recourse to the ordinary so as to present to him the reason why, in their opinion, the *promotor iustitiae* should be led to interpose an appeal for them.[44]

In those cases in which the *promotor iustitiae* acts only after a previous denunciation and the consorts lack the right to at-

[41] Cf. canon 1971, § 1, 2°; *Instructio,* Art. 35, § 1, 2°.

[42] Canon 1971, § 1, 1°. Cf. Aguirre, "De iure accusandi matrimonium" —*Periodica de Re Canonica, Morali, Liturgica* (*Periodica de Religiosis et Missionariis,* Brugis, 1905-1919; *Periodica de Re Canonica et Morali utili praesertim Religiosis et Missionariis,* 1920-1927; *Periodica de Re Canonica, Morali, Liturgica,* 1927—), XXXIV (1945), 285-287 (hereafter referred to as *Periodica*).

[43] Resp. ad III, 3 maii 1945—*AAS,* XXVII (1945), 149.

[44] Wernz-Vidal, *Ius Canonicum,* V, n. 695, p. 902.

tack their marriage, the latter will also lack the right to appeal, and the *promotor iustitiae* alone can institute such an action.[45]

Even after the filing of an appeal the *promotor iustitiae* is not obliged to continue the appeal until the definitive sentence, but may withdraw from the accusation, if afterwards it becomes evident to him that the accusation cannot be sustained in fact or in law.[46]

The words *"ab accusatione recedere,"* which are found in Art. 41, § 4, of the *Instruction,* could refer either to the action or to the process.[47] However, since an action of nullity against a marriage is perpetual—inasmuch as matrimonial causes never become a *res iudicata*—it is evident that the renunciation of the *promotor iustitiae* can refer only to the process. Therefore, when it is said that the *promotor iustitiae* withdraws from the accusation, it is to be understood in the sense of his withdrawing from the process.[48]

Owing to the fact that the permission of the bishop is required for the impugning of the marriage in the cases apart from the type in which the *promotor iustitiae* may act on his own authority, it is only with the permission of the bishop that he can withdraw from them.[49] If the *promotor iustitiae* in such a case were permitted to withdraw on his own authority, he would be setting his judgment against that of the Ordinary who alone is the one authorized to judge the nature and the extent of the scandal. He can withdraw, therefore, only after seeking the consent of the Ordinary. Roberti,[50] who subscribes to this opinion, points out that such an argument is strengthened by a reference to the procedure established for criminal trials, according to which only the bishop can, after the process has begun, order it to be suspended.[51] The parties

45 Cf. Triebs, "De promotore iustitiae in causis nullitatis matrimonii ac praesertim de eius iure accusandi"—*Apollinaris,* X (1937), 407.

46 *Instructio,* Art. 41, § 4. Cf. Cappello, *De Sacramentis,* III, n. 881, p. 427.

47 Roberti, " De recessu ab accusatione matrimonii per promotorem iustitiae"—Apollinaris, XII (1939), 527.

48 Roberti, "De conditione processuali promotoris iustitiae, defensoris vinculi et coniugum in causis matrimonialibus"—*Apollinaris,* XI (1935), 578.

49 *Instructio,* Art. 39, (b).

50 "De recessu ab accusatione matrimonii per promotorem iustitiae"—*Apollinaris,* XII (1939), 528.

51 Cf. canon 1950.

and the *defensor vinculi* must be informed of the renunciation and it must be admitted by the judge.[52]

In regard to the appellate instance, the question immediately arises as to which bishop's consent is necessary, that of the first or that of the second instance. Roberti[53] seems correct in stating that the consent of the bishop of the first instance rather than of the second is the proper one. He argues that the process was begun in the first place on the basis that scandal was to be removed— and such scandal exists or is presumed to exist in the diocese of the first instance. The appellate judge is competent to decide the cause, but the bishop of the diocese of the court of second instance has no authority to be the judge of the scandal in the diocese of first instance. It follows, therefore, writes Roberti, that the judgment whether the process should continue, on the basis of the existing or presumed scandal, belongs to the ordinary of the first instance.[54]

The renunciation in the court of second instance is further subject to the same conditions as in the court of first instance.[55]

When the marriage is attacked by the *promotor iustitiae* in accordance with the provisions of articles 35, § 1, 2°, 38 and 39 of the *Instruction,* the consort who lacks the right to impugn the marriage may appoint an advocate.[56]

If the failure of the *promotor iustitiae* to appeal the case is due to negligence, the parties would have the privilege to request him to do so, or to denounce the nullity anew to the Ordinary.[57]

52 Canon 1740, § 2.

53 "De recessu ab accusatione matrimonii per promotorem iustitiae"—*Apollinaris,* XII (1939), 528.

54 "Art. cit.," *Apollinaris,* XII (1939), 529. "Ideo promotor iustitiae secundae instantiae non potest processui valedicere, ob eiusdem inopportunitatem, sine consensu Ordinarii loci primae instantiae, aut saltem contra eiusdem voluntatem."

55 Canon 1740, § 2.

56 Doheny, *Canonical Procedure in Matrimonial Cases,* p. 107, note 7: "It might well have been in accord with ecclesiastical law to deprive the consort, disqualified from attacking the marriage, of the right to have an advocate. In such an event, the *promotor iustitiae* would have been entrusted with the pleading of the case. Happily, the *Instruction* has seen fit to permit an advocate even to the estopped party," Cf. *Instructio,* Art. 46.

57 *Instructio,* Art. 37, § 4; 40.

ARTICLE IV.

THE RIGHT TO APPEAL AFTER DEATH OF CONSORT

It may sometimes happen that upon the pronouncement of the sentence in the court of first instance, one of the consorts dies. In such a case it is the general rule, according to the norms of canon 1972, that the presumed validity of the marriage can no longer be attacked.

If, while the trial is still in progress in the court of second instance, it becomes established from authentic documents that the death of either of the consorts has taken place, the acts are to be placed in the archives and the court is not to proceed to a decision.[58]

However, if the validity of the marriage should arise as an incidental question, then proofs may be admitted against such presumed validity.[59]

The continuance of the trial in the court of second instance after the death of one of the consorts may be permitted for grave reasons, as for instance in order to safeguard the legitimacy of a child perchance born of an attempted marriage, or in order to acquire an inheritance. Not only the surviving consort, but also the heirs of the deceased, may ask for a continuance of the case, but if the validity of the marriage is to be attacked, it must be only as an incidental question.[60] Even

58 *Instructio,* Art. 222. According to the procedure in the Rota, a decree is made out by the ponens whereby the acts are ordered to be placed in the archives because of the death of one of the consorts. Cf. n. XXI, *Catanen., Nullitatis Matrimonii, ob impotentiam viri,* coram R. P. D. Francesco Roberti —*AAS,* XXXVII (1945), 92.

59 Some authors (cf. Wernz-Vidal, *Ius Canonicum,* VI, n. 698, p. 908; Regatillo, *Ius Sacramentarium,* II, n. 630, p. 416), perhaps misled by the index in the Code, assert that canon 1972 is an example of a *praesumptio iuris et de iure.* Such an opinion, however, is not in conformity with the wording of the canon. The latter explicitly states that proofs are not allowed against the presumed validity of the marriage after the death of either or both of the consorts, *except* as an incidental question. Consequently, if the principal question were, e.g., the legitimacy of the offspring, the validity of the marriage may arise as an incidental question, and direct proofs may be brought against it. Cf. Coronata, *Institutiones Iuris Canonici,* III, n. 1488, p. 427; Vermeersch-Creusen, *Epitome,* III, n. 287, p. 153; Cocchi, *Commentarium,* VII, n. 306, p. 492.

60 *Instructio,* Art. 222. Cf. Coronata, *Institutiones Iuris Canonici,* III, n. 1488, p. 428.

if the cause has not yet reached the court of second instance, the surviving consort or heirs may file and prosecute the appeal.[61]

A noted case involving the rights of inheritance was tried before the Rota in 1922.[62] In this particular case, after the first sentence of nullity, the *defensor vinculi* duly appealed to the Holy See. The husband, however, died within twenty days of the date of the sentence given in the first court, and his brother pressed suit at the Rota to protect the name and hereditary rights of the deceased's collaterals. As the whereabouts of the wife could not be ascertained, the case was introduced in the Rota thus: "An sententia primi gradus, qua nullitas matrimonii declarata fuit, vim rei iudicatae habeat quoad civiles matrimonii effectus, in casu?" The sentence of the Rota was: "Affirmative, seu sententiam primi gradus, qua nullitas matrimonii declarata fuit, vim rei iudicatae habere quoad civiles matrimonii effectus, in casu."

The rights of the *defensor vinculi* in regard to appeals after one or both of the consorts has died differ from the rights of the parties and heirs. According to article 222, § 2 of the Instruction, after one or both of the consorts' death the *defensor vinculi* has neither the right nor the duty to interpose or prosecute an appeal.

61 *Instructio,* Art. 222.

62 *Aegypti, Nullitatis Matrimonii, quaestionis incidentalis de re iudicata, 20 iun. 1922,* coram R. P. D. Ioanne Prior Decano, dec. XIX—*Decisiones,* XIV (1930), 190-198.

CHAPTER SEVEN

INTRODUCTORY STAGE OF THE TRIAL

The introductory stage of the trial in the appellate instance has its preliminaries in the court of first instance, beginning with the rendering of the sentence in the lower tribunal. Because of their intimate connection with the procedure proper to the appellate court, it is thought advisable to indicate the sentences from which an appeal may be taken, the formalities required in lodging an appeal, and finally the transfer of the acts of the lower court to the court of second instance. Official cognizance of the cause begins in the latter court only with the prosecution of the appeal, when the appellant formally petitions the higher court to change the adverse sentence rendered in the lower tribunal.

ARTICLE I. SENTENCES FROM WHICH AN APPEAL MAY BE TAKEN

1. Appeal from a Definitive Sentence

An appeal may be lodged against the definitive sentence of the court of first instance provided that it is a valid sentence. According to canon 1868, § 1, a definitive sentence is one that decides the principal issue of the cause.[1] The sentence referred to here is one which results from a process in which the formal rules of judicial procedure were applied and, therefore, has no reference to the decision which results from an employment of procedural norms used in the informal judicial process.[2] The informal process cannot be used in the lower court, and then be followed by a formal trial in the appellate instance. A trial involving the formal judicial procedure in marriage causes must always begin in a court of first instance, and the same formal rules, *mutatis mutandis,* must be used in the higher tribunal.

[1] Cf. *Instructio,* Art. 196, § 1.
[2] Cf. Canons 1990-1992.

An appeal as a remedy against a judicial sentence must be distinguished from the remedy known as recourse which is used against decrees.[3]

The difference between appeal and recourse involves a knowledge of the difference between judicial and non-judicial jurisdiction. The basis for the distinction between judicial and non-judicial jurisdiction is not so much the nature or source of the power, or even the object toward which it is directed, as the manner or form in which the jurisdiction is exercised. Accordingly, strictly judicial jurisdiction is that which is exercised with the exact observance of all the formalities of legal procedure. The act resulting therefrom is set forth in a sentence, either interlocutory or definitive. Legal redress against such a sentence is called an appeal. Consequently, appeal and sentence are usually correlative terms and connote the fulfillment of complete judicial formalities in the trial of a cause.

On the other hand, non-judicial jurisdiction is exercised when the complete and strict formalities of a judgment are not observed. The resulting act issued in virtue of the exercise of this power is called a decree, and the legal redress against it is usually called recourse.[4]

An appeal may be made only against an unjust sentence, and and not against an invalid one.[5] Against the latter, a complaint of nullity is the proper remedy provided by law.[6]

It should be borne in mind that an invalid sentence is entirely different from one that is absolutely devoid of even a semblance of a sentence. For example, if a priest wrote out a sentence without any previous trial, such would lack even the semblance of a judicial sentence. Against it not even a complaint of nullity would be filed. On the other hand, an invalid sentence is one that is issued by a tribunal and has the semblance of a true sentence, even though it is defective in law for some

[3] With the exception of decrees with the force of a definitive sentence, against which an appeal may be lodged.

[4] Doheny, *Canonical Procedure in Matrimonial Cases,* pp. 142, 143. Cf. McClunn, *Administrative Recourse,* The Catholic University of America Canon Law Studies, n. 240 (Washington, D. C.: The Catholic University of America Press, 1946), pp. 14-16.

[5] Canon 1880, 3°.

[6] Cf. Canons 1892-1897; *Instructio,* Art. 207-211.

reason or other. Against such a sentence a complaint of nullity may be duly raised.[7]

2. Appeal from a Definitive Sentence Joined with a Complaint of Nullity

A brief reference was made in the foregoing discussion concerning the complaint of nullity, the *querela nullitatis,* as a remedy against an invalid sentence. It is necessary at this point to indicate under what conditions it may be cumulatively joined with a definitive sentence and appealed to a higher court.

A complaint of nullity is an action by which an aggrieved party to the trial contends that the judicial sentence is null and void because of some extrinsic substantial defect. It differs from an appeal in that the latter is a formal request of an aggrieved party to a higher court against some intrinsic element, such as the inherent injustice of the lower tribunal.[8]

While a complaint of nullity may be lodged against a sentence which is vitiated either with an irremediable[9] or with a remediable nullity, it is only in reference to the latter that the complaint may be joined with an appeal.[10]

7 Cf. Roberti, *De Processibus,* II, n. 487, p. 222.

8 Cf. Coronata, *Institutiones Iuris Canonici,* III, n. 1417, p. 334; Roberti, *De Processibus,* II, n. 487, p. 222; Lega-Bartoccetti, *Commentarius,* II, n. 2, p. 1015; Wernz-Vidal, *Ius Canonicum,* VI, n. 614, p. 567; Vermeersch-Creusen, *Epitome,* III, n. 241, p. 118; Cocchi, *Commentarium,* VII, n. 232, p. 378; Noval, *De Iudiciis,* n. 657, p. 435. "The complaint of nullity of Canon Law which is called '*querela nullitatis contra sententiam,*' corresponds to the 'motion for a new trial' in the secular courts of the United States."—Woywod, *A Practical Commentary on the Code of Canon Law* (7 ed., edited by Callistus Smith, 2 vols., New York: Joseph F. Wagner, 1943), II, 310.

9 According to canon 1892, a sentence is vitiated with irremediable nullity in the following cases: (a) when it is issued by a tribunal absolutely incompetent or by one that has not the requisite number of judges demanded by canon 1576, § 1; (b) when it has been pronounced in the case of parties, of whom one at least does not enjoy any legal standing in court; (c) when one has prosecuted a case in the name of another without a lawful mandate to do so. Cf. *Instructio,* Art. 207.

10 Lega-Bartoccetti (*Commentarius,* II, n. 2, p. 1029), contrary to other canonists, hold that the complaint of nullity as an action may be joined with the appeal not only with regard to sentences null in consequence of a remediable nullity, but also when the sentence is irremediably null. In the light of canon 1895 and art. 210 of the *Instruction,* such an opinion does not seem to be tenable.

According to canon 1894, a sentence is invalid because of remediable nullity in the following cases: (a) when there was no legal summons; (b) when the sentence does not contain the motives or reasons of the decision; (c) when the signatures prescribed by law are missing; (d) when there has been omitted the indication of the year, of the month, of the day and of the place of the issuing of the sentence.[11]

When the complaint of nullity is proposed together with the appeal, it follows the regulations of law governing appeals. Thus, in accordance with canon 1881, the appeal must be interposed within ten days after the notification of the publication of the sentence before the tribunal which issued the sentence. In accordance with the prescriptions of canon 1883, the appeal must be prosecuted before the appellate tribunal within thirty days after the filing of the appeal, unless the lower court granted a longer period of time.

The complaint of nullity may be brought not only by the parties who think themselves aggrieved, but also by the *defensor vinculi,* or the *promotor iustitiae,* if the latter was engaged in the trial.[12]

When a complaint of nullity is joined with an appeal, the court of second instance, before proceeding with the principal issue, must give a decision as to whether the sentence in the lower court was really null and void. The necessity of such a procedure follows from the fact that an appeal cannot be lodged against an invalid sentence.[13]

In the event that the appellate court finds that the complaint of nullity is to be sustained, then all judicial acts after the sentence, along with the latter, are null and void. Thus, if the sentence of the court of first instance lacked the proper signatures and was appealed to the higher court, the latter tribunal would remand the sentence to the lower court for cor-

[11] Cf.*Instructio,* Art. 209.

[12] Canon 1897. If the complaint of nullity is disjoined from the appeal, it must be introduced in the same tribunal which issued the sentence. In that event, a period of three months is allowed from the date of the publication of the sentence for the lodging of the complaint. Cf. canon 1895; *Instructio,* Art. 210. A further consideration of the complaint of nullity will be found on pp. 155-157.

[13] Canon 1880, 3°.

rection and for the repeating of all the subsequent acts such as the publication of the sentence, the filing of the appeal, etc.[14]

If the proper citations were lacking in the court of first instance, the whole trial in that tribunal would have to be repeated, or one of the following methods could be adopted: (a) one could wait three months for an automatic sanation of the sentence;[15] (b) or one could request a sanation from the Signatura Apostolica.[16]

3. Appeal from Interlocutory Sentences and Decrees with Definitive Force

The judicial sentence is called *definitive* or final, if it settles the principal issue, and *interlocutory* if it decides an incidental cause. All other pronouncements of the judge are called decrees.[17]

As the term indicates, the interlocutory sentence is one which the judge pronounces between the beginning of the trial and the definitive sentence, in order to settle, not the principal cause, but some incidental cause or point which arises and must be decided before the trial can proceed.[18]

The usual remedy against a decree, because of its extra-judicial nature, is recourse. As a general rule, there is no

14 Roberti, "De sententia nullitatis vitio infecta"—*Apollinaris,* IX (1936), 663, 664.

15 Canon 1895; *Instructio,* Art. 210, 211, § 3.

16 Doheny, *Canonical Procedure in Matrimonial Cases,* p. 351.

17 Canon 1868.

18 Lemieux, *The Sentence in Ecclesiastical Procedure,* The Catholic University of America Canon Law Studies, n. 87 (Washington, D. C., The Catholic University of America, 1934), pp. 6, 7; Wernz-Vidal, *Ius Canoncium,* VI, n. 545, pp. 494, 495. According to the strict definition given in canon 1837 and article 187 of the *Instruction,* incidental questions are only those which are proposed after the citation but before the final sentence. Therefore, there are many other matters such as negligence in admitting or rejecting the libellus, or the declaration before the citation alleging the judge's incompetency, which cannot be incidental questions because of the limitation placed by canon 1837. Nevertheless, they resemble such questions in every way except that they are not proposed after the citation and before the final sentence. It seems, therefore, that they should be considered as incidental questions in practical cases. cf. Roberti, *De Processibus,* II, n. 394, pp. 120, 121. Cf. also Torre, *Processus Matrimonialis* (Napoli: M. D'Auria, S. Sedis Apostolicae Typographus, 1947), commentary on Art. 187, p. 121.

appeal from such decrees or from interlocutory sentences.[19] The Code makes an exception to this rule, however, in stating that an appeal is allowed to a higher tribunal from an interlocutory sentence or decree when these have the force of a definitive sentence.[20]

The *Instruction* gives a clear indication of just what is meant by such definitive force.[21] It states that when interlocutory sentences or decrees are of such a nature as to result in a grievance which cannot be rectified by the final sentence, the parties then have the right to appeal to a higher tribunal, as, for instance, if the sentence or decree refuses to admit proofs which really have a bearing on the final sentence. Thus, if in a trial of a matrimonial cause the court should refuse to admit certain proofs that appear to have a vital bearing on the case in the estimation of the parties, of the *defensor vinculi,* or of the *promotor iustitiae,* an appeal can be filed with the higher tribunal. Or, as another example, an appeal could be lodged against an interlocutory sentence or decree which rejected an *exceptio peremptoria,* inasmuch as the injury thus caused could not be repaired by the definitive sentence.[22]

The same judicial formalities are to be observed in appealing against such interlocutory sentences and decrees as against a definitive sentence.[23]

If the definitive force is lacking, the interlocutory decrees may be appealed together with the final sentence.[24]

ARTICLE II. FILING OF THE APPEAL

An appeal may not be lodged against a sentence of the court of first instance until after the publication of the sentence.[25]

19 Wernz-Vidal, *Ius Canonicum,* VI, n. 548, pp. 497, 498; Roberti, *De Processibus,* II, n. 397, p. 123.

20 Canon 1880, 6°;*Instructio,* Art. 214, § 1.

21 Cf. Art. 214, ° 2.

22 Cf. S. R. Rota, *Nullitatis Matrimonii, incidentis de iure appellandi,* 20 iun. 1936, dec. XLII, n. 4—*Decisiones,* XXVIII (1945), 397.

23 Cf. canons 1881-1884.

24 Canon 1880, 6°.

25 Canons 1877; 1881; *Instructio,* Art. 215, § 1.

The appeal may be made in one of two ways: either orally or in writing.[26] If it is interposed orally, it must be done while the judge is sitting in court after the public reading of the sentence. When the appeal is made orally, no definite form is required. Merely to say "I appeal" would be sufficient, if it were an appeal from a definitive sentence. If, however, the appeal is lodged against an interlocutory sentence, the reason for the appeal must be expressed.[27]

When the appeal is made orally, the notary takes it down in writing, but before he signs it he reads it to the appellant.[28]

According to the norms of canon 1877, besides the public reading of the sentence as referred to above, the publication of the sentence may be effected in two other ways, namely: (a) by notifying the parties that the sentence is ready at the chancery of the court and leave is granted to read it and have a copy made, and (b) by sending a copy of the sentence by registered mail.

If either of these methods is followed, the appeal must be filed in a written document within a period of ten days. There is no required form for the written appeal, but it seems that according to canon 1879 the following should be expressed: (a) the name of the appellant, either acting for himself or through a procurator or advocate; (b) the sentence from which the appeal is to be made; (c) the name of the tribunal that gave the sentence; and (d) the indication of the tribunal in which the appeal is to be prosecuted, especially in the event that the appeal is to go to the Holy See instead of to the ordinary court of second instance. If the appeal is to go to the latter, no specific mention need be made of it, for, unless indicated otherwise, appeals are to go to the court immediately superior.[29]

26 Canon 1882. Cf. Muñiz, *Procédimientos Eclesiásticos,* III, n. 469, p. 400; Roberti, *De Processibus,* II, n. 478, p. 211; Coronata, *Institutiones Iuris Canonici,* III, n. 1411, pp. 326, 327; Wernz-Vidal, *Ius Canonicum,* VI, n. 611, p. 563; Lega-Bartoccetti, *Commentarius,* II, n. 9, pp. 988, 989; Vermeersch-Creusen, *Epitome,* III, n. 239, p. 116; Augustine, *A Commentary on Canon Law,* 3. ed. (1930), VII, 321, 322.

27 Coronata, *Institutiones Iuris Canonici,* III, n. 1411, p. 327.

28 Canon 1882. § 2. Cf. Noval, *De Iudiciis,* n. 646, p. 429.

29 Cf. Muñiz, *Procédimientos Eclesiásticos,* III, n. 469, p. 400; Roberti, *De Processibus,* II, n. 478, p. 211; Coronata, *Institutiones Iuris Canonici,* III, n. 1411, p. 327. For examples of formularies of appeal cf. Benedetti, *Ordo Iudicialis,* p. 127; Cappello, *Praxis Processualis,* n. 123, p. 107; Doheny, *Practical Manual for Marriage Cases* (Milwaukee: The Bruce Publishing Co., 1938), p. 218.

This document is to be presented or sent to the court which rendered the decision, and it is to be signed and dated by the notary upon its arrival in the chancery.

If it should happen that the appellant does not know how to write, or if he is lawfully impeded from making a written appeal, an oral petition would suffice. In this event the appellant must go to the tribunal and present his appeal either personally or through his legal representative.[30] Such an appeal is taken down in writing by the notary, after which it is read to the appellant and approved by him.[31]

Apart from the time when the appeal is made orally while the judge is still sitting in court, ten days, equitable time, are permitted for its interposition. This period of time does not begin to elapse until the party knows of his right to appeal and is able to do so.[32]

Canon 34, § 3, 3°,[33] determines the manner in which the ten days are to be computed. In accordance with its norms, the day of publication of the sentence is not counted in the computation of the ten days, and the time expires at the end of the tenth day thereafter. If, however, the tenth day happens to be a judicial holiday, the prorogation is understood to extend to the first court day after the holiday.[34]

This extension is in accordance with the provisions of canon 1635, which states that if the day fixed for a judicial action is a holiday, and the order of the judge does not explicitly state that the court is nevertheless to convene for the trial of cases, the prorogation is understood to extend to the first following day which is not a judicial holiday.

[30] Coronata, *Institutiones Iuris Canonici,* III, n. 1411, p. 327; Muñiz, *Procédimientos Eclesiásticos,* III, n. 469, p. 400.

[31] Canons 1882, § 2; 1707.

[32] Cf. canon 1877.

[33] "Si terminus *a quo* non coincidat cum initio diei, ex. gr., *decimus quartus aetatis annus, annus novitiatus, octiduum a vacatione sedis episcopalis, decendium ad appellandum,* etc., primus dies ne computetur et tempus finiatur expleto ultimo die eiusdem numeri." Cf. Coronata, *Institutiones Iuris Canonici,* III, n. 1410, p. 324.

[34] Wernz-Vidal, *Ius Canonicum,* VI, n. 610, p. 562; Roberti, *De processibus,* II, n. 478, p. 212.

[35] Cf. canon 1247, § 1.

These judicial holidays are all Sundays of the year, holy days of obligation[35] and the last three days of Holy Week. On these days it is forbidden to issue summonses, to have court hearings, to examine the parties and witnesses, to accept proofs, to issue, publish or execute decrees and sentences, unless necessity, Christian charity or the public welfare demand otherwise. In individual cases the judge should decide and announce whether and how far the judicial acts should take place on those days.[36]

ARTICLE III. TRANSFER OF THE ACTS

According to canon 1890, after an appeal has been made, the court to which the appeal has been presented must forward to the court of appeal an authentic copy of the original acts of the *causa*. In a response given by the Pontifical Commission for the Authentic Interpretation of the Code on January 31, 1942, it was stated that the words *acta causae* of canon 1890 include all judicial acts.[37] Consequently, when an appeal has been made, the tribunal *a quo* must send all the judicial acts, both of the *acta causae* and of the *acta processus* to the tribunal *ad quem*.[38]

In the forwarding of the acts to the higher court, they are to be bound in a fascicle, with an index of all the acts and documents, and an affidavit of the notary or chancellor testifying that the copies are exact and complete. If copies cannot be made without great inconvenience, the original acts are to be forwarded with proper precautions. If the acts of the trial are to be forwarded to a place where the vernacular language of the first court is unknown, the acts are to be translated into Latin, due precaution being taken to give a faithful translation. If the acts were not drawn up in the proper form and style, they may be rejected by the superior court; in that case, those responsible for their faulty drafting must have them redrafted and forwarded at their own expense.[39]

36 Cf. canon 1639.

37 *AAS*, XXXIV (1942), 50; Bouscaren, *Digest*, II, 469.

38 Cf. Coronata, *Institutiones Iuris Canonici*, III, n. 1415, p. 330; Cappello, *Praxis Processualis*, n. 124, p. 108; Roberti, *De Processibus*, II, p. 213, note (1); Wernz-Vidal, *Ius Canonicum*, VI, n. 612, p. 564.

39 Canon 1644.

According to the provisions of article 105 of the *Instruction,* when a case is appealed to Rome, the testimony, the acts and documents are to be translated authentically into Latin, French or Italian. If an interpreter is to be employed for the translation, he must be appointed by the tribunal after consultation with the *defensor vinculi,* and he must take the oath to perform his duty faithfully and to keep the secret. With proper authorization, translations will be made by the S. R. Rota, but the expenses for this work will be charged to the parties or the diocesan Curia sending the documents.

In cases of appeal to the Holy See by a party who has received the privilege of gratuitous legal service, the translation of the acts is to be made *ex officio* by the tribunal in which the acts were originally drawn up. Thus, the court of first instance is responsible for the acts drawn up by it, and the tribunal of second instance for its own acts and documents.

It is important to note that the *Instruction* points out that the opinions of the judges are not to be adjoined to the acts of the case, nor are they to be sent to the court of appeal, but should be kept in special archives of the tribunal for at least ten years. Upon the expiration of this period they may be burned.[40]

The secret concerning the discussion held in the tribunal before the pronouncement of the sentence,[41] as well as the secret concerning the votes and opinions given there, must remain inviolable.[42]

Article 203, § 1, which forbids the opinions of the judges to be sent to the court of appeal, terminates a dispute that had existed on this point among canonists. The present ruling sets aside the opinions advanced by Noval,[43] Blat,[44] Roberti,[45] Muñiz[46] and Connolly.[47]

[40] Art. 203, § 1: Vota iudicum actis causae adiungi non debent, neque ad tribunal appellationis sunt transmittenda, sed in speciali archivo secreto servanda, saltem per decennium. Quo elapso fas erit ea comburere.

[41] Canon 1871, § 2; *Instructio,* Art. 198, § 3.

[42] *Instructio,* Art. 203, § 2.

[43] *De Iudiciis,* n. 626, p. 413.

[44] *Commentarium,* Lib. IV, n. 398, p. 378.

[45] "De iure defensoris invisendi scriptas iudicum conclusiones"—*Apollinaris,* I (1928), 189. In the second edition of his *De Processibus,* I (1941), 530, Roberti cites the ruling of the *Instruction* in this regard.

[46] *Procédimientos Eclesiásticos,* III, n. 444, p. 371.

[47] *Appeals,* p. 99.

The rulings of canon 1871, § 2, which state in part "...quae conclusiones actis causae adiungantur, secreto servandae," did not intend to imply that the *conclusiones* or *vota* of the judges could or should be sent with the acts to the court of appeal. Inasmuch as this was sometimes done, and with the approval of many authors, many difficulties and embarrassments arose. Thus the specific ruling of article 203, § 1, was formulated for the sake of averting any difficulties in the future.[48] In this regard the *Instruction* is setting forth a practice which takes its origin from the Rota. From the very beginning the latter tribunal enacted that the *vota* of the judges be placed in secret archives.[49]

ARTICLE IV. THE PROSECUTION OF THE APPEAL

After the appeal has been properly lodged by the appellant, its prosecution must be begun in the appellate court within one month from the time it was filed in the lower tribunal, unless the judge *a quo* has granted a longer period of time.[50] The period of one month is determined according to the norms of canon 34, § 3, 3°. Therefore, the time begins with the first day after the admission of the appeal in the court of first instance. The time is then computed as continuous, not excepting any intervening judicial holidays, but if the last day is a holiday, the time is extended to the next *non feriata* day.[51] The month is calculated according to the calendar.[52]

There are three requirements for the validity of the prosecution of an appeal: (a) that the party petition the services of the higher tribunal for the emendation of the impugned sentence of the lower court; (b) and that he present a copy of the sentence to the appellate court, as well as (c) a copy of the

48 Doheny, *Canonical Procedure in Matrimonial Cases,* pp. 333-337.

49 *Regulae servandae in iudiciis apud S. R. Rotae Tribunal,* 4 aug. 1910, § 178, n. 5—*AAS,* II (1910), 835.

50 Canon 1883.

51 Canon 1635.

52 Cf. canon 34, § 1.

writ of appeal.[53] If the appeal is from an interlocutory sentence, the appellatory *libellus* should also contain the reasons for the appeal.[54]

If the appellant had interposed the appeal orally, the petition of appeal, having been put into writing by the notary, would have to be furnished to the appellant, so that he could present it together with the other necessary documents to the superior tribunal.[55]

If the appellant is unable to obtain a copy of the impugned sentence from the lower court, the month is thereby interrupted, so that a new month begins from that day when the copy is received. The party should inform the court of appeal whenever he is unable to obtain a copy of the sentence from the lower court, and the appellate judge is to compel the judge of the lower tribunal by precept to fulfill his duty as soon as possible.[56]

Although the tribunal *a quo* is obliged to furnish a copy of the sentence, there is no similar obligation to give a copy of the appellatory *libellus* when the appeal was made in written form, since, in that case, the party should have provided himself with it. If, however, the party did not make a duplicate copy, he can require a copy from the tribunal *a quo,* but at his own expense.[57]

Although it is not expressly required by the Code, it is recommended by Coronata[58] and Muñiz[59] that the judge *ad quem* should receive from the judge *a quo* a decree in which is specified the time of the reception of the appeal, whether it conformed to the requirements of law, and the length of time permitted to prosecute it, if more than a month.

[53] Cf. canon 1884, § 1, Coronata *Institutiones Iuris Canonici,* III, n. 1412, p. 328; Roberti, *De Processibus,* II, n. 479, pp. 213, 214; Wernz-Vidal, *Ius Canonicum,* VI, n. 613, p. 564; Noval, *De Iudiciis,* n. 648, p. 430.

[54] Lega-Bartoccetti, *Commentarius,* II, n. 10, pp. 990, 991.

[55] Coronata, *Institutiones Iuris Canonici,* III, n. 1412, p. 328.

[56] Canon 1884. Cf. Roberti, *De Processibus,* II, n. 479, pp. 215, 216; Vermeersch-Creusen, *Epitome,* III, n. 239, p. 117; Coronata, *Institutiones Iuris Canonici,* III, n. 1412, p. 328.

[57] Coronata, *Institutiones Iuris Canonici,* n. 1412, pp. 328, 329.

[58] *Op. cit.,* III, 329.

[59] *Procédimientos Eclesiásticos,* III, n. 470, p. 401.

ARTICLE V. OBLIGATION TO OBSERVE THE "FATALIA LEGIS"

As has already been indicated, the act of appeal comprises two peremptory periods of time within which the right to appeal is to be exercised. The one is the ten day period during which the appeal is to be interposed before the judge who pronounced the sentence, the other the period of one month (unless lawfully extended) during which the prosecution of the appeal must be begun before the judge to whom the appeal is directed. The obligation to observe the *fatalia,* as well as the consequences of the non-observance of them, will now be considered in relation to those who have the right to appeal.

1. The Defensor Vinculi

It has been seen that the *defensor vinculi* is not only obliged to interpose an appeal from the first sentence of nullity, but he is likewise obliged to do so within the period fixed by law.[60] This period of time for the interposition of the appeal is fixed by law as ten days; it cannot be shortened or prolonged by the judge.[61] As a rule it is considered as absolutely peremptory, so that at the termination of that period the right of appeal can no longer be deemed to exist.

An exception to this rule applies to the *defensor vinculi.* In those cases in which he is bound by the mandatory duty to appeal, failure to interpose the appeal within the prescribed time terminates neither the duty nor the right of the *defensor vinculi* to lodge the appeal.

This is evident from the very provisions of canon 1986 which states that, if the *defensor vinculi* fails to appeal within the time fixed by law,[62] he is to be compelled to do so by the judge. The wording of the canon clearly demonstrates that the ten day period does not have a peremptory effect as regards the *defensor vinculi,* inasmuch as the judge is to force him to appeal in the event that he has failed to do so. The *defensor vinculi* is bound to observe the *fatalia legis* only to the extent

60 Canon 1986; *Instructio,* Art. 212, § 2.

61 Canon 1634, § 1.

62 Canon 1881.

that to ignore them without reason would render his actions illicit.[63]

Does the *defensor vinculi* lose his right to urge his appeal if he fails to prosecute it within a month[64] before the court of second instance? The *defensor vinculi* of the court of first instance has the right only of interposing the appeal; the prosecution of it pertains to the *defensor vinculi* of the court of second instance. Nevertheless, both the interposition and the prosecution are but different aspects of the same act—that of appeal.[65]

Since the *defensor vinculi* is strictly bound to interpose an appeal from the first sentence which declares a marriage null, it necessarily follows that the *defensor vinculi* of the higher instance is likewise strictly bound to prosecute such an appeal, even though the periods of time are lacking in peremptory effect.[66] The whole purpose of the law would be defeated if the *fatalia legis* applied to the interposition and not to the prosecution of the appeal in cases of this kind.

The mere transmission of the acts from the court of first instance cannot be said to constitute the prosecution of the appeal.[67] The services of the tribunal receiving the appeal should be invoked for the sake of insuring the integrity of the action.[68]

63 Dolan, *The Defensor Vinculi,* p. 109.

64 Canon 1883; *Instructio,* Art. 215, § 1.

65 Cf. Roberti, "De appellatione defensoris vinculi in causis matrimonialibus."—*Apollinaris,* II (1929), 517.

66 There are no *fatalia* when he is *obliged* to appeal; when he merely has the *right* to appeal, however, he is bound by the *fatalia,* as in canon 1987. Cf. Haring, "Gelten die Notfristen auch für den *defensor vinculi* im Eheprozess?"—*Theologisch-praktische Quartalschrift* (Linz, 1832—), LXXXIII (1930), 597, 598.

67 Cf. canon 1884, § 1.

68 Dolan says in this regard:

> "The *defensor vinculi* of the higher court... does not enter the case until the judge has received the *acta* from the lower court. The *defensor* of the lower court never appears before the higher court, hence the only practical solution will be to submit not only the *acta* but also the appeal of the *defensor.* Prosecution of the appeal, therefore, will be practically automatic in nearly every instance.
>
> "It is the joint duty of both the *defensor vinculi* and the presiding judge to see that all these arrangements are properly carried out as implied by canons 1986, 1890 and 1644.
>
> "Strictly speaking, the *defensor vinculi* himself should see to it that his appeal is presented to the higher court, even though these matters will be taken care of by the Curia itself."—The *Defensor Vinculi,* p. 123.

2. The Parties

The provisions of canon 1886 apply to the consorts who have the right to appeal from an adverse sentence.[69] Accordingly, if they fail to act within the time set for the appeal, in regard either to its interposition or to its prosecution, the appeal is to be considered as deserted. Here the following question naturally arises: In the event that the sentence in the court of first instance stood for the validity of the marriage, and the party or parties failed to observe the *fatalia legis* in filing or prosecuting their appeal, under what conditions may they seek a re-examination of the cause at a later date?

The question here has reference to a retrial of exactly the same cause. If the consorts wish to attack their marriage on new grounds of nullity, then the case comes under the jurisdiction of the court of first instance. Authors generally fail to distinguish between the reintroduction of a cause in which the appeal has been deserted after the sentence for validity in the first instance, and that in which two conformable sentences have been given.

According to the Decretalists before the Code, failure to appeal in the required time had the same effect as two conformable sentences. In other words, the cause could not be reintroduced unless new evidence was brought forward to justify a new trial.[70] This was the rule whether the sentence could or could not become a *res iudicata*. The law did not distinguish.[71] However, as Ciprotti points out,[72] the Code has introduced a change in this procedure. The law now distinguishes between those cases that become a *res iudicata* and those which do not.

69 "Inutiliter elapsis fatalibus appellatoriis sive coram iudice *a quo*, sive coram iudice *ad quem*, deserta censetur appellatio."

70 Panormitanus wrote: ". . . licet sententia in causa matrimoniali non transeat in rem iudicatam, non tamen debet post decem dies quis indifferenter admitti ad probandum contrarium, sed oportet quod allegetur aliqua justa et verisimilis causa iniustitiae, quae habet movere iudicem ad credendum illam iniustam."—*Commentaria,* Tom. IV, c. 7, *de sententia et re iudicata,* nn. 10-11.

71 Reiffenstuel, Lib. II, tit, 27, n. 135: "...appellatio solum potest interponi intra decem dies a die latae sententiae... unde elapso dicto termino decendi appellare volens, non amplius auditur... Istud indistincte verificatur, sive sententia solet transire in rem iudicatam, sive non; cum quoad hoc lex non distinguit." Cf. also Pirhing, Lib. II, tit. 27, n. 51.

72 "Quaestiones de appellatione et peremptione in causis matrimonialibus" —*Apollinaris,* XII (1939), n. 5, pp. 120, 121.

This is clear from a comparison between canons 1902[73] and 1903.[74]

It seems that article 217, § § 1-2 of the *Instructio,* confirms this as the correct procedure, namely, that new evidence is demanded only for the reintroduction of a cause after two conformable sentences, and not in a case in which the appeal was abandoned or abated after only one sentence was pronounced. This article admits as a general rule that inasmuch as matrimonial causes do not become a *res iudicata,* they may be introduced before a higher tribunal, and then adds: "non exceptis casibus in *quibus appellatio defuerit vel deserta aut perempta fuerit.*"

It then gives an exception to this general rule whereby new and important arguments or documents are necessary for the reintroduction of a cause in those cases wherein two concordant sentences have been given.[75]

It seems clear, therefore, that the case of failure to observe the requirements of time regarding appeals is included in the general rule, and not in the exception. Thus, in those cases where the ten days have already elapsed, the appeals can be reintroduced without new arguments or documents, as long as two concordant sentences have not been given. Ciprotti[76] points out that this is also the practice of the S. R. Rota, and states that this tribunal is accustomed to admit appeals against lower courts even after the ten day limit, and also adheres to the principle that such is the procedure except when two concordant sentences have been given.

73 "Res iudicata habetur;

1° Duplici sententia conformi;

2° Sententia intra utile tempus non appellata; aut quae licet appellata coram iudice *a quo,* deserta fuit coram iudice *ad quem;*

3° Sententia definitiva unica, a qua non datur appellatio ad normam can. 1880."

74 "Numquam transeunt in rem iudicatam causae de statu personarum; sed ex duplici sententia conformi in his causis consequitur ut ulterior propositio non debeat admitti, nisi novis prolatis iisdemque gravibus argumentis vel documentis."

75 *Instructio,* Art. 217, § 2.

76 "Art. cit."—*Appollinaris,* XII (1939), n. 5, p. 121.

3. The Promotor Iustitiae

The obligation of the *promotor iustitiae* to observe the *fatalia legis* in regard to the filing and prosecuting of an appeal is similar to that of the consorts who had the right to impugn the validity of their marriage. Consequently there is no law that binds him to appeal from an adverse sentence, or, having filed and prosecuted the appeal, to continue in the proceedings until the definitive sentence.[77]

Although he is a public official like the *defensor vinculi,* he is not legally bound, like the latter,[78] to appeal from an adverse sentence. Consequently, if he fails to interpose the appeal within the ten day limit, or if the *promotor iustitiae* of the court of second instance fails to prosecute the appeal within thirty days, the appeal is considered as deserted.[79]

It is important to note here that it is not the *promotor iustitiae* of the lower court who will be the plaintiff before the appellate tribunal in the prosecution of the appeal; it will be the incumbent of the same office in the higher court who will be called upon to prosecute the case.[80]

According to Roberti, the *promotor iustitiae* of the higher court, although not legally bound to do so, should prosecute the appeal filed in the lower tribunal until it is evident to him that it should be renounced.[81] That the *promotor iustitiae* of the lower court was justified in appealing should be presumed until the contrary is proved. According to the provisions of canon 1740, § 2, however, the *promotor iustitiae* always has the right to renounce the proceedings.[82]

In the event that the *promotor iustitiae* fails to observe the *fatalia legis* and the appeal is deserted, the parties concerned,

77 Cf. S. R. Rota, *Lycien., Nullitatis Matrimonii, incidentis de iure appellandi necnon accusandi matrimonium ex parte promotoris iustitiae,* 27 nov. 1937, coram R. P. D. Andrea Jullien, dec. LXXII—*Decisiones,* XXIX (1945), n. 9, p. 722.

78 Canon 1986; *Instructio,* Art. 212, § 2.

79 Canon 1886.

80 Gynn, *The Promoter of Justice,* The Catholic University of America Canon Law Studies, n. 101 (Washington, D. C.: The Catholic University of America, 1936), p. 174.

81 "De conditione processuali promotoris iustitiae, defensoris vinculi et coniugum in causis matrimonialibus,"—*Appollinaris,* XI (1938), 580.

82 Roberti, "Art. cit."—*Appollinaris,* XI (1938), 580.

if they merely had the right to denounce the marriage, cannot appeal in his place or reintroduce the cause.[83] Inasmuch as they did not have a *"litis consortium"* with the *promotor iustitiae* in attacking the marriage, neither do they enjoy a *"communio appellationis."*[84]

Although the parties have no juridicial right directly to oppose the action of the *promotor iustitiae* in the event that he fails to appeal, nevertheless they may have recourse to the Ordinary, and, in the event of an adverse decree of the latter, to the Sacred Congregation competent for that particular case.[85]

ARTICLE VI. ADMISSION OR REJECTION OF THE APPEAL

The admission or rejection of the appeal in the court of second instance is similar to the procedure regarding the introduction of the *libellus* in the court of first instance.[86]

According to canon 1709, § 1, it is required that, after investigating the matter of judicial competency and the right of the plaintiff to introduce a *libellus,* the judge or tribunal as soon as possible either admit or reject the bill of complaint, giving in the latter case the reasons for so doing. This canon has given rise to various interpretations. Lyons[87] advanced the opinion that " the acceptance or rejection of the petition can be passed on by the official or by an auditor or by the integral tribunal... Usually the official accepts or rejects the petition." Tobin[88] regards the admission of the *libellus* as an act which does not need the concurrence of the tribunal, but favors collegiate action for the rejection of the bill. The same conclusion could be drawn from Roberti's commentary on this

[83] Cf. pp. 85, 86.

[84] S. R. Rota, *Lycien., Nullitatis Matrimonii, incidentis de iure appellandi necnon accusandi matrimonium ex parte promotoris iustitiae,* 27 nov. 1937, coram R. P. D. Andrea Jullien, dec. LXXI—*Decisiones,* XXIX (1945), n. 9, p. 721.

[85] Canon 1601. Cf. S. R. Rota, ibid., p. 720.

[86] Cf. canon 1709, § 1; art. 61, *Instructio.*

[87] *The Collegiate Tribunal of First Instance,* The Catholic University of America Canon Law Studies, n. 78 (Washington, D. C.: The Catholic University of America, 1932), p. 101.

[88] *De Officiali Curiae Dioecesanae* (Romae: Apud Aedes Pontificiae Universitatis Gregorianae, 1936), nn. 338-341.

procedure.[89] For Wernz-Vidal, the advisability of collegiate action would depend to a great extent upon the type of case involved.[90]

In view of the clear wording, however, of article 61,[91] it appears that the afore-mentioned opinions are no longer tenable, so that both the admission or rejection of the *libellus* is a matter for the tribunal. Whereas canon 1709, § 1, states *"iudex vel tribunal,"* article 61 merely says *"tribunal."*[92] Bernardini, in his commentary on the *Instruction* of 1936[93] excepts the case in which the *officialis,* acting in accordance with article 58 of the *Instruction,*[94] is certain of the fraudulent substitution of persons. This view seems justified inasmuch as the *officialis* in such cases seems to be excluding a person from acting rather than taking any judicial action upon the *libellus.* Thus, article 58 should not be regarded as an exception to articles 61 and 62.[95]

In order to forestall any and all undue delay in the admission or rejection of the *libellus,* the court must issue a decree of acceptance or rejection within one month.[96]

If within one month from the presentation of the *libellus* the judge has not issued his decree according to the norms of canon 1709, the party may insist that the judge issue the decree.

89 *De Processibus,* I (Romae, 2. ed., 1941), n. 107, p. 281: "... integro collegio generaliter sunt servanda: admittere ac praesertim reicere petitiones...." Cf. also ibid., note 4.

90 *Ius Canonicum,* VI, n. 375, p. 323.

91 "Tribunal, postquam viderit et rem esse suae competentiae et actori legitimam personam esse standi in iudicio, debet quantocius libellum aut admittere aut reicere, adiectis in hoc altero casu reiectionis causis."

92 Cf. Kealy, *The Introductory Libellus in Church Court Procedure,* The Catholic University of America Canon Law Studies, n. 108 (Washington, D. C.: The Catholic University of America, 1937), p. 51. Torre, in commenting on Art. 61 of the *Instruction,* apparently takes it for granted that the admission or rejection of the libellus is made by the collegiate tribunal. He states: "Si nihil appareat contra competentiam et capacitatem agendi, collegium debet quantocius libellum admittere aut reiicere"—*Processus Matrimonialis,* p. 71.

93 *Apollinaris,* IX (1936), 541.

94 "Officialis curare debet ut constet de personae, quae matrimonium accusat, identitate, iuxta instructionem huius S. C. diei 27 martii 1929." For this *Instruction* cf. *AAS,* XXI (1929), 490.

95 Kealy, *The Introductory Libellus in Church Court Procedure,* p. 58. Cf. Coronata, *Interpretatio Authentica,* resp. ad D. VIII, pp. 384, 385; *Il Monitore Ecclesiastico* (Romae, 1876-), LXIII (1938), 216-217.

96 Canon 1710; *Instructio,* Art. 67.

If the judge is nevertheless silent, the party may, on the lapse of five days after his petition to the judge requesting action, have recourse to the local Ordinary—if he does not act as judge in the case—or to the higher court, to petition that the judge be forced to take action, or that another be appointed in his place to try the action.[97]

This period of a month is taken as it is in the calendar.[98] It is continuous and is computed from the day when the *libellus* was presented, that very day not being counted.[99] The same is true in regard to the period of five days—it is continuous and the first day is not computed.[100]

If the petition is rejected and the decree indicates that such action was taken because of defects that can be corrected, then the appellant, having been notified of the specific defects, can present the amended *libellus* to the court. If this corrected *libellus* is again rejected, then the tribunal must give new reasons for the rejection.[101]

The appellant is always at liberty to have recourse to the higher court within ten days against the rejection of the petition. It is prescribed, further, that the higher tribunal shall give a hearing to the aggrieved party and to the *defensor vinculi,* and shall hand down a prompt ruling on the question of the rejection.[102]

Which is the *superius tribunal* to which recourse may be had from the court of second instance? It appears that ordinarily it is the Rota. If the cause is that in which a non-Catholic is concerned, it would go to the Holy Office. There is no appeal against the decision of the tribunal of the Holy See in matters of this kind.[103]

Recourse does not in any way involve any change in competency. The case remains for trial and under the jurisdiction of the court of first instance, if the question of acceptance or

97 Canon 1710.
98 Canon 34, § 3, 1°.
99 Canon 34, § 3, 3°.
100 Cf. Coronata, *Institutiones Iuris Canonici,* III, n. 1238, p. 146.
101 Cf. canon 1709, § 2; *Instructio,* Art. 62.
102 Canon 1709, § 3.
103 Canon 1880, 7°.

rejection was concerned with that tribunal. When recourse is had to the Holy See from the court of second instance, the trial of the cause remains with the latter court.

The equitable time of ten days[104] is to be computed from the time that the party learns of his right of recourse, or from the time that he is actually able to avail himself of the right. Thus, if the *libellus* was rejected by a tribunal, and the party was ignorant of his right of recourse, he would not forfeit his right after the expiration of ten days. If the party were a prisoner of war, for example, and was unable to press his claim, "the time limit of ten days would not begin to be computed until he was liberated and in a position to lodge the recourse."[105]

ARTICLE VII. EFFECTS OF THE APPEAL

The three effects of an appeal as mentioned by Wernz-Vidal[106] can, as is seen from the practice of the Rota,[107] be applied to appellate procedure in matrimonial trials. The threefold effect is as follows:

(a) *Effectus suspensivus.* The suspensive effect of an appeal ordinarily consists in this—that the jurisdiction of the inferior judge who rendered the decision in the court of first instance is stayed relative to the cause in question and to the execution of the sentence. While it is true that sentences in matrimonial causes are not *executed* in the proper sense, inasmuch as they never become a *res iudicata,*[108] nevertheless the effects of the sentence can become *executivi.* The inferior judge, for the reason that the sentence is *in suspensivo,* cannot carry out these effects until he has been properly authorized to do so by a higher tribunal to which the cause had been appealed.[109]

104 Canon 35.

105 Doheny, *Canonical Procedure in Matrimonial Cases,* p. 139.

106 *Ius Canonicum,* VI, n. 607, pp. 560, 561.

107 Cf. *Rheginen., Nullitatis Matrimonii, incidentis,* 16 iul. 1937, coram R. P. D. Ioanne Teodori, dec. LI, n. 5,—*Decisiones* XXIX (1945), 513, 514.

108 Canon 1903; 1989.

109 For a further discussion on this point cf. Art IV, p. 142 sq.

If the appeal was from an interlocutory sentence, the jurisdiction of the lower judge is suspended until the higher tribunal has rendered a decision on the appealed sentence. It follows, therefore, that the judge of the court of first instance cannot proceed further in the trial of the principal issue until a decision has been reached on the interlocutory sentence by the appellate tribunal in regard to the incidental cause.

(b) *Effectus devolutivus.* The effect of an appeal which connotes a devolution in matrimonial causes implies that not only the judgment concerning the justice of the appeal is referred to the superior judge, but also the merits of the cause as appealed, *"tamquam ad iudicem competentem."*[110]

Due to the fact that the court of second instance is the legally established court to receive appeals from specified courts of first instance, it follows that, after an appeal has been directed to the higher tribunal, the competency and jurisdiction enjoyed by the lower courts devolves to the court of second instance.

(c) *Remedium attentatorum.* Although the *remedium attentatorum* is given by Wernz-Vidal[111] as a third effect of the appeal, it should rather be considered as a direct result and consequence of the suspensive effect of the appeal.[112]

The principle mentioned in canon 1889, § 1, *"lite pendente, nihil innovetur,"* follows from the fact that the jurisdiction of the inferior judge has been stayed, so that he is to be regarded as incompetent relative to the cause appealed.[113]

An appeal is pending from the very moment that a sentence is rendered in the court of first instance in matrimonial causes, even before any appeal is filed against the sentence. This is a consequence of the fact that as soon as the verdict is communicated to the parties, through the publication of the

110 Cf. S. R. Rota, *Rheginen, Nullitatis Matrimonii, incidentis,* 16 iul. 1937, coram R. P. D. Ioanne Teodori, dec. LI, n. 5—*Decisiones,* XXIX (1945), 514. The effect here mentioned is not the same as *"in devolutivo tantum,"* whereby, according to canon 1889, the execution of the sentence is not suspended, Cf. Wernz-Vidal, *Ius Canonicum,* VI, n. 607, p. 560.

111 *Loc. cit.*

112 Lega-Bartoccetti, *Commentarius,* II, n. 6, p. 1006.

113 Roberti, *De Processibus,* II, n. 476, pp. 208, 209.

sentence,[114] the term of ten days[115] is allowed for the placing of an appeal, and the cause will continue to pend until it is terminated either by the expiration of ten days or because of the judgment of a higher tribunal acting in accordance with the principles governing appellate procedure. For example, a cause ceases to pend after two conformable sentences of nullity in which no further appeal was lodged by the *defensor vinculi.*[116]

According to canon 1854, attempts to prejudice the rights of the parties in a case pending in court may not be made by one of the parties or by the judge; they may not, without the consent of the party concerned, make any changes (*innovationes*) as to the object or right in controversy, or as to the terms or periods of the time assigned by law or by the judge for the performance of certain judicial acts.

To qualify as an *attentatum,* the act must be prejudicial or detrimental to one of the parties concerned. It is also called an *innovatio,* since it alters the judicial status of the object.[117] All attempts of this kind are null and void *ipso iure.*[118]

A brief review of a matrimonial cause, tried before the Rota in 1937[119] regarding an incidental question, will help to illustrate some of these principles.

The plaintiff, being deprived of any further services of his advocate, legitimately selected another. This new advocate petitioned the court to bring in new proofs in accordance with the provisions of canons 1786 and 1861, § 1. His petition being rejected, the advocate properly lodged an interlocutory appeal to the Rota.

While this appeal was still pending, the lower court proceeded to a definitive sentence in regard to the principal issue. The Rota decided that not only was this sentence of the lower court null and void, but also all the judicial acts, inasmuch as

114 Canon 1877.

115 Canon 1881.

116 Canon 1987; *Instructio,* Art. 220.

117 Augustine, *A commentary on Canon Law,* 3. ed. (1930), VII, p. 298.

118 Canon 1855, § 1.

119 *Rheginen., Nullitatis Matrimonii, incidentis,* 16 iul. 1937, coram R. P. D. Ioanne Teodori, dec. LI—*Decisiones,* XXIX (1945), pp. 511-515.

they were *attentata,* and were rendered invalid from the day on which the interlocutory appeal was lodged.[120]

The object of an innovation may concern real as well as personal action. Thus an *innovatio* is forbidden in matrimonial cases which are pending on the score of a diriment impediment, so that the parties must not be separated or be denied their matrimonial rights until the case is settled.[121]

The authority exercised by the court in accordance with the provision of article 223 of the *Instruction* is not an *innovatio*. According to the provisions of this article,[122] if either or both of the consorts should attempt marriage after the nullity of the marriage has been affirmed by the court of the first instance, or by the courts of both the first and the second instance, but against which an appeal has been filed, the tribunal is to decree *ex officio,* or upon the instance of the *defensor vinculi,* the prohibition of the exercise of the right, until the definitive sentence is rendered, in accordance with the provisions of canon 1672, § 3.

In virtue of the provisions of the latter canon, the sequestration of a thing and the prohibition to exercise a right can be decreed by the judge *ex officio,* especially upon the instance of the *promotor iustitiae* or of the *defensor vinculi,* as often as the public good seems to require it.

Due to the fact that a marriage bond is not considered dissolved after only one sentence of nullity, the consorts are forbidden to attempt another marriage until they are properly

120 "Principium autem praecipuum de attentatis est quod sint ipso iure nulla; et cum per appellationem iurisdictio suspendatur in iudice inferiori, tribuatur vero iudici superiori, hic, perdurante appellatione, videre debet de innovationibus, si quae hoc temporis spatio introducantur in praeiudicium partis appellantis, et consequenter, si casus ferat, omnia ad pristinum statum revocare. Dubium prae oculis tantum habet sententiam latam a Tribunali Rheginen. die 12 novembris 1936, quia haec gravamen intulit praecipuum parti appellanti; sed ex dictis apparet quomodo et alia acta posita a praedicto Tribunali a die appellati decreti diei 28 septembris 1936 usque ad diem prolatae sententiae, quaeque sint in partis appellantis praeiudicium, sint ipso iure nulla."—S. R. Rota, *dec. cit.—Decisiones,* XXIX (1945), 514, 515.

121 Augustine, *A Commentary on Canon Law,* 3. ed. (1930), VII, 299.

122 "Si alteruter vel uterque coniux post primam vel duplicem conformem sententiam affirmativam pro nullitate, a qua appellatum sit, matrimonium attentaverit, collegii erit decernere, *ex officio* vel instante vinculi defensore, inhibitionem exercitii iuris, ad tramitem can. 1672 § 3, usque ad definitivam sententiam."

authorized to do so by the Church. If the *defensor vinculi* files no appeal after the second sentence which confirms the first sentence of nullity, the parties are free to marry after the expiration of ten days from the date of the declaration of the sentence.[123]

If the *defensor vinculi* files an appeal after two concordant sentences of nullity, and later abandons the appeal, the parties are free to marry only after being notified by a decree of the tribunal that said appeal had been waived or abated.[124]

ARTICLE VIII. THE CITATIONS AND THE LITIS CONTESTATIO

1. The Necessity of the Citations

After the appeal has been admitted by the court of second instance, the party opposing the appeal must be summoned to appear in court.[125]

While it is true that any formal summons of a person to appear in court when served by the duly constituted authority of the tribunal is a citation,[126] this article will be concerned with the strict meaning of a citation,[127] whereby the defendant, the *defensor vinculi* or the *promotor iustitiae,* if he attacked the marriage, are summoned into court for the express purpose of contesting the appeal.[128]

Although the Code does not explicitly state that such citations are necessary in the court of second instance, nevertheless it is clearly indicated in canon 1595, wherein it is stated that the court of appeal is to follow the same rules, *accomodatae ad rem,* as in the lower court, and in canon 1891, § 1, in which

123 Canon 1987; *Instructio,* Art. 220.

124 *Instructio,* Art. 221, § 3. For a further consideration of the procedure following two concordant sentences of nullity, cf. pp. 152-155.

125 Cf. canon 1711, § 1.

126 Cf. Roberti, *De Processibus,* I (Romae, 1926), n. 288, pp. 435, 436; Coronata, *Institutiones Iuris Canonici,* III, n. 1239, p. 147; Wernz-Vidal, *Ius Canonicum,* VI, n. 380, p. 327; Lega-Bartoccetti, *Commentarius,* II, n. 3, p. 525; Cocchi, *Commentarium,* VII, n. 113, pp. 197, 198; Vermeersch-Creusen, *Epitome,* III, n. 145, p. 65.

127 "Stricte citatio est prima vocatio rei conventi in iudicium."—Coronata, *Institutiones Iuris Canonici,* III, n. 1239, p. 147. Cf. also Roberti, *De Processibus,* I (Romae, 1926), n. 288, p. 435.

128 Cf. *Instructio,* Art. 74, § 1.

a new *contestatio litis* is required. The latter necessarily presupposes the issuance of the proper summons to those who have a right to contest the suit.[129]

Article 213 of the *Instruction* of 1936, after pointing out that the court of second instance proceeds *eodem modo et ratione* as the court of first instance, makes special mention of the fact that the citations are not to be omitted in the appellate tribunal.

The very nature of the process demands that the party contesting the appeal be summoned,[130] just as in the first instance when the defendant was duly served with a citation.[131] The appellate process constitutes a new trial, a new examination of the evidence, and a new sentence.

If the necessary citations were omitted, the resulting sentence would be vitiated with remediable nullity according to the provisions of canon 1894, 1°.[132] If the summons did not contain all of the requirements mentioned in canon 1715, or if it has not been legally served, both the summons and the acts of the process are null and void.[133]

If the contending parties appear in court of their own accord, it is not necessary to issue a formal summons. In such an event the notary should make a special note of the fact that the parties appeared in court on their own initiative.[134]

129 Cf. *Querela Nullitatis et Nullitatis Matrimonii,* 10 aug. 1929, coram R. P. D. Massimi, dec. L, n. 2—*Decisiones,* XXI (1937), 428; Torre, *Processus Matrimonialis,* p. 147, Art. 213.

130 Coronata, *Institutiones Iuris Canonici,* III, n. 1240, p. 148; Lega-Bartoccetti, *Commentarius,* II, n. 4, p. 525; Wernz-Vidal, *Ius Canonicum,* VI, n. 383, p. 330; Coronata, *Interpretatio Authentica,* p. 374, under canon 1894.

131 Cf. "Citazione in Sede di Appello"—*Il Monitore Ecclesiastico* (Romae: 1876—), 5. Serie, Vol. VII (47. of entire collection, 1935), 240.

132 For an example of a sentence declared null and void by the Rota due to the fact that the citation of the *pars conventa* was lacking, cf. *Culmen., Querelae Nullitatis et Nullitatis Matrimonii,* 30 jan., coram R.P.D. Arcturo Wynen, dec. VIII— *Decisiones,* XXVIII (1944), p. 80.

133 Canon 1723; *Instructio,* Art. 84.

134 Canon 1711, § 2; *Instructio,* Art. 74, § 2. The provisions relating to the *defensor vinculi* are found in canon 1587.

In case a duly sommoned party fails to appear, the court may proceed to the declaration of contumacy in accordance with the rulings of canons 1842-1851.[135]

In addition to the proper citation to the appellee and the *defensor vinculi,* the appellant should also be informed of the summons, so that he likewise may appear before the judge on the day and hour specified.

Instead of being served on the parties, the summons may be sent to the procurator or to the advocate of the parties in accordance with the provisions of article 74, § 4, of the *Instruction.* This is especially more convenient in the court of second instance.

If the marriage was impugned by the *promotor iustitiae ex officio,*[136] he must be cited for the validity of the appellate trial, in order that the interests of the public good may not be unprotected.[137] The *Instruction* specifies that in such an event the two consorts must also be summoned.[138]

Due to the fact that the citations are thus necessary in the court of second instance, the requirements governing their proper serving and the resulting judicial consequences are to be strictly adhered to in accordance with the norms for the similar procedure in the court of first instance.[139]

2. The Litis Contestatio

After the petition of appeal has been admitted by the tribunal and the necessary citations duly served, the next step in the process is definitely to determine the point at issue through the *litis contestatio.*[140]

According to canon 1726, the joining of issue, or the *litis contestatio,* is effected by the formal denial on the part of the

135 Cf. *Instructio,* Art. 89-91.

136 Canon 1971, § 1, 2°.

137 Glynn, *The Promoter of Justice,* p. 174. Cf. Dalpiaz, "Consultationes," n. V—*Apollinaris,* VIII (1935), 139, 140.

138 Art. 75: "Si causa instituatur agente *ex officio* promotore iustitiae, ambo coniuges citandi sunt." If this citation is omitted, the sentence is invalid by way of remediable nullity. Cf. Doheny, *Canonical Procedure in Matrimonial Cases,* p. 159.

139 Cf. canons 1711-1725; *Instructio,* Art. 74-86.

140 Cf. Coronata, *Institutiones Iuris Canonici,* III, n. 1250, p. 156.

defendant of the allegation of the plaintiff, made with the intention of contesting the case before the judge.[141]

It is apparently this meaning of the *litis contestatio* that Wernz-Vidal had in mind when they wrote that the *litis contestatio* is not necessary in the appellate instance, inasmuch as the cause remains the same as in the first instance, and that the *litis contestatio* was not extinguished by the sentence of the judge in the lower tribunal.[142]

The more common view, however, among the authors is that the *litis contestatio,* in view of canon 1891, § 1, is to be observed.[143]

Roberti points out that the *litis contestatio* may consist either in *"statuendo obiecto seu materia iudicii, aut in determinandis terminis controversiae aut in concordatione dubiorum."*[144] It is in the latter sense that the *litis contestatio* consists in the appellate instance, that is, in the *"concordatio duborium.*[145]

While it is true that this procedure is not as important in the second instance as in the lower tribunal,[146] nevertheless article 213 of the *Instruction,* in speaking of the procedure in the court of second instance explicitly points out that it is to be constituted in the same manner and with the same formalities as in the first instance, *non omissis citationibus et dubii concordatione."*

The purpose of the *litis contestatio* is that the *animus litigandi* of the parties concerned be made evident, and that they know the scope of the *obiectum litis.*[147]

141 Cf. Wernz-Vidal, *Ius Canonicum,* VI, n. 396, p. 340; Roberti, *De Processibus,* I (Romae, 1926), n. 301, p. 452; Coronata, *Institutiones Iuris Canonici,* III, n. 1250, p. 157; Lega-Bartoccetti, *Commentarius,* II, nn. 1, 2, pp. 545, 546; Cocchi, *Commentarium,* VII, n. 117, pp. 206, 207; Vermeersch-Creusen, *Epitome,* III, n. 148, p. 67; Connolly, *Appeals,* p. 168.

142 *Ius Canonicum,* VI, n. 399, p. 344.

143 Cf. Roberti, *De Processibus,* I (Romae, 1926), n. 301, p. 454; Cocchi, *Commentarium,* VII, n. 229, p. 376; Noval, *De Iudiciis,* n. 655, p. 434.

144 *De Processibus,* I (Romae, 1926), n. 301, p. 453. Roberti arrives at this conclusion from a consideration of the provisions of canons 1726; 1727; 1728.

145 Cf. *Instructio,* Art. 88.

146 Hanssen, "De sanctione nullitatis in processu canonico"—*Apollinaris,* XII (1939), 251.

147 Cf. Hanssen, "De sanctione nullitatis in processu canonico"—*Apollinaris,* XI (1938), 396.

Unless these are clearly determined, the trial cannot proceed. Thus article 88 of the *Instruction* states that the concordance of the doubt should take place before the presiding judge, and that the discussion is to center about the point as to whether the nullity of the marriage is clearly established in the specific case by reason of the charges alleged. Hence, the formula to be used is: "An constet de matrimonii nullitate in casu." The specific grounds upon which the plea of nullity is based should likewise be stated.[148] Unless the precise grounds are indicated, for example, *ex capite vis et metus,* the *obiectum litis* is not definitely determined. As a result considerable confusion may result in the process, especially in the briefs of the procurator-advocate, the *defensor vinculi,* and in the sentence.

If the marriage is attacked on several grounds, they should be distinctly and separately stated,[149] and in the sentence disposition is to be made of each one of these points.

The procedure to be followed in the session of the *litis contestatio* is not complicated. No formalities are necessary. The parties, or their legal representatives, appear before the judge and a notary, the dubium is properly formulated, and the grounds upon which the trial is to take place are set forth. A record of this is then inserted in the acts of the case.[150]

The presence of the *defensor vinculi,* although seemingly implied in article 89, § § 1, 2, of the *Instruction,* is not of a strict obligation relative to the *litis contestatio.* In view of the fact that at times both consorts request a declaration of the nullity of their marriage, it could seem that the duty of contesting the charges and allegations would rest upon the *defensor vinculi* at the time of the issue in pleading; however, due to the fact that his special duty in the subsequent steps of the case is concerned with the safeguarding of the marriage bond, there seems to be no indispensable need of his intervention at the time of the *litis contestatio.* It is the practice of the Rota, how-

148 The same procedure is followed in the Rota, as is evident from the *Normae* of 1934, §77: 1. Formula dubii referre debet ipsum controversiae meritum, cauto ne excedantur limites quaestiones appellatae vel commissae.

2. In causis nullitatis matrimonii, sueta dubii formula est "an constet de matrimonii nullitate in casu."—*AAS,* XXVI (1934), 469, 470.

149 Cf. *Instructio,* Art. 88.

150 Canon 1727. Cf. Doheny, *Practical Manual for Marriage Cases,* Ch. XXVI, pp. 152-156.

ever, to cite the *defensor vinculi* and the parties or their attorneys for the *concordatio dubii.*[151]

It is not essential for the validity of the *litis contestatio* that the parties appear at the same time before the judge, or even that they appear singly. It is sufficient if by letters or successive letters they indicate their intention to litigate, and that they are sufficiently cognizant of the point or points at issue in the trial. This correspondence should be inserted in the acts by the notary.

Hanssen points out[152] that even the formalities of written correspondence and the placing of the letters in the acts are not so essential that the trial would otherwise be null and void. The trial would still be valid if it is apparent from the acts that the parties have the *animus litigandi,* and that they sufficiently understand the object of the trial. Such can even be demonstrated from the *libellus* and the citations—so that the *concordatio dubii is* but a further confirmation of what is already contained in the *libellus* and the citations.[153] This is especially true when the defendant is contumacious and the judge acts *ex officio,* at the request of the other party, in formulating the doubt.[154]

When the parties are in agreement as to the form of the *formula dubiorum,* it is always to be approved by the presiding judge.[155] In the event that the parties disagree about the form of the *formula dubiorum,* the collegiate tribunal is to determine the form *ex officio.*[156]

In matrimonial trials the *formula dubiorum* would rarely be a cause of disagreement.[157]

The date of the *litis contestatio* is important, for it constitutes the point of time from which the length of the trial is computed. Canon 1620 states that cases may not be protracted in the court of second instance beyond one year.

151 Doheny, *Canonical Procedure in Matrimonial Cases,* p. 171.

152 "De sanctione nullitatis in processu canonico"—*Apollinaris,* XI (1938), 396.

153 Roberti, *De Processibus,* I (Romae, 1926), n. 301, p. 453.

154 Canon 1729, § 1; *Instructio,* Art. 89, § 2.

155 Canon 1729, § 2; *Instructio,* Art. 92, § 1.

156 Canon 1729, § 3; *Instructio,* Art. 92, § 2.

157 Doheny, *Canonical Procedure in Matrimonial Cases,* p. 177.

According to a letter of the Sacred Congregation of the Sacraments of July 1, 1932, it is apparent that greater insistence will be placed upon this ruling than in the past.[158]

If, through the fault of the judges, a tribunal fails to give its decision in a case within one year, the provisions of Canon 1625 may be invoked against the offending judges. The canon states in part that judges who cause injustice or harm to the parties are liable for damages and can be punished by the Ordinary even to the extent of removal from office. The proceedings against such judges may be instituted either at the request of the parties or *ex officio.* If a bishop is at fault, the matter may be referred to the Sacred Consistorial Congregation.[159]

It is important to note that the *litis contestatio* in the court of second instance is to concern itself only with the cause as it was appealed from the tribunal of first instance.[160] Otherwise the appellate tribunal would be overstepping the limits of its competency in attempting to decide on an action of which the lower court had not yet taken cognizance.[161]

Thus, if the appealed cause were concerned only with *impotentia* as a basis of the alleged nullity, the court of second instance could not act, as such, on a new cause such as, e.g., *vis et metus.* This follows from the fact that the appellate court is competent *ratione gradus,* which implies that its competency is limited to the causes as already tried in the lower tribunal.[162]

As previously explained,[163] under certain conditions a new cause may be introduced in the appellate instance after the trial has begun to pend. But then the latter tribunal must try the new cause as a court of first instance.

158 *Litterae ad Excellentissimos Archiepiscopos, Episcopos atque locorum ordinarios: De Tractatione causarum matrimonialium—AAS,* XXIV (1932), 272.

159 Cf. Canon 248, § 3.

160 Canon 1891, § 1.

161 Cf. Augustine, *A Commentary on Canon Law,* 3. ed. (1930), VII, 327, note 14.

162 Roberti, *De Processibus,* II, n. 480, p. 216; Cocchi, *Commentarium,* VII, n. 229, p. 376; Wernz-Vidal, *Ius Canonicum,* VI, n. 613, p. 566.

163 Cf. pp. 62-64.

CHAPTER EIGHT

PROBATORY STAGE OF THE TRIAL

ARTICLE I. THE INTRODUCTION OF NEW PROOFS

An appeal from the court of first instance is not to be considered as a complaint against a lower tribunal, but rather as a legal petition to a higher court in which it is asked that the case be adjudged anew and that a second thorough examination be made of it because of the hardship resulting to the party from the unfavorable sentence in the lower court.

This concept of the ecclesiastical system of courts must be thoroughly understood if one is properly to differentiate it from the procedure usually followed in secular courts. In the courts of cassation of continental Europe the decision of the lower tribunal is examined with a view to approving or disapproving of the manner in which procedural laws were applied. Through this method of cassation the higher court is superior in authority to the first court, since it can quash the decision of the lower tribunal.[1]

Such is not the purpose of the Church's courts of second instance.[2] While it is true that the latter may well indicate and correct errors of procedure made in the lower tribunal, its real function is to study and decide the case "ut causa novo ac pleniori examini subiiciatur."[3]

All the proofs which were brought forward in the court of first instance are sent to the higher tribunal after an appeal to the latter has been legitimately lodged.[4]

[1] Cf. Doheny, *Canonical Procedure in Matrimonial Cases,* p. 355.

[2] Cf. Benedictus XIV, const. *"Dei miseratione,"* 3 nov. 1741, § § 3, 5, 8, 11, 14—*Fontes,* n. 318; ep. encycl. *"Nimiam licentiam,"* 18 maii 1743, § 7—*Fontes,* n. 337.

[3] Roberti, *De Processibus,* II, n. 467, p. 197. Cf. Coronata, *Institutiones Iuris Canonici,* II, n. 1408, p. 320.

[4] Canon 1890.

The sentence in the court of second instance may be based exclusively upon this evidence, or, under certain conditions, the introduction of new proofs may be permitted. Very often the cause has been so sufficiently well instructed in the court of first instance that no further testimony is considered as necessary in the appellate tribunal. The testimony that had already been judicially taken and accepted by the lower tribunal has the same legal value in the higher court.[5] Consequently there is no obligation on the latter tribunal to re-interrogate witnesses or experts if it considers as sufficient their testimony already given in the court of first instance.

No special problem arises, therefore, in the probatory period if the same evidence is used as was produced in the lower tribunal. Consequently, this article will be concerned only with the procedure relating to the introduction of new proofs in the appellate instance.

Canon 1891, in allowing for the admission of new documents and new proofs in the court of second instance, states that the regulations of canons 1786[6] and 1861[7] are to be followed.

The procedural rules contained in these two canons are concerned with the examining of witnesses after the publica-

5 "In iudicio appellationis ad novum examen revocatur causa quae non est funditus et denuo instruenda sed per se, novum examen cadit in pristinae instantiae acta, et nova instructio non admittitur nisi probetur hanc non fuisse sufficienter expletam et documenta seu probationes adhuc desiderari ad plenam causae cognitionem."— Lega-Bartoccetti, *Commentarius,* II, n. 1, p. 1007. cf. also Roberti, *De Processibus,* II, n. 482, p. 217; Connolly, *Appeals,* p. 172.

6 "Post evulgatas testificationes, testes iam auditi denuo super iisdem articulis ne interrogentur, neque novi testes admittantur, nisi caute et ex gravi ratione in causis quae numquam transeunt in rem iudicatam; ex gravissima ratione in ceteris; et in quolibet casu omni fraudis et subornationis periculo remoto; altera parte audita, et requisito voto promotoris iustitiae vel defensoris vinculi, si hi iudicio intersint; quae omnia iudex decrete suo definiat."

7 § 1. "Post conclusionem in causa novas probationes inhibentur, nisi agatur de causis quae nunquam transeunt in rem iudicatam, aut de documentis nunc primum repertis, aut de testibus qui antea ob legitimum impedimentum tempore utili induci non potuerunt.

§ 2. Si novas probationes admittendas censeat, id decernat iudex, audita altera parte, cui congruum tempus concedat ut novas probationes cognoscere et se defendere possit; aliter iudicium nullius est momenti."

tion of the testimony,[8] and with the admission of new proofs after the *conclusio in causa.*[9]

These norms must be accommodated not only to second instance procedure, but also to cases which never become irrevocably adjudged, to which category matrimonial causes *de vinculo* belong.

Hence, it can be said that new evidence may be produced in the appellate instance in matrimonial causes under the following conditions: (a) there must be a grave cause for its introduction; (b) the danger of fraud and subornation must be removed; (c) when one party introduces new evidence, the other party must be heard; (d) new evidence is admitted by decree; and (e) the other party must be given a sufficient amount of time to study these new proofs and to offer a defense against them.[10]

Thus, whereas causes that become irrevocably adjudged require a *causa gravissima* before new proofs may be admitted, matrimonial causes require only a *causa gravis,* e.g., the introduction of a document that had previously been lost.[11]

The danger of fraud and subornation must be removed. Neither the Code nor the *Instruction* determine in detail just how this is to be accomplished. It seems however, that the judge could determine that by considering the character of the persons to be examined and the nature of their testimony. In cases of doubt the judge may be obliged to secure more information about the credibility of the witnesses from the pastor or the acquaintances.[12]

According to canon 1861, § 2, if the judge believes that the new proofs should be admitted, he must, before deciding to admit them, give a hearing to the opponent and allow him

8 Canon 1786.

9 Canon 1861.

10 Cf. Noval, *De Iudiciis,* n. 656, p. 434.

11 Augustine, *A Commentary on Canon Law* 3. ed. (1930), VII, 233, 234. Cf. Muñiz, *Procédimientos Eclesiásticos,* III, n. 299, p. 237, note 2.

12 Cf. *Instructio,* Art. 138. If these witnesses were suborned and told falsehoods under oath, they would be guilty of perjury. The penalty for such is personal interdict for laymen, and suspension for clerics. Cf. canon 1743, § 3; *Instructio,* Art. 121, § 3.

sufficient time to acquaint himself with the new proofs and to offer a defense against them; otherwise the trial is invalid.

Two conditions therefore are stated in the second paragraph of this canon: (a) that the opposite party be heard before the judge admits new proofs, and (b) that the opposite party be given sufficient time to become cognizant of the new proofs and to defend himself against them. At the end of the second condition the canon concludes with the nullifying phrase: *"aliter iudicium nullius est momenti."*

The question that arises here is whether both of these conditions must be met for the forestalling of the nullifying effect. Authors agree that at least the second condition is essential, that is, that the opposing party must be given sufficient time to become acquainted with the new proofs and to offer a defense against them.[13]

In regard to the first condition, however, Ciprotti[14] maintains that nullity results if the judge admits proofs without hearing the other party first, even though the second condition is fulfilled.

There is no doubt that, if the judge refuses to hear the opposite party before he admits new proofs, he is violating the provisions of canon 1861, § 2, and is at least acting illicitly. In the following arguments Ciprotti attempts to prove that the judge, when acting in this fashion, is proceeding not only illicitly, but also invalidly, with the result that the trial is rendered null and void.

In his first argument he maintains that § 2 of canon 1861 must be taken as a unit. Each clause is to be considered as essential, with the consequence that the violation of any one of the conditions stated will result in the nullity of the trial. He states that this interpretation is evident from an examination of the text and context, and that the incidental phrase, *"cui congruum tempus concedat ut novas probationes cognos-*

[13] Roberti, *De Processibus,* II, n. 438, p. 161; Wernz-Vidal, *Ius Canonicum,* VI, n. 580, pp. 528, 529; Vermeersch-Creusen, *Epitome,* III, n. 224, p. 106.

[14] "De novis probationibus post conclusionem in causa"—*Apollinaris,* XII (1939), 110-112.

cere et se defendere possit," should not carry more weight than the principal proposition, *"audita altera parte."*[15]

In answer to the argument that the second paragraph of canon 1861 must be taken as a unit, reference should be made to the *Instruction* of 1936, regarding this particular point of procedure. In § 3 of article 178, the *Instruction* states:

> "Collectis novis probationibus, ab instructore moneantur partes et vinculi defensor eisque praestituatur congruum tempus ut probationes ipsas perpendere et impugnare possint; aliter iudicium est nullius momenti."

The *Instruction,* therefore, does not incorporate the phrase *"audita altera parte,"* but merely states that the trial is null and void if, after the proofs have been obtained by the court, the parties and the *defensor vinculi* are not informed of this fact by the auditor, and if they are not given sufficient time to study and impugn these proofs.[16]

If the condition, *audita altera parte,* were set up as a condition essential for the validity of the trial, it seems that it should have appeared thus in this article of the *Instruction,* and with the same nullifying clause attached.

Most of the authors fail to take up this problem. They merely quote the canon. Doheny's treatment of the question indicates that the condition, *audita altera parte,* is not an essential condition whose lack of fulfillment would entail nullity for the trial.[17] He touches on the point whether the trial would be invalid "if the parties, though not canonically informed by the auditor, nevertheless had an opportunity to examine and even to impugn the new proofs, if they so wished." He continues: "Our opinion is that in this case the trial is

[15] "Art. cit."—*Apollinaris,* XII (1939), 111. "Verum animadvertendum est praescriptum canonis 1861, § 2, esse quiddam unum, nec posse normam in incidentali locutione expressam potiorem haberi quam normam quae statuitur in propositione principali; interpretatio autem illius paragraphi, secundum propriam verborum significationem in textu et contextu consideratam, secumfert ut nullitas semper habeatur, quotiescumque eiusmodi praescripta violentur."

[16] Ciprotti maintains that this argument, based on the silence of the *Instruction* as to the phrase *"audita altera parte,"* would mean the derogation of part of the Code, and thus would militate against the very purpose of the *Instruction.* It seems more correct to state, however, that in this particular point of procedure the *Instruction* is not derogating the Code, but simply clarifies what may have been doubtful before.

[17] *Canonical Procedure in Matrimonial Cases,* pp. 303, 304.

valid since the rights of the parties and the *defensor vinculi* were safeguarded despite the reprehensible neglect on the part of the auditor in failing to give due notice. A parity seems to be found in canon 1587 [18] which states that the acts are valid in cases where the *promotor iustitiae* or the *defensor vinculi* are present at a session, even if they had not been summoned."[19]

Since the evident purpose of the invalidating clause is intended as a guarantee of equal judicial protection, Doheny seems justified in arguing *a pari* from canon 1587 that the trial would be valid if the parties, though not legally informed of the new proof, nevertheless actually examined it and had the opportunity of refuting it.

That the failure to hear the other party before admitting new proofs would not necessarily mean a resultant invalid trial is also evident from Augustine's commentary on this canon. He states: "... the judge must deliberate whether the new evidence is to be admitted or not, and if he decides to admit it, he must issue a decree to that effect, after having heard the other party, viz., the one who has not produced new evidence. This same party must *then* (italics supplied) under penalty of nullity of the trial, be given sufficient time to take cognizance of the new evidence and to prepare his defense."[20]

The same conclusion may be drawn from Roberti, who apparently does not consider the condition *audita altera parte,* as one of the essential requirements set under pain of nullity.[21]

In his second argument, Ciprotti[22] attempts to show, in the event that the foregoing argument proved unconvincing,

18 § 1. "In causis in quibus eorum praesentia requiritur, promotore iustitiae aut vinculi defensore non citato, acta irrita sunt, nisi ipsi, etsi non citati, revera interfuerunt.

§ 2. Si legitime citati aliquibus actibus non interfuerint, acta quidem valent, verum postea eorum examini subiicienda omnino sunt ut ea omnia sive voce sive scriptis possint animadvertere et proponere quae necessaria aut opportuna iudicaverint."

19 *Loc. cit.*

20 *A Commentary on Canon Law* 3. ed. (1930), VII, 303.

21 *De Processibus,* II, n. 438, p. 161: "At alteri parti semper terminus concedendus est ad contrariam proponendam probationem ut se defendere possit; aliter iudicium nullius est momenti." Cf. also Lega-Bartoccetti, *Commentarius,* nn. 10, 11, pp. 909, 910.

22 "Art. cit."—*Apollinaris,* XII (1939), 112.

that a judge who acts in the manner above described, that is, *inaudita altera parte,* at least commits an *attentatum.*[23]

Contending that the enumeration in canon 1854, as to what constitutes an *attentatum,* is not all-inclusive, Ciprotti accepts Roberti's definition that "quaelibet perversio ordinis processualis in praeiudicium partium facta potest attentatum constituere."[24] He argues, therefore, that this definition applies in this case, and as a result the judge commits an *attentatum* with the consequent effect of nullity.[25]

It must be admitted that, if a judge admits evidence *inaudita altera parte* he violates the procedural order, but to constitute an *attentatum,* according to the definition of Roberti as accepted by Ciprotti, it must also be *in praeiudicium partium facta.*

It is difficult to see, however, how the rights of the parties are prejudiced, at least to the extent that an *attentatum* would be allegedly committed if they are given an opportunity to rebut the new arguments. The right in question here is the *ius defensionis,* which is an essential condition in any trial. It is the apparent intention of canon 1861, § 2, to safeguard that right when it attaches the clause: *"aliter iudicium nullius est momenti."* Thus, even if the other party is not heard before the new proofs are formally admitted, but he is nevertheless given a sufficient amount of time to acquaint himself with the new evidence and to defend himself against it, it seems that the right of defense is thus adequately safeguarded. Under such circumstances it seems that an *attentatum* is not committed, despite the neglect of the proper procedural order on the part of the judge.[26]

23 Cf. canon 1854: "Attentatum est quidquid, lite pendente, aut altera pars adversus alteram aut ipse iudex adversus alterutram vel utramque partem innovat, parte dissentiente et in eius praeiudicium; sive innovatio respiciat litis materiam, salvo tamen praescripto can. 1672, 1673, sive respiciat terminos partibus a iure vel a iudice assignatos ad ponendos certos actus iudiciales."

24 *De Processibus,* II, n. 431, p. 154.

25 Canon 1855, § 1: "Attentata sunt ipso iure nulla."

26 "Non omnes inoboedientiae partium aut negligentiae iudicum attentatum constituunt, quamvis et partes possint a iudice reprehendi, et iudices possint a superioribus puniri (can. 1625, § § 1, 2). Attentatum committitur tantum quando haec diriguntur in damnum aliorum. E.g., si iudex antequam labatur terminus ad comparendum partem contumacem declaret, committit attentatum; si statuto tempore pars vel iudex omiserint actum ponere, committunt simplicem inoboedientiam vel negligentiam."—Roberti, *De Processibus,* II, n. 430, p. 152.

ARTICLE II. THE RIGHT TO BRING IN CONTRARY PROOFS

When one party is permitted to bring in new proofs, what restrictions are placed upon the opposite party in putting up a defense against such new proofs? If new witnesses are brought in, for example, is the judge within his rights in refusing the opposite party to bring in new witnesses?

The discussion of this question has reference only to the proper interpretation of canon 1862, § 2, and not to the provisions of other canons whereby the judge is empowered to admit or reject certain kinds of proofs.[27]

The text of canon 1862, § 2,[28] does not authorize the judge to restrict or in any way to determine what means of defense may be employed by the party defending himself against new proofs brought in by the opposing party. Accordingly, he cannot limit the defense to simple animadversions to the exclusion of contrary proofs. Such a restriction in a case wherein the testimony of witnesses constitutes the only effective means of defense would be tantamount to a denial of the *ius defensionis*. The powers of the judge seem to be clearly determined by this canon; he decrees whether or not the new evidence should be admitted,[29] and when it is admitted he determines the time sufficient for the preparation of a defense. He is obliged to concede the opportunity for a defense, and is not authorized to prescribe what particular kind or manner of defense must or may be employed.[30]

According to Ciprotti, however, a judge in a diocesan court would not violate the provisions of canon 1861, § 2, if he refused to admit contrary proofs, e.g., by witnesses, provided that he granted the other party sufficient time to study the new proofs and to proffer animadversions concerning them.[31] He

27 Cf. canon 1749; *Instructio*, Art. 95.

28 "Si novas probationes admittendas censeat, id decernat iudex, audita altera parte, cui congruum tempus concedat ut novas probationes cognoscere et se defendere possit; aliter iudicium nullius est momenti."

29 It is noteworthy that the authority of the presiding judge is sufficient for the admitting of new proofs. However, if he rejects them, recourse may be had to the collegiate tribunal. Cf. *Instructio*, Art. 178, §2.

30 Cf. Król, *The Defendant in Contentious Trials*, p. 151.

31 "Quapropter, si iudex non admittat ut pars, ad se defendendum contra novas probationes, contraria probatione, e.g., testibus, utatur, non violat can. 1861, § 2, dummodo congruum ipsi tempus concedat ut novas probationes cognoscere et contra eas animadvertere possit"—"De novis probationibus post conclusionem in causa"—*Apollinaris*, XII (1939), 113.

argues that canon 1861, § 2, does not determine in what sense the judge should allow sufficient time in order that the party defend himself, and from this he concludes that the canon does not specify what particular type of defense is to be admitted.[32]

Thus, inasmuch as that is left to the prudent decision of the judge, the law is not violated if he admits, for example, only written animadversions against the new proofs. Ciprotti goes on to say that by such a decision and action on the part of the judge the right of defense is not taken away from the party, since the latter can still use the method provided in canon 1861, § 2, for the introduction of new proofs, but that for this, a new decree of the judge is necessary.

In answer to this argument of Ciprotti, it seems that he is placing an unwarranted restriction upon the words of canon 1861, § 2, "*ut novas probationes cognoscere et se defendere possit.*" It is difficult to conceive how the right to determine the manner of defense logically follows from the right to determine the time of defense, especially since the law makes no distinction with reference to the manner of defense. That the opposing party is not forbidden to use any legitimate means of defense, and can therefore introduce contrary proofs by witnesses, etc., is evident from the comments on this matter by Wernz-Vidal,[33] Muñiz[34] and Roberti.[35]

Furthermore, Ciprotti's statement that contrary proofs could be admitted only through a decree on the part of the judge does not find support in the canons. A decree is necessary with regard to the admission of new proofs, but not in regard to the defense against such admitted proofs.

[32] *Loc. cit.*: "Nam revera canon 1861, § 2, non determinat quo sensu iudex debeat congruum concedere tempus ut pars se defendere possit, quaenam videlicet defensionis ratio sit admittenda; propterea id iudicis prudenti arbitrio reliquitur, nec violatur lex a iudice qui e.g. solas scriptas animadversiones contra novas probationes admittat."

[33] *Ius Canonicum,* VI, n. 580, p. 529: "Quod ius alterius partis *libere* (italics supplied) impugnandi novam adductam probationem, perinde si fit in periodo probatoria nondum clausa, adeo sacrum est, ut si facultas concessa non fuit, iudicium nullitatis vitio inficiatur."

[34] *Procédimientos Ecclesiásticos,* III, n. 416, p. 345: "... se da vista de ella a la parte contraria para que la impugne como si aún corriera el período probatorio."

[35] *De Processibus,* II, n. 438, p. 161: "At alteri parti semper terminus concedendus est ad contrarium proponendam probationem ut se defendere possit."

Ciprotti offers a second argument in support of his opinion, based on a comparison between the norms of the Rota and those established for diocesan tribunals. According to the *Normae* of the Rota of 1934,[36] article 121 does not speak of granting time to the other party *"ut se defendere possit,"* as is done in canon 1861, § 2, but states *"tantum ut super illis* [*i.e. probationibus*] *suas animadversiones conficere valeat."* He states that if one admits a difference between the relevant clauses affecting the Rota and the inferior tribunals to the extent that the clause, *"se defendere possit,"* allows the admission of contrary proofs in the diocesan tribunals, while in the Rota only *"animadversiones"* are permitted, one would acknowledge too great a difference between the rights of the parties concerned in the two procedures. Ciprotti believes that the discrepancy is obviated if one concedes that the clause, *"ut se defendere possit"* is to be interpreted as meaning the same as the clause *"suas animadversiones conficere valeat."*[37]

In reply, it must be stated that the procedural norms of the Rota and those mentioned in the Code are too clear and specific to allow for an attempt to make one the equivalent of the other. Ciprotti tries to explain the diversity as being more apparent than real, on the grounds that it is hard to conceive of inferior tribunals as obliged to grant greater rights of defense than are found in the *Normae* governing the Rota.[38]

At least according to the phraseology of the two norms, however, a great deal of difference does exist between them. To try to harmonize them would result in doing violence to the provisions of the Code. It is not intended that the procedure in the Rota should be at all times identical with that given in the Code. Bernardini, in commenting on the force of the *Normae S. Romanae Rotae Tribunalis,*[39] states that the

36 *AAS,* XXVI (1934), 478.

37 "De novis probationibus post conclusionem in causa"—*Apollinaris,* XII (1939), 113.

38 "Art. cit."—*Apollinaris,* XII (1939), 113: "Nec secus facile intelligeretur gravis differentia quae adesset inter iudicium apud S. R. Rota et iudicium apud inferiora tribunalis: nimia enim esset diversitas si ius proponendi contrarias probationes coram inferioribus tribunalibus daretur, quod coram S. R. Rota non concedatur."

39 *Apollinaris,* VII (1934), 430.

Normae of 1934 are not merely *iuxta* or *praeter Codicem,* but that sometimes they even derogate the Code.[40]

If the two procedures must be harmonized, it indeed seems more proper, in view of canon 1555, § 2, to interpret the provision of the Rota in the light of the norms of the Code, rather than vice versa.

It likewise cannot be argued that the *Instruction* of 1936 made any change in this regard. It is true, however, that article 178, § 3, of the *Instruction* used the words: *"ut probationes ipsas perpendere et impugnare possint"* instead of the terminology, *"ut novas probationes cognoscere et se defendere possit"* of canon 1861, § 2.[41] Yet the meaning is apparently the same in either case, so that full liberty is granted for the presenting of contrary proofs. The *Instruction,* like the Code, places no restriction upon that liberty.

40 *Loc. cit.*: "...non est putandum novas normas constituere iura merae executionis Codicis, ideoque semper iuxta vel praeter Codicem esse; eaedem enim non tantum aptant Rotali stilo generali Codicis, sed ipsis aliquando immo saepius derogant; ex quo fit ut in Rota adhuc dentur instituta iuridica quae singularia sint relate ad processum iuris communis, et procedura libri IV Codicis tunc tantum applicetur cum desint speciales normae Rotae vel illae ad ius commune sese remittant."

41 Cf. Ciprotti, "art. cit."—*Apollinaris,* XII (1939), 113: "Ac denique si alia esset recta interpretatio illius locutionis (*ut... se defendere possit*), non intelligeretur quare in art. 178, § 3, Instructionis S.C. de Sacramentis ea locutio mutata sit in alia verba: ut probationes ipsas perpendere et impugnare possint; nam Sacra Congregatio, ut diximus, noluit Codici derogare; ergo censuit haec verba verbis Codicis omnino aequivalere."

CHAPTER NINE

CONCLUDING STAGE OF THE TRIAL

ARTICLE I. THE SENTENCE

Although the tribunal of the court of second instance is said to confirm or reverse the sentence of the lower tribunal, it is more correct to say that it judges the cause on its own merits, independently of the decision of the court of first instance.[1]

When all the testimony and proofs have been presented, upon the submission of the briefs of the advocates, and of the animadversions of the *defensor vinculi,* and when the publication of the process, of the conclusion, and of the discussion of the case have taken place according to law, the tribunal must then examine, appraise and evaluate all the proofs of the case so as to attain the moral certainty necessary for a decision.[2]

The procedure in formulating the sentence in the appellate instance follows, in general, the norms prescribed for the court of first instance.[3] Consequently, only a brief review of that procedure will be given here.

Each of the judges shall submit his written conclusions on the merits of the case and his reasons in law and in fact which led him to these conclusions. The latter are to be appended to the acts and kept secret.[4]

Each judge shall offer his conclusions in accordance with the rules of precedence, beginning with the *ponens* or *relator.* A moderate discussion of the case should then take place under the guidance of the presiding judge of the collegiate tribunal,

1 Cf. Roberti, *De Processibus,* II, n. 485, p. 219; Lemieux, The *Sentence in Ecclesiastical Procedure,* p. 95; Connolly, *Appeals,* p. 182; Labouré Byrnes, *Procedure,* p. 114.

2 Canon 1869. Cf. Doheny, *Canoical Procedure in Matrimonial Cases,* p. 321. Cf. also *Instructio,* Art. 197.

3 Cf. canons 1868-1874; *Instructio,* Art. 198-202. Cf. also Hanssen, "De sanctione nullitatis in processu canonico,"—*Apollinaris,* XII (1939), 251.

4 *Instructio,* Art. 198, § 2.

especially for the sake of deciding what is to be determined in the dispositive part of the sentence.[5]

Any judge may change his original conclusion during the course of the discussion, but the reasons for doing so should be briefly indicated in the same written opinion.[6]

If the judges are unwilling or unable to pronounce the final sentence, the decision may be deferred to another meeting after thus duly recording: "The decision will be rendered at the next meeting." The postponement is not to extend beyond the period of one week.[7]

The notary in charge of the register of cases may communicate orally the decision of the case to the parties and present them with a copy of it if requested, provided that the collegiate tribunal has not decreed that the decision is to be kept secret until the time of the formal publication of the sentence,[8] in which case the *ponens* shall determine by decree the time of the publication. This notification of the sentence in no wise affects the computation of the lapse of time for the filing of a further appeal.[9]

The sentence is to be published as soon as possible, not more than one month from the day when the case was decided, unless the collegiate tribunal has determined upon a longer period of time for some grave reason.[10] It should be drawn up in Latin by the *ponens,* unless this task has been assigned for some just cause to some other judge in the discussion.[11]

The sentence should contain mention of the motives, both in fact and in law, upon which the dispositive part of the sentence is based. The motives are to be selected by the drafter of the sentence from those which the individual judges adduced during the course of the discussion, unless it has been previously decided by the majority of the judges which motives

[5] *Instructio,* Art. 198, § 3.

[6] *Instructio,* Art. 198, § 4.

[7] Canon 1871, § 5; *Instructio* Art. 198, § 5. Cf. Noval, *De Iudiciis,* n. 626, p. 413.

[8] Cf. canon 1625, § § 2, 3.

[9] *Instructio,* Art. 199.

[10] *Instructio,* Art. 200, § 1.

[11] *Instructio,* Art. 200, § 2.

are to be incorporated in the sentence. The latter is to be submitted to each of the judges for his approval and signature.[12]

Although the appellate tribunal may incorporate in its sentence the reasons and motives contained in that of the lower tribunal, nevertheless it would seem that an invalid sentence would be rendered by the court of second instance if, instead of listing any *motiva,*[13] it merely referred to those already given by the court of first instance.[14] Such a nullity, however, would be remediable.[15]

The sentence ought to be rendered with the invocation of the Divine Name always appearing in the beginning. Then it should state respectively the names of the judges of the tribunal, the names of the appellant, of the appellee, of the procurators and advocates, with their domiciles properly indicated, and the names of the *defensor vinculi* and of the *promotor iustitiae,* if the latter has taken part in the trial.

Next in order it should state briefly the facts of the case, the sentence given in the court of first instance, and the date on which this sentence was rendered. At the conclusion of this narration is stated the doubt in accordance with the formula as drawn up by the tribunal, usually: *"An constet de nullitate matrimonii in casu."* The grounds upon which the marriage is attacked should also be clearly indicated. They will be the same as those given in the *concordatio dubii* as formulated in the court of second instance.

The dispositive part of the sentence should then follow, preceded by the reasons upon which the decision is based, both in fact and in law.[16]

12 *Instructio,* Art. 200, § §3-5.

13 Cf. Canons 1873, § 1, 3°; 1874, §4.

14 Hanssen, "De sanctione nullitatis in processu canonico,"—*Apollinaris,* XII (1939), 251.

15 Canon 1894, 2°; *Instructio,* Art. 209, 2°.

16 The Code indicates that the motives *in facto* are to precede the motives *in iure*—cf. Canons 1605, § 1; 1871, § 2; 1873, § 1, 3°. However, the reverse form is in common use, as is evident from the practice of the Rota. This seems to be the more practical method, although the order may be changed. Cf. Roberti, *De Processibus,* II, n. 457, p. 187, note (2).

This part of the sentence is concluded in solemn language with the formal decision which states: *"Constare de matrimonii nullitate in casu"* or *"Non constare de matrimonii nullitate in casu,"* as the facts and law warrant. A separate decision must be given for each *dubium* if more than one *dubium* was to be considered.

Next follows the assessment of the fees and the expenses of the case. The sentence should conclude with an indication of the day on which, and of the place at which, it was rendered, and with the signatures of all the judges and also of the notary. The executory decree should also be subjoined.[17]

The opinions of the judges should not be incorporated in the acts of the case, nor are they to be sent to the higher tribunal if an appeal is made,[18] but should be kept for ten years in special secret archives. Upon the expiration of this period they may be burned.

Inviolable secrecy must be observed concerning the discussion which takes place preparatory to the rendering of the sentence, and likewise as to the votes and opinions expressed therein.[19]

In the event that the collegiate tribunal is of the opinion that the nullity of the marriage has not yet been proved from the points adduced, but thinks that it can be proved by means of a supplementary elaboration of the case, it should pronounce: *"Dilata et compleantur acta"* or *"Coadiuventur probationes."* Instructions should be given secretly for the supplementary investigation of the case, after consultation with the *defensor vinculi.*[20]

[17] Cf. canon 1874; *Instructio,* Art. 202. The various decisiones of the Rota furnish an excellent pattern as to the proper form in which a sentence should be written.

[18] It is to be noted that Art. 203, § 1, of the *Instruction* states that the opinions of the judges, in contradistinction to the conclusions referred to in Article 198, § 2, are not to be adjoined to the acts. Cf. Doheny, *Canonical Procedure in Matrimonial Cases,* pp. 335, 336.

[19] *Instructio,* Art. 203.

[20] *Instructio,* Art. 201.

ARTICLE II. JUDICIAL EXPENSE

The sentence of the appellate court must not only indicate the costs of the trial in the court of second instance, but it must also review the assessments and taxing costs of the lower court. This is necessary owing to the fact that not only the merits of the cause are included in the sentence of the court of first instance but also the indication of the party or parties who are to pay for the expenses of the trial; the appeal from the sentence has placed both matters before the appellate court.[21]

No distinct appeal is allowed against the decision of the court in regard to the assessed expenses, but an appeal from the sentence of the principal question of the case carries with it an appeal from the decision about expenses.[22]

When no appeal is made, the party who considers himself aggrieved may file an objection within ten days before the same judge who rendered the sentence, and he, in turn, may reconsider the matter and adjust or reduce the amount of the assessment.[23]

In regard to the payment of expenses, the general norm as given by the Code[24] and the *Instruction*,[25] is that the parties ought to be obliged to offer some financial remuneration unless they are exempted from this obligation by a grant of gratuitous legal assistance. In reference to the specific amounts that should be paid, every tribunal should have a list and register of fees, drafted by the provincial council or at a meeting of the bishops, stipulating the amount to be paid by the parties for the different judicial acts and the remuneration to be given to the advocates and procurators;[26] the cost designated for the translation and transcription of documents; the fees for the ex-

21 Labouré-Byrnes, *Procedure*, pp. 114, 115. Cf. also Coronata, *Institutiones Iuris Canonici*, n. 1433, p. 354; Roberti, *De Processibus*, II, n. 537, p. 277; Wernz-Vidal, *Ius Canonicum*, VI, n. 647, p. 595; Vermeersch-Creusen, *Epitome*, III, n. 248, p. 124; Cocchi, *Commentarium*, VII, n. 247, pp. 397, 398.

22 Canon 1913; *Instructio*, Art. 236, § § 3, 4.

23 Canon 1913, § 1; *Instructo*, Art. 236, § 3.

24 Canon 1908.

25 Art. 232.

26 For the remuneration and gratuitous patronage of advocates and procurators, cf. Hogan, *Judicial Advocates and Procurators*, pp. 171-179.

amination of these documents and the attestation to their genuineness; and likewise for transcripts of documents from archives.[27]

The presiding judge may decree that a sufficient amount of money be deposited in the treasury of the tribunal in order to defray judicial expenses, the fees of the experts, if there is need of expert assistance, and for the remuneration of witnesses. This deposit of money may be increased during the course of the trial, if this appears necessary to the presiding judge. Although this sum is ordinarily deposited by the plaintiff, the presiding judge has the authority to determine whether and in what proportion a deposit should be made by the other party, should the latter intervene in the case. A peremptory period of time may be designated for a party who refuses to deposit the money prescribed.[28]

The tribunal has the right to determine in the definitive sentence whether the expenses are to be defrayed by the appellant alone, or partly also by the other party, whenever the latter intervenes in the case. The tribunal is also to determine the proportion of the expenses to be born by both parties, if the payments are to be divided.

If the *patrocinium gratuitum* or only a reduction of the fees to be paid had been granted in the court of first instance, the procedure of investigating the necessity of granting such a favor is not repeated in the appellate court if the same exemption or reduction is asked.[29]

An attestation to the granting of such gratuitous legal service or to the reduction of expenses should be sought from the lower tribunal.

[27] Cf. canon 1909, § 1; *Instructio,* Art. 233; Roberti, "De expensis iudicialibus pro exequendis litteris rogatoriis"—*Apollinaris,* X (1937), 278, 279.

[28] Cf. Canon 1909, § 2; *Instructio,* Art. 235.

[29] Coronata, *Institutiones Iuris Canonici,* III, n. 1435 p. 357; Wernz-Vidal, *Ius Canonicum,* VI, n. 652, pp. 599-600. In the event that a gratuitous patronage had been denied, it seems that the aggrieved party could have recourse to the bishop or to the superior judge. Cf. Roberti, *De Processibus,* II, n. 543, p. 282. Cf. also D'Angelo, "De gratuito patrocinio"—*Apollinaris,* II (1929), 514-516.

Whenever the party receives a total[80] or only a partial exemption from the payment of expenses, the advocate is always to be designated *ex officio.*[81]

If, when a total or partial exemption from judicial expenses has been granted, it afterwards comes to light in the course of the trial, either from the acts of the case or from new documents, that the alleged poverty or the presumed just right to a gratuitous service has been non-existent, the collegiate tribunal, either *ex officio,* or upon the request of the *defensor vinculi,* or of the *promotor iustitiae,* if the latter is engaged in the case, should revoke the exemption or reduction.[82] It may be possible that the financial status of the party or parties has changed considerably since the time the sentence was given in the court of first instance.

Whenever a case is appealed to the Rota and an exemption from payment of court expenses or a reduction of fees is to be accorded, the diocesan tribunal transmitting the case should attest to the party's financial condition. This document, properly phrased, signed, and sealed, should be adjoined to the acts.[83]

It should be noted, therefore, that even if the *defensor vinculi* files the appeal to the S. R. Rota or to the Holy Office, the parties must nevertheless pay the expenses incurred in the trial, unless they have been accorded gratuitous legal assistance or a reduction of fees.[84]

The *Instruction* of 1936 asks that great care be taken in regard to the control and surveillance over expenses on the part of the tribunal. It deems such a precaution necessary for three principal reasons:[85] (a) lest the judicial expenses be unduly increased by unnecessary and superfluous acts; (b) lest the parties be unjustly burdened with the fees and expenses of the

[80] Cf. Roberti, *De Processibus,* II, n. 544, p. 282.

[81] Cf. canon 1916, § 1; *Instructio,* Art. 237, § § 1, 2. Apparently this appointment is to be made by the presiding judge.

[82] *Instructio,* Art. 239.

[83] *Normae,* a. 1934, § 179—*AAS,* XXVI (1934), 490.

[84] Cf. canon 1908; *Instructio,* Art. 232; Doheny, *Canonical Procedure in Matrimonial Cases,* p. 363.

[85] Art. 234.

experts, and these costs should be determined by the presiding judge according to the custom prevailing in the civil courts for similar services; and (c) lest the attorneys and advocates extort any payments for fees and expenses other than those approved in the list of rates effective in the court, so that if the party requests, the presiding judge shall determine by decree the amount to be paid.

These same precautions and safeguards could well serve the appellate court in reviewing the costs levied by the lower tribunal.

A letter of the Sacred Congregation of the Sacraments under date of July 1, 1932, states than an annual report on the handling of matrimonial cases is obligatory on bishops and other Ordinaries of places, and that an account must be given regarding the amount of money which is required to be deposited in the judicial tribunal by the parties; a statement of the taxes and fees which have to be paid for each case, including the honoraria of the advocates and experts, if any; and also what provision is made for gratuitous service to the poor according to canons 1908-1916.[36]

ARTICLE III. PUBLICATION OF THE SENTENCE

The sentence is to be published as soon as possible, not more than one month from the day when the case was decided, unless the collegiate tribunal has determined upon a longer period of time for some grave reason.[37]

This publication of the sentence may be made in one of three ways: [38]

[36] *Litterae ad Excellentissimos Archiepiscopos, Episcopos atque locorum ordinarios*: *De Tractatione causarum matrimonialium—AAS*, XXIV (1932), 272, 273.

[37] *Instructo,* Art. 200, § 1.

[38] Canon 1877; *Instructio,* Art. 204, § 1. Cf. Roberti, *De Processibus,* II, n. 458, p. 189; Coronata, *Institutiones Iuris Canonici,* III, n. 1405, pp. 316, 317; Wernz-Vidal, *Ius Canonicum,* VI, n. 596, p. 546; Lega-Bartoccetti, *Commentarius,* II, nn. 1-8, pp. 963-966; Vermeersch-Creusen, *Epitome,* III, n. 233, pp. 111, 112; Cocchi, *Commentarium,* VII, n. 220, p. 361; Benedetti, *Ordo Iudicialis,* p. 116, 117, note 2; Lemieux, *The Sentence in Ecclesiastical Procedure*, p. 90. For examples of the three types of formulas that may be used for the publication of the sentence, cf. Cappello, *Praxis Processualis,* n. 122, pp. 106, 107.

1. By summoning the parties to hear the solemn reading of the sentence by the judge sitting in court;

2. By notifying the parties that the sentence is available at the chancery of the tribunal and that they are authorized to read it and request a copy of it;

3. Wherever the custom prevails, by sending a copy of the sentence to the parties by registered mail in accordance with the rulings of canon 1719. By the provisions of this canon, a signed receipt must be obtained certifying that the letter was duly received.

The sentence should also be communicated to the *defensor vinculi,* and the *promotor iustitiae,* if the latter was engaged in the case. It should likewise be communicated to the appellee who has remained contumacious.[39]

If the party had an attorney, he also may be notified; this, however, is not a necessary requirement.[40]

In its regulations regarding the publication of the sentence, the *Instruction* makes no distinction between the first and second instance. It appears, therefore, that the tribunal of second instance, just as the lower court, notifies the parties or the attorneys directly of the sentence, rather than indirectly through the court of first instance as intermediary.[41]

Notification of the sentence is also sent to the Ordinary of the diocese in which the case was tried in first instance, and it is his duty, either personally or through a delegate, to carry out the effects of the sentence as prescribed by the superior tribunal.[42]

In the event that a further appeal is to be made, it would be well for the judge to notify the parties that the time for doing so is computed from the day of the notification of the sentence.[43] This is important because of the fact that the ten day period permitted for the lodging of the appeal is equitable

39 *Instructio,* Art. 204, § 2.

40 *Instructio,* Art. 204, § 3. Cf. Cappello, *Praxis Processualis,* n. 122, p. 108.

41 Doheny, *Canonical Procedure in Matrimonial Cases,* p. 338.

42 Cf. canon 1920, § 1.

43 Cf. canon 1881.

time,[44] and thus does not begin to elapse until the party is cognizant of his right to appeal.[45]

According to the provisions of article 199 of the *Instruction*[46] the notary in charge of the register of cases of the tribunal may notify the parties of the decision even before the formal publication of the sentence. He may do this by oral communication, or he may give them a copy of the decision if they so desire it, provided that the tribunal does not decree that the decision is to be kept secret until the formal publication of the sentence. In the latter case the *ponens* is to mention this fact regarding secrecy in his decree, and should indicate the reason for it. It is important to note that this notification to the parties has no effect upon the interval of time for the lodging of a further appeal,[47] as the ten day limit for the interposing of the appeal begins only with the formal publication of the sentence.[48]

ARTICLE IV. EXECUTION OF THE EFFECTS OF THE SENTENCE

Sentences *de statu personarum* do not *per se* require execution, but require rather an execution of the effects of the sentence. In this sense, then, after two conformable sentences for nullity have been pronounced and the time for the appeal has elapsed, the sentence becomes *executiva.*[49]

While it is true that the appellate court will return its verdict to the court of first instance, including a bill of ex-

[44] Canon 35.

[45] *Instructio,* Art. 204, § 4. Cf. Coronata, *Institutiones Iuris Canonici,* III, n. 1410, p. 324.

[46] "Causae decisionem notarium protocollo addictus partibus oretenus communicare valet, eiusdemque decisionis exemplar, si petatur, tradere, dummodo collegium decisionem secreto servandum esse non decreverit usque ad formalem sententiae publicationem: quo in casu id ponens suo decreto statuat. Haec communicatio nullam vim habet quoad decursum temporis pro appellatione interponenda."

[47] The *Instruction* is here following the practice of the S. R. Rotae. Cf. *Regulae servandae in iudiciis apud S. R. Rotae tribunal,* 4 aug. 1910, § 179—*AAS,* II (1910), 835.

[48] Canon 1881.

[49] Lemieux, *The Sentence in Ecclesiastical Procedure,* p. 108. Cf. Regatillo, *Ius Sacramentarium,* II, n. 662, p. 430. The clause usually employed by the Rota is *"Sententia facta est executiva."*

pense,[50] the responsibility of carrying out the main effects of the sentence lies with the court of second instance. The formalities which remain to be considered in that regard are: (1) the notification sent to the Ordinary of the place in which the marriage was celebrated; (2) the annotation of nullity in the parochial records and registers.

1. Notification to the Ordinary

According to article 224 of the *Instruction,*[51] after the second sentence for the nullity of the marriage has been announced to the parties as provided in article 204, § 1, and ten days have elapsed without an appeal by the *defensor vinculi,* the presiding judge is bound to give notice thereof to the Ordinary of the place where the marriage was celebrated.

It will be noticed that this article does not distinguish between the presiding judge of the first and of the second instance. It seems clear, however, from the context, that the reference is to the presiding judge of the court that rendered the last sentence in favor of nullity and, therefore, to the presiding judge of the court of second instance. Article 224 thus gives a more expeditious method of procedure in this regard than that which some authors, from their interpretation of canon 1988,[52] set forth.[53] According to these authors, the court of second instance is to notify the Ordinary of the place where the case was first tried, and the latter was to be responsible for the sending of the notification of the sentence to the Ordinary of the place where the marriage was celebrated. While it is true that perhaps in most cases the Ordinary of the court of

[50] Cf. Canon 1920, § 1; Vaughn, *Constitutions for Diocesan Courts,* The Catholic University of America Canon Law Studies, n. 210 (Washington, D. C.: The Catholic University of America Press, 1944), p. 114.

[51] "Post duplicem sententiam pro nullitate matrimonii partibus denunciatam iuxta praescriptum art. 204, § 1, et intra decem dies a defensore vinculi non appellatam, praeses tenetur eam notificare Ordinario loci, ubi matrimonium celebratum fuit." Cf. canons 1987; 1988.

[52] "Decreta matrimonii nullitate, Ordinarius loci curare debet, ut de ea mentio fiat in baptismorum et matrimoniorum regestis, ubi matrimonii celebratio consignata invenitur."

[53] Lemieux, *The Sentence in Ecclesiastical Procedure,* p. 108; Labouré-Byrnes, *Procedure,* p. 116; Cocchi, *Commentarium,* VII, n. 306, p. 491.

first instance is also the Ordinary of the place in which the marriage was contracted, it is not always so.

The sending of the notification directly from the court of second instance to the Ordinary of the place in which the marriage was celebrated, would, according to the provisions of the *Instruction,* obviate a too circuitous method of notification when the court of first instance is used only as an intermediary.

Article 224 of the *Instruction* presumes that the notice of the sentence has been communicated to the parties as prescribed by article 204, § 1. As was previously explained,[54] this notification of the sentence is sent directly by the court of second instance to the parties, instead of indirectly through the court of first instance.

2. Annotation of Nullity in Parish Records and Registers

Article 225 of the *Instruction*[55] obliges the Ordinary of the place where the marriage was celebrated to direct the rector of the parish in which the ceremony was performed duly to make an annotation in the parochial records of the sentence of nullity of the marriage and of any prohibitory clauses, e.g., in the cases of impotence, that may have been decreed. If either or both consorts were baptized in that parish, proper annotation should also be made in the baptismal records.

The rector of the parish is thereupon bound to make the proper annotations as commanded in the aforementioned registers in regard to the sentence of nullity and of any pro-

[54] Cf. pp. 141.

[55] § 1. "Ordinarius loci praedicti obligatione adstringitur iniungendi quantocius rectori paroeciae, ubi matrimonii celebratio est paroecialibus regestis consignata, ut de sententia nullitatis ac de vetitis forsan statutis, ex. gr. in causis impotentiae, in iis faciat mentionem necnon in baptizatorum regesto, si in ea paroecia uterque vel alteruter coniux fuerit baptizatus.

§ 2. Rector autem paroeciae tenetur sententiam nullitátis ac vetita forte statuta statim adnotare in praedictis regestis et, si uterque vel alteruter coniux alibi baptizatus fuit, parochum vel parochos loci baptismi collati monere de prolata nullitatis sententia, ac de vetitis forte statutis, ut haec in renatorum libro ipsi adnotent, necnon de iis a se peractis certiorem quam primum reddere proprium Ordinarium."

hibitory clauses that may have been decreed. If either or both consorts were baptized elsewhere, then he is to send to the pastor or pastors of the place of baptism a notice of the judgment of nullity and of the prohibitions which may have been decreed, so that these pastors may enter the record in their baptismal registers. The pastor must, as soon as possible, notify his own Ordinary of what he has done.[56]

Article 225 of the *Instruction* is but a detailed sequel of canons 470, § 2; 1103; and 1988. It is the rigid policy of the Church that complete records be kept in regard to baptisms and marriages. Because of the great importance of the declaration of the nullity of a marriage and its effects, the *Instruction* demands that diligent care be observed in seeing that it is properly recorded. The primary responsibility for the fulfillment of this duty rests upon the Ordinary of the place where the marriage was celebrated, and he in turn is to see that the pastor or rector of the church where the ceremony took place properly carries out the prescriptions of the law.[57]

In view of the provisions of the *Instruction* in article 225, it must be observed that the records of the church where the marriage was celebrated rarely have an indication of the places of baptism of the contracting parties unless they were actually baptized in that parish. As a result it would be difficult for the rector of the parish to obtain this information. Doheny[58] recommends that the "presiding judge, in notifying the Ordinary of the place where the marriage was celebrated, should also send information as to the dates and places of baptism. All these records are in the acts of the case and are easily available. This courtesy would obviate innumerable difficulties and would tend to facilitate and expedite the work of the proper annotations in the parochial registers."

56 Cf. Regatillo, *Ius Sacramentarium,* II, n. 663, p. 431.

57 Doheny, *Canonical Procedure in Matrimonial Cases,* p. 375; Cappello, *Praxis Processualis,* n. 126, p. 109. If the pastors are culpably negligent in fulfilling their duty as specified in article 225, they may be punished in accordance with the norm of canon 2383, which states that a pastor is to be punished for his negligence in these matters by his proper Ordinary according to the gravity of the fault. Cf. also canon 2406.

58 *Op. cit.,* p. 375.

It should be noted that the execution of the effects of the sentence as just now noted is concerned only with the formalities after two concordant sentences of nullity have been pronounced, and from which no further appeal has been taken by the *defensor vinculi.* However, a sentence becomes *executiva* whenever no further litigation in the cause is demanded by law, or whenever the option of further legal redress is not taken advantage of, or whenever such redress has been deserted, even thought it had been invoked at some earlier time.[59]

When two conformable sentences of nullity have not been obtained, the execution of the effects of the sentence is concerned mainly with the notification of the sentence to the lower court and to the parties, and the amount to be paid for the expenses of the trial.

[59] For example, cf. *Florentina, Nullitatis Matrimonii,* 9 maii 1936, coram R. P.D. Andrea Jullien, dec. XXXXIII—*Decisiones,* XXVIII (1936), 319.

CHAPTER TEN

LEGAL REDRESS AGAINST THE SENTENCE

ARTICLE I. FURTHER APPEAL

1. When Second Sentence Differs from the First

If the sentence in the court of first instance affirmed the validity of the marriage, and the court of second instance gave a sentence of nullity, then the *defensor vinculi* is bound to appeal to a court of third instance according to the procedure previously treated[1] regarding the appeal from a sentence of nullity in the court of first instance.[2]

An appeal filed by a party does not exempt the *defensor vinculi* from filing a separate appeal.[3]

If the first sentence was for nullity and the second for the validity of the marriage, the parties have a right to file a further appeal if they so desire.[4] The same right belongs to the *promotor iustitiae* if he is engaged in the case.

While it is clear that the *defensor vinculi* is not bound to appeal from such a sentence of validity, nevertheless it is not certain whether he is permitted to do so. The authors are not in agreement as to the procedure permissible in such a case. Wernz-Vidal,[5] Cappello,[6] Chelodi[7] and Payen[8] concede both to the parties and to the *defensor vinculi* the right to appeal when the first sentence stood for the nullity and the second for the validity of the impugned marriage. Dolan, after an analysis of the various opinions, seems justified in arguing

[1] Cf. Art. II, pp. 81-83; Art V, pp. 103, 104.

[2] Canon 1986; *Instructio,* Art. 212, § 2. Cf. Coronata, *Institutiones Iuris Canonici,* III, n. 1498, p. 436; Wernz-Vidal, *Ius Canonicum,* V, n. 703, p. 914; Cappello, *De Sacramentis,* III, n. 886, p. 434; Cocchi, *Commentarium,* VII, n. 304, pp. 489, 490; Dolan, *The Defensor Vinculi,* pp. 101, 110.

[3] *Instructio,* Art. 212, § 3.

[4] Canon 1879; *Instructio,* Art. 212, § 1.

[5] *Ius Canonicum,* V, n. 703, p. 914.

[6] *De Sacramentis,* III, n. 886, p. 434.

[7] *Ius Matrimoniali Iuxta Codicem Iuris Canonici* (3. ed., Trento, 1921), p. 195.

[8] *De Matrimonio,* III, n. 2715, p. 567.

from the very nature of the office and duties of the *defensor vinculi* that the latter is "neither obliged nor authorized to appeal."[9]

He further states: "The *defensor vinculi* in first instance obeyed the law of canon 1906 when he appealed from the sentence of nullity. The *defensor* in second instance brought the case to a successful termination, and he has no need to have recourse to a remedy against the sentence, since the cause for validity has been sustained, and has not been prejudiced in any way. Nor can any harm come to the status of the marriage through the abstinence of the *defensor vinculi* from appealing. The parties cannot remarry, though it is true they may appeal, but in this event the *defensor vinculi* of the next instance would take up the defense of the marriage, and this is exactly what would have happened if the *defensor vinculi* himself had interposed the appeal."[10]

This opinion is in full accord with the pre-Code legislation ever since the issuance of the Constitution "*Dei miseratione*" of Benedict XIV, on November 4, 1741.[11]

It should also be pointed out that the *Instruction* of 1936 has indicated no different interpretation of the Code in this regard.

2. When Sentences of First and Second Instances are Conformable

A. *Meaning of "two conformable sentences."*

Causes that involve the personal status of individuals never become a *res iudicata*,[12] and matrimonial causes are among those included in this category.[13]

[9] *The Defensor Vinculi*, p. 113. Cf. Gasparri, *De Matrimonio*, II, n. 1287, p. 310; Lanier, *Guide Pratique de la Procédure Matrimoniale en Droit Canonique* (Parisiis, 1927), p. 31.

[10] *Op. cit.*, pp. 110, 111.

[11] N. 8: "Itaque si a iudice pro matrimonii validitate iudicabitur, et nullus sit, qui appellet, ipse i.e. defensor etiam ab appellatione se abstineat; idque etiam servetur, si a iudice secundae instantiae pro validitate matrimonii fuerit iudicatum, postquam iudex primae instantiae de illius nullitate sententiam pronuntiaverat..."—*Fontes*, n. 318.

[12] Canon 1903; *Instructio*, Art. 217, § 1.

[13] Canon 1989; *Instructio*, Art. 217, § 1.

Such causes, however, do attain the status of a *quasi res iudicata* after the declaration of two conformable sentences.[14]

The proper understanding of this principle is important because of the subsequent procedure following two such sentences. The *defensor vinculi* is freed of the obligation to interpose an appeal against a sentence of nullity only after the pronouncement of two conformable sentences;[15] and apart from the right of the *defensor vinculi* to a further appeal as mentioned in canon 1987, the further consideration of a cause after two conformable sentences may be permitted only after new and important documents are furnished.[16]

It was clear from the pre-Code legislation and was so understood by the authors, that two conformable sentences meant essentially that they were based upon the same grounds of nullity. Thus, by the mere fact that the courts of first and second instance rendered a decision of nullity in the same marriage case, it did not necessarily follow that the two sentences were conformable. Such a situation would arise under the following circumstances. After the court of first instance granted a sentence of nullity on only one of two grounds alleged, e.g., *ex capite vis et metus,* the *defensor vinculi* properly lodges his appeal to a higher court. The court of second instance also finds the marriage invalid, but on the other of the two grounds alleged, i.e., *ex capite impotentiae.* Thus two sentences have been validly handed down, but on different grounds. That sentences such as these can not be regarded as conformable was clear from the Constitution *"Dei miseratione"* of Benedict XIV, in which he declared that the marriage bond should in no case be considered as dissolved *"nisi duo iudicata, vel resolutiones, aut sententiae penitus similes et conformes, a quibus neque pars, neque defensor matrimonii crediderit appellandum, emanaverint."*[17]

Accordingly, two sentences could hardly be classified as *"conformes"* and *"penitus similes"* unless their identity were

14 Canon 1903. Cf. Cappello, "Utrum conformes ad normam cann. 1903 et 1987 dicendae sint duae sententiae de nullitate matrimonii latae, si eiusdem nullitas declarata fuerit ex diverso capite."—*Periodica,* XX (1931), 20*-28*.

15 Canon 1903; *Instructio,* Art. 220. Cf. Dolan, *The Defensor Vinculi,* p. 116.

16 Canon 1903; *Instructio,* Art. 217, § 2.

17 N. 14—*Fontes,* n. 318.

based on the same grounds of nullity.[18] The same conclusion is evident from the writings of Schmalzgrueber (1663-1735)[19] and Pirhing (1606-1674).[20]

No real change in this doctrine has been made by the law of the Code; hence, canons 1903, 1987 and 1989 must be understood in the light of the pre-Code law.[21] It should also be noted that no change in this interpretation is contained in the *Instruction* of 1936.[22]

B. *Further appeal after two conformable sentences.*

After the pronouncement of the second sentence in favor of the nullity of the marriage, the *defensor vinculi* of the court of second instance is free to appeal or not to appeal the cause. The law leaves the decision to his own conscience,[23] entirely depending on whether he believes the sentence to be in accord with truth or at variance with it. It seems, therefore, that the *defensor vinculi* is bound to appeal from a second sentence confirming the nullity of the marriage only when he believes that there is a reasonable probability that the marriage is actually valid.[24]

18 Cappello, *De Sacramentis,* III, n. 887, p. 440.

19 Lib. II, tit. 28, n. 5.

20 Lib. II, tit. 5, n. 12.

21 Canon 6, 2°.

22 Cf. *Instructio,* Art. 217, § 2; 218, § § 1, 2. For a detailed development and analysis of this interpretation cf. Dolan, *The Defensor Vinculi,* pp. 116-119, and Cappello, *De Sacramentis,* III, n. 887, pp. 434-441.

23 Canon 1987; *Instructio,* Art. 221, § 1.

24 What if the *defensor vinculi,* overly zealous in the performance of his office, should lodge a further appeal without any reason for doing so? Owing to the fact that the decision is left entirely to the *defensor vinculi* himself, no one can limit his rights in that regard. The parties have no authority to do so, and neither has the judge, inasmuch as he must act only in accordance with the prescriptions of the law. Apparently the only recourse left to the parties, according to Roberti, would be to petition a tribunal of the Holy see, usually the Rota, in an effort to determine whether or not that tribunal's *defensor vinculi* intends to prosecute the appeal. Cf. "De facultatibus defensoris vinculi quoad appellationem"—*Appollinaris,* IX (1936), 311. If the appeal seems futile to him, he will not prosecute it, thus saving the time and expense of a new trial. Although the *defensor vinculi* of the court of third instance is bound by his office to use proper diligence in determining whether appeals from the lower courts, after two sentences of nullity, should be subject to another trial, nevertheless the aforementioned petition of the parties may induce him to greater promptness and care in rejecting the appeal as soon as possible. No other recourse seems available to the parties in a matter that is left entirely to the conscience of the *defensor vinculi.*

If the *defensor vinculi* does decide to appeal after the second sentence of nullity, the cause will be tried by the Rota or the Holy Office. It should be noted, however, that even if the *defensor vinculi* of the court of second instance files an appeal, it can nevertheless be waived by the *defensor* of the tribunal of the Holy See.[25]

If the *defensor vinculi* fails to prosecute the appeal within one month from the time that it is filed,[26] the appeal is considered as waived.[27]

If no procedural act has taken place within the course of a year[28] the court may declare the cause abated. The parties should be notified without delay by means of a decree of the court that the appeal was waived or abated in the court of third instance. As soon as they receive this notification, they are free to marry.[29]

Thus the rights of the parties to marry as contained in article 221 of the *Instruction* are clearly differentiated from the provisions in that regard in article 220.[30] According to the latter article, if the *defensor vinculi* files no appeal after the second conformable sentence of nullity of the marriage, the parties are free to marry after the expiration of ten days from the date of the notification of the sentence. On the other hand, in accordance with article 221, if the *defensor vinculi* does file

25 For an example of this cf. n. XIX, *Indianopolitana—Nullitatis Matrimonii, ob clandestinitatem,* coram R.P.D. Henrico Cariazzo: "Patres de turno, decreto diei 21 novembris 1944 acceptarunt renunciationem defensoris vinculi S. R. Rotae, declarantis se recedere ab appellatione, quam defensor vinculi tribunalis secundae instantiae interposuit adversus secundam sententiam quae prime sententiae conformis erat."—*AAS,* XXXVII (1945), 92.

26 Canon 1883; *Instructio,* Art. 215, § 1.

27 Canon 1886; *Instructio,* Art. 221, § 2.

28 Cf. canons 1736; 1737. Cf. n. VII, *Tergestina, Nullitatis Matrimonii, ob vim et metum* [13 maii 1944], coram R.P.D. Jullien—*AAS,* XXXVII (1945), 90.

29 *Instructio,* Art. 221, § 3: In casu autem desertionis, partibus ius est ad novas nuptias convolare, habita notificatione decreti quo collegium statuerit appellationem desertam (cfr. can. 1886), vel peremptam (cfr. cann. 1736, 1737) habendam esse.

30 "Post secumdam sententiam, quae matrimonii nullitatem confirmaverit, si defensor vinculi gradu appellationis pro sua conscientia non crediderit esse appellandum, ius coniugibus est, decem diebus a sententiae denunciatione elapsis, novas nuptias contrahendi." Cf. canon 1987.

an appeal, the parties are free to marry only after they have received a decree of the tribunal of the court of third instance which states that the appeal had been waived or abated.[31]

ARTICLE II. REINTRODUCTION OF CAUSE AFTER TWO CONFORMABLE SENTENCES

The preceding discussion was concerned only with an appeal after two conformable sentences of nullity. Such a remedy was shown to be available to the *defensor vinculi* of the court of second instance, not the parties, if he felt in conscience that the cause should be subjected to another trial. If he decides that this further redress is necessary, he is bound to observe the usual procedure demanded on lodging and prosecuting an appeal.[32] In the event that he fails to observe the *fatalia legis* either in regard to the court *a quo*[33] or the court *ad quem*[34] the appeal is considered as deserted.[35] He is therefore not compelled to appeal as in the case after the first sentence of nullity.[36]

It is important to note that a similar right to a further appeal, under the same conditions, is not granted to the parties.

Inasmuch as matrimonial causes *de vinculo* do not become a *res iudicata,*[37] however, what further action is available to the parties after two conformable sentences, and to the *defensor vinculi,* in the event that he either failed to appeal or deserted an appeal after two conformable sentences of nullity?

[31] It would appear that the process is not terminated in the court of third instance by the mere withdrawal from the appeal by the *defensor vinculi* of that tribunal. The requirements for a judicial renunciation are that it must be made in writing, accepted by the parties, and admitted by a decree of the judge (cf. canon 1740, § 2). It would seem, therefore, that these requirements must be met in the event the *defensor vinculi* withdraws from the appeal in the court of third instance. Cf. Roberti, "De facultatibus defensoris vinculi quoad appellationem"—*Apollinaris,* IX (1936), 311.

[32] *Instructio,* Art. 221, § 1.

[33] Canon 1881.

[34] Canon 1883.

[35] Canon 1886.

[36] Canon 1986; *Instructio,* Art. 212, § 2.

[37] Canons 1903; 1989; *Instructio,* Art. 217, § 1.

Further litigation in such cases is provided for in the Code,[38] but is more clearly outlined in the *Instruction* of 1936. Accordingly article 217 states:

§ 1. Cum sententiae in causis matrimonialibus numquam transeunt in rem iudicatam, causae ipsae retractari poterunt coram tribunali superiori, non exceptis casibus in quibus appellatio defuerit vel deserta aut perempta fuerit.

§ 2. Sed ex duplici sententia conformi in his causis consequitur ut ulterior propositio non debeat admitti, nisi novis prolatis iisdemque gravibus argumentis vel documentis.

Thus, according to the provisions of this article, inasmuch as matrimonial causes never become irrevocably adjudged, they may be reintroduced before a higher tribunal, not even excepting the cases in which no appeal had been previously made, or when the appeal had been waived or abated. However, in these cases it follows that from two concordant sentences no further litigation should be admitted unless new and important arguments or documents are furnished.[39]

It is noteworthy to point out that neither the Code nor the *Instruction* refers to this further consideration of the cause as an appeal, but as an *"ulterior propositio."*[40] Thus, to differentiate it from an appeal, the term "reintroduction" will be used here in reference to this particular procedure.[41]

When a cause is reintroduced, it must be done so in a court of higher instance than that in which it was last tried. It is similar to an appeal in this respect.[42] The two procedures differ, however, in that the peremptory periods of time as demanded in an appeal are not required in the reintroduction of a cause.[43]

38 Canons 1989; 1903.

39 Cf. canons 1903; 1989.

40 Canon 1903; *Instructio,* Art. 217, § 2. Cf. Benedetti, *Ordo Iudicialis,* p. 126, note 2.

41 Cf. Doheny, *Canonical Procedure in Matrimonial Cases,* p. 364.

42 *Instructio,* Art. 217, § 1; Coronata, *Institutiones Iuris Cononici,* III, n. 1500, p. 437; Torres, *Processus Matrimonialis,* pp. 150, 151, commentary on Art. 217. Cf. P.C.I., resp. 16 iun. 1931: "An vi canonis 1989 eadem causa matrimonialis ab uno tribunali iudicata, ab alio tribunali eiusdem gradus iterum iudicari possit? R. Negative."—*AAS,* XXIII (1931), 353.

43 Roberti, *De Processibus,* II, n. 512, p. 250.

Another difference is that the appeal may be lodged without any new evidence, whereas a reintroduction of a cause, after two conformable sentences, is not to be admitted unless new and important evidence warrants it, *"nisi novis prolatis iisdemque gravibus argumentis vel documentis."*[44]

Article 217, § 3, of the *Instruction* explains that such new arguments or documents need not be *gravissima,*[45] and thus not necessarily the most cogent;[46] and much less must they be of such a nature that they would demand peremptorily a decision contrary to the previous one. The new arguments or documents, however, should give evidence of solid probability.[47]

According to Roberti, a wide interpretation may be given to *nova argumenta.*[48] They include therefore proofs of any kind, and may refer to facts already brought forward in previous instances but not sufficiently proved, or even to a deeper consideration of proofs already produced.

Because of the nature and importance of matrimonial causes and the obligation to adjudge them properly, jurisprudence is very benign in admitting a new examination of a cause in which the marriage bond is involved.[49]

The cogency of this new evidence is to be decided, not by the court of second instance, but by the tribunal of the third instance upon consultation with the *defensor vinculi.*[50] Although article 217, § 3, of the Instruction does not specify to which tribunal the *defensor vinculi* belongs, regarding the required consultation in this matter, it seems obvious that it refers

[44] Canons 1903; 1989; *Instructio,* Art. 217, § 2. Cf. Wernz-Vidal, *Ius Canonicum,* V. n. 703, pp. 914, 915.

[45] Thus Labourné-Byrnes are inexact in stating "... according to canon 1903, this can be done only if new and *very serious* [italics supplied] proofs or documents can be furnished as the basis of a new trial."—*Procedure,* p. 118.

[46] Cf. Acta Tribunalium, Sacra Romana Rota, *Dioecesis Z., Nullitate Matrimonii, incidentis,* 19 maii 1919—*AAS,* XIII (1921), 547.

[47] For examples of cases not permitted to be reintroduced before the S. R. Rota, cf. *AAS,* XXVI (1934), 125, n. I; *AAS,* XXII (1931), 105, n. II.

[48] *De Processibus,* II, n. 511, pp. 249, 250.

[49] Thus Roberti remarks: "Practice iurisprudentia, cum in discrimen ius divinum dubitat inveniri, valde benigna est in novis examinibus admittendis."—*De Processibus,* II, n. 511, p. 250.

[50] *Instructio,* Art. 217, § 3.

to the *defensor* of the court of third instance. Since the decision regarding the probative value of these documents and arguments rests with the tribunals of the Holy See, a great burden and responsibility is lifted from the court of second instance.[51]

When a new examination of the cause is requested, there should be formulated a *libellus*[52] in which the reasons will be indicated as the basis upon which the request is made. If the Rota should reject the petition, recourse could be taken to the Signatura Apostolica.[53]

ARTICLE III. COMPLAINT OF NULLITY

The procedure in introducing a complaint of nullity, the *querela nullitatis,* against a sentence in the court of second instance follows the norms for the same legal redress against an invalid sentence in the lower tribunal. Consequently, only a brief review of the essential provisions will be noted here.

In attacking a sentence because of alleged invalidity, it is necessary to keep in mind the distinction between nullity which is remediable and that which is irremediable. When a sentence is vitiated with irremediable nullity according to the norms of canon 1892,[54] an action of complaint of nullity may be presented within thirty years of the publication of the sentence to the tribunal which rendered the decision.[55] The day of publication is not computed in the period of thirty years.[56]

[51] Doheny, *Canonical Procedure in Matrimonial Cases,* p. 365.

[52] Cappello, *Praxis Processualis,* n. 129, p. 111.

[53] Roberti, *De Processibus,* II, n. 512, p. 250. For an example of recourse to the Signatura Apostolica in this regard, cf. Acta Tribunalium Sacra Romana Rota, *Dioecesis Z., Nullitatis matrimonii, incidentis,* 19 maii 1919—*AAS,* XIII (1921), 546-548.

[54] "Sententia vitio insanabilis nullitatis laborat, quando:

1° Lata est a iudice absolute incompetente vel in tribunali collegiali a non legitimo iudicum numero contra praescriptum can. 1576, § 1;

2° Lata est inter partes, quarum altera saltem non habet personam standi in iudicio;

3° Quis nomine alterius egit sine legitimo mandato.

Cf. *Instructio,* Art. 207.

[55] Canon 1893; *Instructio,* Art. 208.

[56] Coronata, *Institutiones Iuris Canonici,* III, n. 1417, p. 335.

An exception of nullity, however, being perpetual by its very nature, may be presented at any time before any competent tribunal.[57]

The complaint of nullity, whether in the form of an action or of an exception, may be proposed by the parties, by the *defensor vinculi,* or by the *promotor iustitiae,* if the latter is engaged in the case.[58] When the question of such nullity is introduced before the tribunal, the *promotor iustitiae,* although not legally obliged to do so, should be present at the preceedings, even though he has not taken part in the trial. The reason for this is based on the fact that such a matter pertains to the public good.[59]

The mere expiration of time can in no way sanate the irremediably invalid sentence. There is likewise no possibility of appeal to the Rota or to the Holy Office. The only possibility of a sanation lies with the Signatura Apostolica, and consequently all such requests should be directed to that tribunal.[60]

In the event that the sentence is one of remediable nullity according to the provisions of canon 1894,[61] the complaint of

[57] Canon 1667; 1893; *Instructio,* Art. 208. Cf. Wernz-Vidal, *Ius Canonicum,* VI, n. 619, p. 570.

[58] It appears in virtue of art. 44, § 2, and art. 50 of the *Instruction,* that the procurator may also propose the complaint of nullity to the court, unless the mandate authorizing him to represent the parties has been expressly or tacitly revoked. This opinion is held by Coronata, *Institutiones Iuris Canonici,* III, n. 1420, p. 339; Wernz-Vidal, *Ius Canonicum,* VI, n. 617, p. 569; Muñiz, *Procédimientos Eclesiásticos,* III, n. 498, p. 425; Doheny, *Canonical Procedure in Matrimonial Cases,* p. 347; against Roberti, *De Processibus,* II, n. 500, p. 234.

[59] Cf. Coronata, *Institutiones Iuris Canonici,* III, n. 1419, pp. 337, 338; Wernz-Vidal, *Ius Canoncium,* VI, n. 620, p. 570, note (9); Muñiz, *Procédimientos Eclesiásticos,* III, n. 500, p. 427, note (1); Roberti, *De Processibus,* II, n. 500, p. 234. For examples of petition of the *querela nullitatis* and the decree of the tribunal in regard to its admission, cf. Benedetti, *Ordo Iudicialis,* pp. 122, 123.

[60] Doheny, *Canonical Procedure in Matrimonial Cases,* p. 351. For an example of a sanation of this kind cf. *Vicariatus Apostolicus de Loango, Nullitatis Matrimonii,* 31 iul. 1928, coram R.P.D. Iosepho Florczak, dec. XXXVII, nn. 1, 8—*Decisiones,* XX (1936), 342, 346.

[61] "Sententia vitio sanabilis nullitatis laborat, quando:

1° Legitima defuit citatio;

2° Motivis seu rationibus decidendi est destituta, salvo praescripto can. 1605;

3° Subscriptionibus caret iure praescriptis;

4° Non refert indicationem anni, mensis, diei et loci quo prolata fuit.

nullity may be proposed either together with the appeal within ten days to a higher tribunal, or separately and alone within three months from the time of the publication of the sentence. If the latter course is followed, the complaint must be presented to the court which rendered the sentence.[62] If the party fears that the tribunal may be prejudiced because of its pronouncement of the sentence of nullity, and consequently thinks that it is suspect, he may demand that other judges be substituted in the same tribunal.[63]

When the complaint of nullity is joined with the appeal, it is sent with the latter to the court of third instance, that is, to the Rota or to the Holy Office.

The court of second instance may retract and correct the sentence itself, but it must do so within the time set by law.[64]

If the complaint of nullity has not been introduced by the parties, by the *defensor vinculi,* or by the *promotor iustitiae,*[65] or if it has not been corrected by the court within the time limits set by the law,[66] the sentence is considered as automatically sanated after the lapse of three months.[67]

It should be remembered, however, that this automatic sanation after three months applies only to those sentences which were vitiated with a remediable nullity, and not to those which were invalid in consequence of an accompanying irremediable nullity.

62 Canon 1895; *Instructio,* Art. 210.

63 Canons 1615, 1896; *Instructio,* Art. 211. § 4. Cf. Vermeersch-Creusen, *Epitome,* III, n. 242, p. 119.

64 Canon 1897 § 2; *Instructio,* Art. 210; 211, § 2. Cf. Wernz-Vidal, *Ius Canonicum,* VI, n. 622, p. 572.

65 Canon 1897; *Instructio,* Art. 211, § 1.

66 Canons 1895; 1897; *Instructio,* Art. 210, 211, § 2.

67 *Instructio,* Art. 211, § 3.

CONCLUSIONS

1. The ordinary court of second instance is competent *ratione gradus.*

2. When a new cause has been introduced into the court of second instance according to the provisions of article 219, § 2, of the *Instruction* of 1936, it should be tried by this tribunal, acting as a court of first instance, as a separate and distinct cause from that appealed from the lower tribunal. An appeal from the sentence on the new grounds of nullity would go either to the appellate court of the tribunal that rendered the sentence or to Rome. The latter's courts would not enjoy such exclusive competency over it that it would have to be appealed there directly.

3. If a question of disputed competency should arise between two metropolitan tribunals, or between a metropolitan see and a suffragan see, or between sees subject to the Holy See, the conflict is to be settled by the Legate of the Holy See, if there is one, or by the Signatura Apostolica. The appellate tribunals mentioned in canon 1594, § § 2, 3, are thus excluded.

4. A cause in the court of second instance must be judged by a tribunal of at least three judges; otherwise the sentence is vitiated by irremediable nullity. The acts of the process, however, are valid.

5. Consorts who are legally prevented from impugning their marriage are likewise prevented from the right to appeal.

6. The advocate as well as the procurator has the right and duty to appeal unless the party has expressly refused to permit him to do so.

7. The *promotor iustitiae* is not legally bound to appeal from an adverse sentence. If he does appeal, he may withdraw from the process if he finds that the impugning of the validity of the marriage cannot be sustained in fact or in law. The judgment, however, as to whether the process should continue, on the basis of scandal, belongs to the Ordinary of the court of first instance.

8. The continuance of the trial in the court of second instance after the death of one of the consorts may be permitted for grave reasons, as, for instance, in order to safeguard the legitimacy of a child perchance born of an attempted marriage, or in order to acquire an inheritance. Not only the surviving consort, but also the heirs of the deceased, may ask for a continuance of the case, but if the validity of the marriage is to be attacked it must be only as an incidental question.

9. The admission or rejection of the appeal pertains to the collegiate tribunal.

10. The citations are as necessary in the court of second instance as in the lower tribunal.

11. New evidence is demanded only for the reintroduction of a cause after two conformable sentences, and not in a case in which the appeal was abandoned or abated after only one sentence had been pronounced, or after a second sentence that did not conform to the first.

12. Before the introduction of new proofs in the ordinary court of second instance, it is not necessary under pain of nullity of the trial that the opposite party first be heard, as long as the latter is given sufficient time, after the introduction of such proofs, to be cognizant of the new proofs and to put up a defense against them.

13. Under the provisions of canon 1861, § 1, the judge is not permitted, as a general rule, to limit the defense against new proofs to mere animadversions; he must permit contrary proofs if they are offered.

14. Notification of the sentence is to be sent directly by the court of second instance to the parties, instead of indirectly through the court of first instance.

15. In the reintroduction of a cause after two conformable sentences, a wide interpretation may be given to *nova argumenta.* They include, therefore, proofs of any kind, and may refer to facts already brought forward in previous instances but not sufficiently proved, or even to a deeper consideration of proofs already produced.

BIBLIOGRAPHY

SOURCES

Acta Apostolicae Sedis, Commentarium Officiale, Romae, 1909—

Acta et Decreta Concilii Plenarii Baltimorensis Tertii, A.D. MDCCCLXXIV, Baltimorae: Typis Joannis Murphy Sociorum, 1886.

Bruns, H. Theodorus, *Canones Apostolorum et Conciliorum Saeculorum IV-V-VI-VII,* 2 vols., Berolini, 1839.

Bouscaren, T. Lincoln, *The Canon Law Digest,* 2 vols., Milwaukee: Bruce Publishing Co., 1934-1943.

Codex Iuris Canonici Fontes, cura Emi Petri Card. Gasparri editi, 9 vols., Romae (postea Civitate Vaticana): Typis Polyglottis Vaticanis, 1923-1939. (Vols. VII, VIII, IX, ed. cura et studio Emi Iustiniani Card. Serédi).

Codex Iuris Canonici Pii X Pontificis iussu digestus Benedicti XV auctoritate promulgatus, Romae: Typis Polyglottis Vaticanis, 1917.

Coronata, Matthaeus Conte a, *Interpretatio Authentica Codicis Iuris Canonici et circa Ipsum Sanctae Sedis Iurisprudentia,* 1916-1940, Taurini-Marietti, 1940.

Corpus Iuris Canonici, editio Lipsiensis II post Aemilii Ludovici Richteri curas instruxit Aemilius Friedberg, Lipsiae: Ex Officina Bernhardi Tauchnitz, 1879-1881; ed. anastatice repetita, 1928.

Corpus Iuris Civilis, editio stereotypa, 3 vols., Berolini: apud Weidmannos, 1928-1929, Vol. I, ed. 15., *Institutiones,* recognovit P. Krueger, 1929; *Digesta,* ed. 15., recognovit T. Mommsen, retractavit P. Krueger, 1929; Vol. II, ed., 10., *Codex Iustinianus,* recognovit et retractavit P. Krueger, 1929; Vol. III, ed. 5., *Novellae Constitutiones,* recognovit R. Schoell; opus Schoellii morte interceptum absolvit G. Kroll, 1928.

Corpus Scriptorum Ecclesiasticorum Latinorum, 68 vols., Vindobonae: apud C. Geroldi Filium Bibliopolam Academiae, 1866-1877; Hoelder, Pichler, Tempsky, 1888—

Decretales D. Gregorii Papae IX, una cum glossis Restitutae, Romae, 1582.

Decretum Gratiani Emendatum et Notationibus illustratum una cum glossis, Romae, 1582.

Didascalia et Constitutiones Apostolorum, ed. F. X. Funk, 2 vols., Paderbornae, 1905.

Ecclesiae Occidentalis Monumenta Iuris Antiquissima Canonum et Conciliorum Graecorum Interpretationes Latinae, edidit Cuthbertus Hamilton Turner, 2 vols., Oxonii, 1899-1930.

Hardouin, Jean, *Acta Conciliorum et Epistolae Decretales ac Constitutiones Summorum Pontificum,* 12 vols., Parisiis, 1714-1715.

Jaffé, Ph., *Regesta Pontificum Romanorum ab condita Ecclesia ad annum post Christum natum MCXCVIII,* 2. ed., correctam et auctam auspiciis Guglielmi Wattenbach, curaverunt F. Kaltenbrunner, P. Ewald, S. Loewenfeld, 2 vols. in I, Lipsiae, 1885-1888.

Lex Romana Visigothorum, ed., Gustavus Haenel, Leipsig, 1849.

Liber Sextus Decretalium, una cum Clementinis et Extravagantibus earumque glossis restitutis, Romae, 1582.

Mansi, Joannes, *Sacrorum Conciliorum Nova et Amplissima Collectio,* 53 vols. in 60, Parisiis, 1901-1927.

Monumenta Germaniae Historica, Epistolae, Tom. II, *Gregorii I Papae Registrum Epistolarum,* 2 parts, ed. Paulus Ewald et Ludovicus M. Hartman, Berolini, 1891-1899.

Monumenta Germaniae Historica, Epistolae, Tom. VIII, *Karolini Aevi,* Fasc. I. *Hincmari Archiepiscopi Remensis Epistolarum pars prima,* Berolini apud Weidmannos, 1939.

Monumenta Germaniae Historica, Legum Sect. III, Concilia Aevi Merovingici, Tom. I, recensuit Friedericus Maasen, Hannoverae, 1893.

Monumenta Germaniae Historica, Leges, 5 vols., Vols., I-IV ed. G. Pertz; Vol. V ed. G. Pertz, G. Waitz, H. Brunner, Hannoverae, 1835-1889.

Potthast, Augustus, *Regesta Pontificum Romanorum inde ab anno post Christum natum 1198 ad annum 1304,* 2 vols., Berolini, 1874-1875.

Sacrae Romanae Decisiones seu Sententiae quae... prodierunt anno 1909-1938, 30 vols., Romae: Typis Vaticanis, 1912-1945.

Theodosiani Libri XVI cum Constitutionibus Sirmondianis, ediderunt Th. Mommsen et Paulus M. Meyer, 3 vols., Berolini, 1905.

Thesaurus Resolutionum Sacrae Congregationis Concilii, 167 vols., Romae, 1718- 1908.

REFERENCE WORKS

Augustine, Charles, *A Commentary on the New Code of Canon Law,* 8 vols., St. Louis: B. Herder and Co., Vol. II, 4 ed., 1923; Vol. V, 1919; Vol. VII, 3. ed., 1930.

Bassibey, R., *Le Mariage devant les Tribunaux Ecclésiastiques, Procedure Matrimoniale Generale,* Paris: Librairie Religieuse H. Oudin, 1899.

Bellarmine, R., *Opera Omnia,* 2. ed., 8 vols., Neapoli: Xisto Riario Sforza, 1872.

Benedetti, Ivo, *Ordo Iudicialis Processus Canonici Super Nullitate Matrimonii Instruendi,* 2. ed., Taurini: Marietti, 1938.

Bernardus Papiensis, *Summa Decretalium,* ed. E.A.T. Laspeyres, Ratisbonae, 1860.

Biondi, Biondo, *Appunti intorno alla Sentenza nel Processo Civile Romano,* Pavia: Successori Fratelli Fusi, 1929.

Blat, Albertus, *Commentarium Textus Codicis Iuris Canonici,* Lib. IV, De Processibus, Romae, 1927.

Bouix, D., *Tractatus de Judiciis Ecclesiasticis,* 2. ed., 2 vols., Parisiis, 1866.

Buckland, W. W., *A Text Book of Roman Law from Augustus to Justinian,* 2. ed., Cambridge: University Press, 1921.

Burke, Thomas J., *Competence in Ecclesiastical Tribunals,* The Catholic University of America Canon Law Studies, n. 14, Washington, D.C.: The Catholic University of America, 1922.

Cappello, Felix M., *Praxis Processualis,* Taurini-Romae: Marietti, 1940.

———, *Tractatus Canonico-Moralis de Sacramentis,* III, Pars II, *De Matrimonio,* 4. ed., Romae: Apud Aedes Universitatis Gregorianae, 1939.

Chelodi, Ioannes, *Ius Matrimoniale iuxta Codicem Iuris Canonici,* 3. ed., Trento 1921.

Cicognani, Amleto Giovanni, *Canon Law,* authorized English version by J. O'Hara and F. Brennan, Philadelphia: Dolphin Press, 1934.

Cocchi, Guidus, *Commentarium in Codicem Iuris Canonici,* VII, 3. ed., Taurini: Marietti, 1940.

Connolly, Thomas A., *Appeals,* The Catholic University of America Canon Law Studies, n. 79, Washington, D. C.: The Catholic University of America, 1932.

Corbett, P., *The Roman Law of Marriage,* Oxford: Clarendon Press, 1930.

Coronata, Matthaeus Conte a, *Institutiones Iuris Canonici,* III, *De Processibus,* 2. ed., Taurini: Marietti, 1941.

Costa, Emilio, *Profilo Storico del Processo Civile* Romano, Roma, 1918.

De Luca, Ioannes Baptista, *Theatrum Veritatis et Justitiae,* 16 vols., Coloniae Agrippinae, 1706.

De Smet, Aloysius, *De Sponsalibus et Matrimonio,* Brugis, 1909.

———, *Tractatus Theologico-Canonicus de Sponsalibus et Matrimonio,* 4. ed., Brugis: Car. Beyaert, 1927.

Devoti, Ioannes, *Institutionum Canonicarum Libri IV,* 3 vols., Romae, 1827.

Doheny, William, *Canonical Procedure in Matrimonial Cases,* I, *Formal Judicial Procedure,* Milwaukee: Bruce Publishing Co., 1938.

———, *Practical Manual for Marriage Cases,* Milwaukee: Bruce Publishing Co., 1938.

Dolan, John, *The Defensor Vinculi, His Rights and Duties,* The Catholic University of America Canon Law Studies, n. 85, Washington, D. C.: The Catholic University of America, 1934.

Durandus (Durantis) Guglielmus, *Speculum Iuris,* 3 vols., Venetiis, 1577.

Eichmann, Eduard, *Das Prozessrecht des Codex Iuris Canonici,* Paderborn: Schöningh, 1921.

Engelmann, Arthur, and Millar, Robert, *A History of Continental Civil Procedure,* Boston: Little, Brown and Co., 1927.

Esmein, A., *Le Mariage en Droit Canonique,* 2. ed., 2 vols., Paris: Librairie du Recueil Sirey, 1929- 1935. Vol. I, ed. R. Génestal, 1929; Vol. II, ed. R. Génestal—. Dauvillier, 1935.

Feeney, Thomas, *Restitutio in Integrum,* The Catholic University of America Canon Law Studies, n. 129, Washington, D. C.: The Catholic University of America Press, 1941.

Feije, Henricus, *De Impedimentis et Dispensationibus Matrimonialibus,* 3. ed., Lovanii, 1885.

Ferraris, Lucius, *Prompta Biblioteca Canonica, Iuridica, Moralis, Theologica necnon Ascetica, Polemica, Rubricistica, Historica,* 9 vols., Romae, 1885-1889.

Gasparri, Petrus, *Tractatus Canonicus de Matrimonio,* ed. nova ad mentem Codicis Iuris Canonici, 2 vols., Romae: Typis Polyglottis Vaticanis, 1932; also ed. tertia, 2 vols., Parisiis, 1904.

Glynn, John C., *The Promoter of Justice,* The Catholic University of America Canon Law Studies, n. 101, Washington, D. C.: The Catholic University of America, 1936.

Hostiensis (Henricus de Segusio), *In Quinque Libros Decretalium Commentaria,* 5 vols., Venetiis, 1581.

Hefele, Charles Joseph, and Leclerq, H., *Histoire des Conciles,* 10 vols. in 19, Paris: Letouzey et Ané, 1907-1938.

Hogan, James J., *Judicial Advocates and Procurators,* The Catholic University of America Canon Law Studies, n. 133, Washington, D. C.: The Catholic University of America Press, 1941.

Jolowicz, H. F., *An Historical Introduction to the Study of Roman Law,* Cambridge: University Press, 1932.

Joyce, George H., *Christian Marriage,* London: Sheed and Ward, 1933.

Kay, Thomas H., *Competence in Matrimonial Procedure,* The Catholic University of America Canon Law Studies, n. 53, Washington, D. C.: The Catholic University of America, 1929.

Kealy, John J., *The Introductory Libellus in Church Court Procedure,* The Catholic University of America Canon Law Studies, n. 108, Washington, D. C.; The Catholic University of America, 1937.

Kennedy, Edwin J., *The Special Matrimonial Process in Cases of Evident Nullity,* The Catholic University of America Canon Law Studies, n. 93, Washington, D. C.: The Catholic University of America, 1935.

Król, John J., *The Defendant in Contentious Trials,* The Catholic University of America Canon Law Studies, n. 146, Washington, D. C.: The Catholic University of America Press, 1942.

Labouré, T., and Byrnes, W., *Procedure in the Diocesan Matrimonial Courts of First Instance,* New York: Benziger Bros., 1928.

Lanier, C. Henri, *Guide Pratique de la Procédure Matrimoniale en Droit Canonique,* Parisiis, 1927.

Laurin, Franciscus, *Introductio in Corpus Iuris Canonici,* Friburgi Brisgoviae, 1889.

Lega, Michael, *Praelectiones de Iudiciis Ecclesiasticis,* 4 vols., Romae, 1896-1901.

———, *Praelectiones de Iudiciis Civilibus,* 2. ed., Romae, 1905.

Lega, M., and Bartoccetti, V., *Commentarius in Iudicia Ecclesiastica iuxta Codicem Iuris Canonici,* II, Romae: Anonima Libraria Cattolica Italiana, 1939.

Lemieux, Delisle, A., *The Sentence in Ecclesiastical Procedure,* The Catholic University of America Canon Law Studies, n. 87, Washington, D. C.: The Catholic University of America, 1934.

Lyons, Avitus, E., *The Collegiate Tribunal of First Instance,* The Catholic University of America Canon Law Studies, n. 78, Washington, D. C.: The Catholic University of America, 1932.

Mansella, Joseph, *De Impedimentis ac de Processu Iudiciali in Causis Matrimonialibus,* Romae, 1881.

McClunn, Justin, D., *Administrative Recourse,* The Catholic University of America Canon Law Studies, n. 240, Washington, D. C.: The Catholic University of America Press, 1946.

Migne, P. J., *Patrologiae Cursus Completus, Series Graeca,* 161 vols., Parisiis, 1856-1866.

———, *Patrologiae Cursus Completus, Series Latina,* 221 vols., Parisiis, 1844-1864.

Muñiz, T., *Procédimientos Eclesiásticos,* 2. ed., 3 vols., Sevilla, 1925.

Noval, Ioseph, *Commentarium Codicis Iuris Canonici,* Liber IV, *De Processibus,* Pars I, *De Iudiciis,* Augustae Taurinorum-Romae, 1920.

Panormitanus, Abbas (Nicholaus de Tudeschis), *Commentaria in Quinque Libros Decretalium,* 8 vols., Venetiis, 1588.

Payen, G., *De Matrimonio in Missionibus ac Potissimum in Sinis Tractatus Practicus et Casus,* 2. ed., 3 vols., Zi-ka-wei: Typographia T'ou-Sé Wé, 1935-1936.

Pellegrini, Carolus, *Praxis Vicariorum,* Venetiis, 1696.

Pirhing, Ernricus, *Ius Canonicum in V Libros Decretalium,* 5 vols., Dilingae, 1674.

Regatillo, Eduardus F., *Ius Sacramentarium,* 2 vols., Santander: Sal Terrae, 1945-1946.

Reiffenstuel, Anacletus, *Jus Canonicum Universum,* 6 vols., Romae, 1831-1835.

Roberti, Franciscus, *De Processibus,* 2 vols., Romae: Apud Aedes Facultatis Iuridicae ad S. Apollinaris, 1926; Vol. I, 2. ed., Romae: Apud Custodiam Librariam Pontificii Instituti Utriusque Iuris, 1941.

Santi, Franciscus, *Praelectiones Iuris Canonici,* ed. M. Leitner, 4. ed., 3 vols., Ratisbonae, 1903-1905.

Scaccia, Sigismundus, *Tractatus de Appellationibus,* 3. ed., Coloniae, 1717.

Schmalzgrueber, Franciscus, *Jus Ecclesiasticum Universum,* 5 vols. in 12, Romae, 1843-1845.

Smith, S. B., *Elements of Ecclesiastical Law,* Vol. II, *Ecclesiastical Trials,* 5. ed., New York, 1892.

———, *The Matrimonial Process in the United States,* New York, 1895.

Sohm, Rudolph, *The Institutes of Roman Law,* translated by James C. Leslie, 3. ed., Oxford: Clarendon Press, 1907.

Tobin, Thomas, *De Officiali Curiae Diocesanae,* Romae: Aud Aedes Pontificiae Universitatis Gregorianae, 1936.

Torre, Ioannes, *Processus Matrimonialis,* Napoli: M. D'Auria, 1936.

Van Hove, A., *Commentarium Lovaniense in Codicem Iuris Canonici,* Vol. I, Tom. I, *Prolegomena,* 2. ed., Mechliniae-Romae: H. Dessain, 1945.

Vaughn, William E., *Constitutions for Diocesan Courts,* The Catholic University of America Canon Law Studies, n. 210, Washington, D. C.: The Catholic University of America Press, 1944.

Vermeersch, A.-Creusen, J. *Epitome Iuris Canonici,* III, 6. ed., Mechliniae-Romae: H. Dessain, 1946.

Vismara, Giulio, *Episcopalis Audientia,* Pubblicazioni della U. Cattalica del Sacro Cuore, 2. serie, Scienze Giuridiche, n. LIV, Milano: Vita e Pensiero, 1937.

Vlaming, Th. M., *Praelectiones Iuris Matrimonii,* 3. ed., 2 vols., Bussum in Hollandia, 1919-1921.

Wenger, Leopold, *Institutes of the Roman Law of Civil Procedure,* revised ed. translated by Otis H. Fisk, New York: Veritas Press, 1940.

Wahrmund, Ludwig, *Quellen zur Geschichte des römisch-kanonischen Processes im Mittelalter,* Innsbruck: Verlag der Wagner'schen Universitäts-Buchhandlung, 1905-1928.

Wernz, Franciscus, *Ius Decretalium,* 6 vols. in 10, Vol. IV, *Ius Matrimoniale,* 2. ed., Prati, pars prima, 1911; pars secunda, 1912; Vol. V, *De Iudiciis Ecclesiasticis,* 3. ed., Prati, 1914.

Wernz, Franciscus, and Vidal, Petrus, *Ius Canonicum,* Vol. V, *Ius Matrimoniale,* 3. ed., a. P. Philippo Aguirre recognita, Romae: Apud Aedes Universitatis Gregorianae, 1946; Vol. VI, *De Processibus,* Romae: Apud Aedes Universitatis Gregorianae, 1927-1928.

Woywod, Stanislaus, *A Practical Commentary on the Code of Canon Law,* 7. ed., edited by Callistus Smith, 2 vols., New York: Joseph F. Wagner, 1943.

Zaccaria, A., *Anti-Febbronio,* 2. ed., Cesena, 1770.

PERIODICALS

Analecta Juris Pontificii, Romae, 1855-1869; Parisiis, 1872-1891.

Apollinaris, Romae, 1928-1940.

Jurist, The, Washington, D. C., 1941—

Jus Pontificium, Romae, 1921—

Monitore Ecclesiastico, II, Romae, 1876—

Periodica de Religiosis et Missionariis, Brugis, 1905-1919; *Periodica de Re Canonica et Morali utili Praesertim Religiosis et Misionariis,* 1920-1927; *Periodica de Re Canonica, Morali, Liturgica,* 1927—

Revista Española de Derecho Canónico, Salamanca, 1946—

Theologisch-praktische Quartalschrift, Linz, 1832—

PRINCIPAL ARTICLES

Aguirre, P., "De Iure Accusandi Matrimonium"— *Periodica,* XXXIV (1945), 285-287.

Cabreros, M., "Apelación contra la sententia del juez delgado"—*Revista Española de Derecho Canónico,* I (1946), 105-133.

Cappello, F. M., "Utrum conformes ad normam can. 1903 et 1987 dicendae sint duae sententiae de nullitate matrimonii latae, si eiusdem nullitas declarata fuerit ex diverso capite"—*Periodica,* XX (1931), 20*-28*.

Ciprotti, P., "Quaestiones de appellatione et peremptione in causis matrimonialibus"—*Apollinaris,* XII (1939), 115-123.

———, "De novis probationibus post conclusionem in causa"—*Apollinaris,* XII (1939), 110-113.

D'Angelo, S., "De gratuito patrocinio"—*Apollinaris,* II (1929), 514-516.

Dalpiaz, V., "An in altera instantia causae de qua in can. 1917, § 1, n. 2, requiratur ad validitatem interventus promotoris iustitiae, etiamsi defensor vinculi appellationem interposuit"—*Apollinaris,* VIII (1935), 139-140.

Hanssen, A., "De sanctione nullitatis in processu canonico"—*Apollinaris,* XI (1938), 381-403; XII (1939), 198-251.

Haring, J., "Gelten die Notfristen auch für den *defensor vinculi* im Eheprozess?"—*Theologisch-praktische Quartalschrift,* LXXXIII (1930), 597, 598.

Roberti, F., "De nullitate sententiae ob defectum habilitatis ad accusandum matrimonium"—*Apollinaris,* XII (1939), 415-417.

———, "De recessu ab accusatione matrimonii per promotorem iustitiae"—*Apollinaris,* XII (1939), 527-530.

———, "De condicione processuali promotoris iustitiae, defensoris vinculi et coniugum in causis matrimonialibus"—*Apollinaris,* XI (1938), 575-584.

———, "De sententia nullitatis vitio infecta"—*Apollinaris,* IX (1936), 662-664.

———, De appellatione defensoris vinculi in causis matrimonialibus"—*Apollinaris,* II (1929), 516-518.

———, "De facultatibus defensoris vinculi quoad appellationem"—*Apollinaris,* IX (1936), 310-311.

———, "De iure defensoris vinculi invisendi scriptas iudicum conclusiones" *Apollinaris* I (1928), 188-189.

———, "De expensis iudicialibus pro exsequendis litteris rogatoriis"—*Apollinaris,* X (1937), 278-279.

Toso, A., "De munere promotoris iustitiae matrimonium accusantis"—*Jus Pontificium,* XVIII (1938), 3-9.

———, "De matrimonio accusando vel denunciando"—*Jus Pontificium,* XVII (1937), 5-12.

Triebs, F., "De promotore iustitiae in causis nullitatis matrimonii ac praesertim de eius iure accusandi"—*Apollinaris,* X (1937), 395-407.

ABBREVIATIONS

AAS—*Acta Apostolica Sedis*

C.—*Codex* (Iustinianus)

D.—*Digestum* (Iustinianus)

Decisiones—*S. Romanae Rotae Decisiones seu Sententiae*

Fontes—*Codicis Iuris Canonici Fontes*

I.—*Institutiones* (Iustinianae)

Jaffé—*Regesta Pontificium Romanorum* (edited by Ewald, Kaltenbruner, Loewenfeld)

Mansi—*Sacrorum Conciliorum Nova et Amplissima Collectio*

MGH—*Monumenta Germaniae Historica*

MPG—*Migne, Patrologia, Series Graeca*

MPL—*Migne, Patrologia, Series Latina*

N.—*Novellae* (Iustinianae)

P.C.I.—*Pontificia Commissio ad Codicis Canones authentice interpretandos*

Potthast—*Regesta Pontificium Romanorum*

S.C.C.—Sacra Congregatio Concilii

S.C. de Prop. Fide—Sacra Congregatio de Propaganda Fide

S.C. de Sacr.—Sacra Congregatio de Sacramentis

S.C.S. Off.—Sacra Congregatio Sancti Officii

ALPHABETICAL INDEX

BIOGRAPHICAL NOTE

Loras Thomas Lane was born at Cascade, Iowa, October 19, 1910. He received his primary and high school education at St. Martin's Parochial School of Cascade. From there he entered Notre Dame University, South Bend, Indiana, and was graduated in June, 1932, with the degree of Ph. B. in Foreign Commerce. In June, 1933, he received the Bachelor's degree in Liberal Arts from Loras College, Dubuque, Iowa. In the fall of that year he was assigned to take up his theological studies at the Pontifical Gregorian University in Rome, Italy. He obtained the degree of Licentiate in Sacred Theology from that institution in July, 1937. In 1940 he was appointed to the faculty of Loras College of Dubuque, where he served as Instructor in Spanish and Economics. In 1944, after a year of graduate work in Spanish at the University of Iowa, he enrolled in the School of Canon Law at The Catholic University of America. There he was awarded the degree of Bachelor in Canon Law in May, 1945, and the degree of Licentiate in Canon Law in June, 1946.

CANON LAW STUDIES*

1. Freriks, Rev. Celestine A., C.PP.S., J.C.D., Religious Congregations in Their External Relations, 121 pp., 1916.

2. Galliher, Rev. Daniel M., O.P., J.C.D., Canonical Elections, 117 pp., 1917.

3. Borkowski, Rev. Aurelius L., O.F.M., J.C.D., De Confraternitatibus Ecclesiasticis, 136 pp., 1918.

4. Castillo, Rev. Cayo, J.C.D., Disertación Histórico-Canónica sobre la Potestad del Cabildo en Sede Vacante o Impedida del Vicario Capitular, 99 pp., 1919 (1918).

5. Kubelbeck, Rev. William J., S.T.B., J.C.D., The Sacred Penitentiaria and Its Relation to Faculties of Ordinaries and Priests, 129 pp., 1918.

6. Petrovits, Rev. Joseph, J.C., S.T.D., J.C.D., The New Church Law on Matrimony, X-461 pp., 1919.

7. Hickey, Rev. John J., S.T.B., J.C.D., Irregularities and Simple Impediments in the New Code of Canon Law, 100 pp., 1920.

8. Klekotka, Rev. Peter J., S.T.B., J.C.D., Diocesan Consultors, 179 pp., 1920.

9. Wanenmacher, Rev. Francis, J.C.D., The Evidence in Ecclesiastical Procedure Affecting the Marriage Bond, 1920 (Printed 1935).

10. Golden, Rev. Henry Francis, J.C.D., Parochial Benefices in the New Code, IV-119 pp., 1921 (Printed 1925).

11. Koudelka, Rev. Charles J., J.C.D., Pastors, Their Rights and Duties According to the New Code of Canon Law, 211 pp., 1921.

12. Melo, Rev. Antonius, O.F.M., J.C.D., De Exemptione Regularium, X-188 pp., 1921.

13. Schaaf, Rev. Valentine Theodore, O.F.M., S.T.B., J.C.D., The Cloister, X-180 pp., 1921.

14. Burke, Rev. Thomas Joseph, S.T.D., J.C.D., Competence in Ecclesiastical Tribunals, IV-117 pp., 1922.

15. Leech, Rev. George Leo, J.C.D., A Comparative Study of the Constitution "Apostolicae Sedis" and the "Codex Juris Canonici," 179 pp., 1922.

16. Motry, Rev. Hubert Louis, S.T.D., J.C.D., Diocesan Faculties According to the Code of Canon Law, II-167 pp., 1922.

17. Murphy, Rev. George Lawrence, J.C.D., Delinquencies and Penalties in the Administration and the Reception of the Sacraments, IV-121 pp., 1924.

18. O'Reilly, Rev. John Anthony, S.T.B., J.C.D., Ecclesiastical Sepulture in the New Code of Canon Law, II-129 pp., 1923.

19. Michalicka, Rev. Wenceslas Cyrill, O.S.B., J.C.D., Judicial Procedure in Dismissal of Clerical Exempt Religious, 107 pp., 1923.

*—All published numbers of this series are available from the Catholic University of America Press, 621 Michigan Ave., N.E., Washington 17, D.C., except the following: nn. 1-114 inclusive, 116, 118, 120, 122, 123, 136, 162 and 198.

20. Dargin, Rev. Edward Vincent, S.T.B., J.C.D., Reserved Cases According to the Code of Canon Law, IV-103 pp., 1924.

21. Godfrey, Rev. John A., S.T.B., J.C.D., The Right of Patronage According to the Code of Canon Law, 153 pp., 1924.

22. Hagedorn, Rev. Francis Edward, J.C.D., General Legislation on Indulgences, II-154 pp., 1924.

23. King, Rev. James Ignatius, J.C.D., The Administration of the Sacraments to Dying Non-Catholics, V-141 pp., 1924.

24. Winslow, Rev. Francis Joseph, O.F.M., J.C.D., Vicars and Prefects Apostolic, IV-149 pp., 1924.

25. Correa, Rev. Jose Servelion, S.T.L., J.C.D., La Potestad Legislativa de la Iglesia Católica, IV-127 pp., 1925.

26. Dugan, Rev. Henry Francis, A.M., J.C.D., The Judiciary Department of the Diocesan Curia, 87 pp., 1925.

27. Keller, Rev. Charles Frederick, S.T.B., J.C.D., Mass Stipends, 167 pp., 1925.

28. Paschang, Rev. John Linus, J.C.D., The Sacramentals According to the Code of Canon Law, 129 pp., 1925.

29. Piontek, Rev. Cyrillus, O.F.M., S.T.B., J.C.D., De Indulto Exclaustrationis necnon Saecularizationis, XIII-289 pp., 1925.

30. Kearney, Rev. Richard Joseph, S.T.B., J.C.D., Sponsors at Baptism According to the Code of Canon Law, IV-127 pp., 1925.

31. Bartlett, Rev. Chester Joseph, A.M., LL.B., J.C.D., The Tenure of Parochial Property in the United States of America, V-108 pp., 1926.

32. Kilker, Rev. Adrian Jerome, J.C.D., Extreme Unction, V-4125 pp., 1926.

33. McCormick, Rev. Robert Emmett, J.C.D., Confessors of Religious VIII-266 pp., 1926.

34. Miller, Rev. Newton Thomas, J.C.D., Founded Masses According to the Code of Canon Law, VII-93 pp., 1926.

35. Roelker, Rev. Edward G., S.T.D., J.C.D., Principles of Privilege According to the Code of Canon Law, XI-166 pp., 1926.

36. Bakalarczyk, Rev. Richards, M.I.C., J.U.D., De Novitiatu, VIII-208 pp., 1927.

37. Pizzuti, Rev. Lawrence, O.F.M., J.U.L., De Parochis Religiosis, 1927. (Not Printed.)

38. Bliley, Rev. Nicholas Martin, O.S.B., J.C.D., Altars According to the Code of Canon Law, XIX-132 pp., 1927.

39. Brown, Mr. Brendan Francis, A.B., LL.M., J.U.D., The Canonical Juristic Personality with Special Reference to its Status in the United States of America, V-212 pp., 1927.

40. Cavanaugh, Rev. William Thomas, C.P., J.U.D., The Reservation of the Blessed Sacrament, VIII-101 pp., 1927.

41. Doheny, Rev. William J., C.S.C., A.B., J.C.D., Church Property: Modes of Acquisition, X-118 pp., 1927.

42. Feldhaus, Rev. Aloysius H., C.PP.S., J.C.D., Oratories, IX-141 pp., 1927.

43. Kelly, Rev. James Patrick, A.B., J.C.D., The Jurisdiction of the Simple Confessor, X-208 pp., 1927.

44. Neuberger, Rev. Nicholas J., J.C.D., Canon 6 or the Relation of the Codex Juris Canonici to the Preceding Legislation, V-95 pp., 1927.

45. O'Keefe, Rev. Gerald Michael, J.C.D., Matrimonial Dispensations, Powers of Bishops, Priests, and Confessors, VIII-232 pp., 1927.

46. Quigley, Rev. Joseph A. M., A.B., J.C.D., Condemned Societies, 139 pp., 1927.

47. Zaplotnik, Rev. Johannes Leo, J.C.D., De Vicariis Foraneis, X-142 pp., 1927.

48. Duskie, Rev. John Aloysius, A.B., J.C.D., The Canonical Status of the Orientals in the United States, VIII-196 pp., 1928.

49. Hyland, Rev. Francis Edward, J.C.D., Excommunication, Its Nature, Historical Development and Effects, VIII-181 pp., 1928.

50. Reinmann, Rev. Gerald Joseph, O.M.C., J.C.D., The Third Order Secular of Saint Francis, 201 pp., 1928.

51. Schenk, Rev. Francis J., J.C.D., The Matrimonial Impediments of Mixed Religion and Disparity of Cult, XVI-318 pp., 1929.

52. Coady, Rev. John Joseph, S.T.D., J.U.D., A.M., The Appointment of Pastors, VIII-150 pp., 1929.

53. Kay, Rev. Thomas Henry, J.C.D., Competence in Matrimonial Procedure, VIII-164 pp., 1929.

54. Turner, Rev. Sidney Joseph, C.P., J.U.D., The Vow of Poverty, XLIX-217 pp., 1929.

55. Kearney, Rev. Raymond A., A.B., S.T.D., J.C.D., The Principles of Delegation, VII-149 pp., 1929.

56. Conran, Rev. Edward James, A.B., J.C.D., The Interdict, V-163 pp., 1930.

57. O'Neill, Rev. William H., J.C.D., Papal Rescripts of Favor, VII-218 pp., 1930.

58. Bastnagel, Rev. Clement Vincent, J.U.D., The Appointment of Parochial Adjutants and Assistants, XV-257 pp., 1930.

59. Ferry, Rev. William A., A.B., J.C.D., Stole Fees, V-136 pp., 1930.

60. Costello, Rev. John Michael, A.B., J.C.D., Domicile and Quasi-Domicile, VII-201 pp., 1930.

61. Kremer, Rev. Michael Nicholas, A.B., S.T.B., J.C.D., Church Support in the United States, VI-136 pp., 1930.

62. Angulo, Rev. Luis, C.M., J.C.D., Legislación de la Iglesia sobre la intención en la applicación de la Santa Misa, VII-104 pp., 1931.

63. Frey, Rev. Wolfgang Norbert, O.S.B., A.B., J.C.D., The Act of Religious Profession, VIII-174 pp., 1931.

64. Roberts, Rev. James Brendan, A.B., J.C.D., The Banns of Marriage, XIV-140 pp., 1931.

65. Ryder, Rev. Raymond Aloysius, A.B., J.C.D., Simony, IX-151 pp., 1931.

66. Campagna, Rev. Angelo, Ph.D., J.U.D., Il Vicario Generale del Vescovo, VII-205 pp., 1931.

67. Cox, Rev. Joseph Godfrey, A.B., J.C.D., The Administration of Seminaries, VI-124 pp., 1931.

68. GREGORY, REV. DONALD J., J.U.D., The Pauline Privilege, XV-165 pp., 1931.

69 DONOHUE, REV. JOHN F., J.C.D., The Impediment of Crime, VII-110 pp., 1931.

70. DOOLEY, REV. EUGENE A., O.M.I., J.C.D., Church Law on Sacred Relics, IX-143 pp., 1931.

71. ORTH, REV. CLEMENT RAYMOND, O.M.C., J.C.D., The Approbation of Religious Institutes, 171 pp., 1931.

72. PERNICONE, REV. JOSEPH M., A.B. J.C.D., The Ecclesiastical Prohibition of Books, XII-267 pp., 1932.

73. CLINTON, REV. CONNELL, A.B., J.C.D., The Paschal Precept, IX-108 pp., 1932.

74. DONNELLY, REV. FRANCIS B., A.M., S.T.L., J.C.D., The Diocesan Synod, VIII-125 pp., 1932.

75. TORRENTE, REV. CAMILO, C.M.F., J.C.D., Las Procesiones Sagradas, V-145 pp., 1932.

76. MURPHY, REV. EDWIN J., C.PP.S., J.C.D., Suspension Ex Informata Conscientia, XI-122 pp., 1932.

77. MACKENZIE, REV. ERIC F., A.M., S.T.L., J.C.D., The Delict of Heresy in its Commission, Penalization, Absolution, VII-124 pp., 1932.

78. LYONS, REV. AVITUS E., S.T.B., J.C.D., The Collegiate Tribunal of First Instance, XI-147 pp., 1932.

79. CONNOLLY, REV. THOMAS A., J.C.D., Appeals, XI-195, pp., 1932.

80. SANGMEISTER, REV. JOSEPH V., A.B., J.C.D., Force and Fear as Precluding Matrimonial Consent, V-211 pp., 1932.

81. JAEGER, REV. LEO A., A.B., J.C.D., The Administration of Vacant and Quasi-Vacant Episcopal Sees in the United States, IX-229 pp., 1932.

82. RIMLINGER, REV. HERBERT T., J.C.D., Error Invalidating Matrimonial Consent, VII-79 pp., 1932.

83. BARRETT, REV. JOHN D. M., S.S., J.C.D., A Comparative Study of the Councils of Baltimore and the Code of Canon Law, IX-223 pp., 1932.

84. CARBERRY, REV. JOHN J., PH.D., S.T.D., J.C.D., The Juridical Form of Marriage, X-177 pp., 1934.

85. DOLAN, REV. JOHN L., A.B., J.C.D., The Defensor Vinculi, XII-157 pp., 1934.

86. HANNAN, REV. JEROME D., A.M., S.T.D., LL.B., J.C.D., The Canon Law of Wills, IX-517 pp., 1934.

87. LEMIEUX, REV. DELISE A., A.M., J.C.D., The Sentence in Ecclesiastical Procedure, IX-131 pp., 1934.

88. O'ROURKE, REV. JAMES J., A.B., J.C.D., Parish Registers, VII-109 pp., 1934.

89. TIMLIN, REV. BARTHOLOMEW, O.F.M., A.M., J.C.D., Conditional Matrimonial Consent, X-381 pp., 1934.

90. WAHL, REV. FRANCIS X., A.B., J.C.D., The Matrimonial Impediments of Consanguinity and Affinity, VI-125 pp., 1934.

91. WHITE, REV. ROBERT J., A.B., LL.B., S.T.B., J.C.D., Canonical Ante-Nuptial Promises and the Civil Law, VI-152 pp., 1934.

92. HERRERA, REV. ANTONIO PARRA, O.C.D., J.C.D., Legislación Ecclesiástica sobre el Ayuno y la Abstinencia, XI-191 pp., 1935.

93. KENNEDY, REV. EDWIN J., J.C.D., The Special Matrimonial Process in Cases of Evident Nullity, X-165 pp., 1935.

94. MANNING, REV. JOHN J., A.B., J.C.D., Presumption of Law in Matrimonial Procedure, XI-111 pp., 1935.

95. MOEDER, REV. JOHN M., J.C.D., The Proper Bishop for Ordination and Dimissorial Letters, VII-135 pp., 1935.

96. O'MARA, REV. WILLIAM A., A.B., J.C.D., Canonical Causes for Matrimonial Dispensations, IX-155 pp., 1935.

97. REILLY, REV. PETER, J.C.D., Residence of Pastors, IX-81 pp., 1935.

98. SMITH, REV. MARINER T., O.P., S.T.Lr., J.C.D., The Penal Law for Religious, VIII-169 pp., 1935.

99. WHALEN, REV. DONALD W., A.M., J.C.D., The Value of Testimonial Evidence in Matrimonial Procedure, XIII-297 pp., 1935.

100. CLEARY, REV. JOSEPH F., J.C.D., Canonical Limitations on the Alienation of Church Property, VIII-141 pp., 1936.

101. GLYNN, REV. JOHN C., J.C.D., The Promoter of Justice, XX-337 pp., 1936.

102. BRENNAN, REV. JAMES H., S.S., M.A., S.T.B., J.C.D., The Simple Convalidation of Marriage, VI-135 pp., 1937.

103. BRUNINI, REV. JOSEPH BERNARD, J.C.D., The Clerical Obligations of Canons 139 and 142, X-121 pp., 1937.

104. CONNOR, REV. MAURICE, A.B., J.C.D., The Administrative Removal of Pastors, VIII-159 pp., 1937.

105. GUILFOYLE, REV. MERLIN JOSEPH, J.C.D., Custom, XI-144 pp., 1937.

106. HUGHES, REV. JAMES AUSTIN, A.B., A.M., J.C.D., Witnesses in Criminal Trials of Clerics, IX-140 pp., 1937.

107. JANSEN, REV. RAYMOND J., A.B., S.T.L., J.C.D., Canonical Provisions for Catechetical Instruction, VII-153 pp., 1937.

108. KEALY, REV. JOHN JAMES, A.B., J.C.D., The Introductory Libellus in Church Court Procedure, XI-121 pp., 1937.

109. McMANUS, REV. JAMES EDWARD, C.SS.R., J.C.D., The Administration of Temporal Goods in Religious Institutes, XVI-196 pp., 1937.

110. MORIARITY, REV. EUGENE JAMES, J.C.D., Oaths in Ecclesiastical Courts, X-115 pp., 1937.

111. RAINER, REV. ELIGIUS GEORGE, C.SS.R., J.C.D., Suspension of Clerics, XVII-249 pp., 1937.

112. REILLY, REV. THOMAS F., C.SS.R., J.C.D., Visitation of Religious, VI-95 pp., 1938.

113. MORIARITY, REV. FRANCIS E., C.SS.R., J.C.D., The Extraordinary Absolution from Censures, XV-334 pp., 1938.

114. CONNOLLY, REV. NICHOLAS P., J.C.D., The Canonical Erection of Parishes, X-132 pp., 1938.

115. DONOVAN, REV. JAMES JOSEPH, J.C.D., The Pastor's Obligation in Prenuptial Investigation, XII-322 pp., 1938.

116. HARRIGAN, REV. ROBERT J., M.A., S.T.B., J.C.D., The Radical Sanation of Invalid Marriages, VIII-208 pp., 1938.

117. BOFFA, REV. CONRAD HUMBERT, J.C.D., Canonical Provisions for Catholic Schools, VII-211 pp., 1939.

118. Parsons, Rev. Anscar John, O.M.Cap., J.C.D., Canonical Elections, XII-236 pp., 1939.

119. Reilly, Rev. Edward Michael, A.B., J.C.D., The General Norms of Dispensation, XII-156 pp., 1939.

120. Ryan, Rev. Gerald Aloysius, A.B., J.C.D., Principles of Episcopal Jurisdiction, XII-172 pp., 1939.

121. Burton, Rev. Francis James, C.S.C., A.B., J.C.D., A Commentary on Canon 1125, X-222 pp., 1940.

122. Miaskiewicz, Rev. Francis Sigismund, J.C.D., Supplied Jurisdiction According to Canon 209, XII-340 pp., 1940.

123. Rice, Rev. Patrick William, A.B., J.C.D., Proof of Death in Prenuptial Investigation, VIII-156 pp., 1940.

124. Anglin, Rev. Thomas Francis, M.S., J.C.D., The Eucharistic Fast, VIII-183 pp., 1941.

125. Coleman, Rev. John Jerome, J.C.D., The Minister of Confirmation, VI-153 pp., 1941.

126. Downs, Rev. John Emmanuel, A.B., J.C.D., The Concept of Clerical Immunity, XI-163 pp., 1941.

127. Esswein, Rev. Anthony Albert, J.C.D., Extrajudicial Penal Powers of Ecclesiastical Superiors, X-144 pp., 1941.

128. Farrell, Rev. Benjamin Francis, M.A., S.T.L., J.C.D., The Rights and Duties of the Local Ordinary Regarding Congregations of Women Religious of Pontifical Approval, V-195 pp., 1941.

129. Feeney, Rev. Thomas John, A.B., S.T.L., J.C.D., Restitutio in Integrum VI-169 pp., 1941.

130. Findlay, Rev. Stephen William, O.S.B., A.B., J.C.D., Canonical Norms Governing the Deposition and Degradation of Clerics, XVII-279 pp., 1941.

131. Goodwine, Rev. John, A.B., S.T.L., J.C.D., The Right of the Church to Acquire Property, VIII-119 pp., 1941.

132. Heston, Rev. Edward Louis, C.S.C., Ph.D., S.T.D., J.C.D., The Alienation of Church Property in the United States, XII-222 pp., 1941.

133. Hogan, Rev. James John, A.B., S.T.L., J.C.D., Judicial Advocates and Procurators, XIII-200 pp., 1941.

134. Kealy, Rev. Thomas M., A.B., Litt.B., J.C.D., Dowry of Women Religious, IX-152 pp., 1941.

135. Keene, Rev. Michael James, O.S.B., J.C.D., Religious Ordinaries and Canon 198, V-164 pp., 1942.

136. Kerin, Rev. Charles A., S.S., M.A., S.T.B., J.C.D., The Privation of Christian Burial, XVI-279 pp., 1941.

137. Louis, Rev. William Francis, M.A., J.C.D., Diocesan Archives, X-101 pp., 1941.

138. McDevitt, Rev. Gilbert Joseph, A.B., J.C.D., Legitimacy and Legitimation, X-247 pp., 1941.

139. McDonough, Rev. Thomas Joseph, A.B., J.C.D., Apostolic Administrators, X-217 pp., 1941.

140. Meier, Rev. Carl Anthony, A.B., J.C.D., Penal Administrative Procedure Against Negligent Pastors, XI-240 pp., 1941.

141. Schmidt, Rev. John Rogg, A.B., J.C.D., The Principles of Authentic Interpretation in Canon 17 of the Code of Canon Law, XII-331 pp., 1941

142. Slafkosky, Rev. Andrew Leonard, A.B., J.C.D., The Canonical Episcopal Visitation of the Diocese, X-197 pp., 1941.

143, Swoboda, Rev. Innocent Robert, O.F.M., J.C.D., Ignorance in Relation to the Imputability of Delicts, IX-271 pp., 1941.

144. Dube, Rev. Arthur Joseph, A.B., J.C.D., The General Principles for the Reckoning of Time in Canon Law, VIII-299 pp., 1941.

145. McBride, Rev. James T., A.B., J.C.D., Incardination and Excardination of Seculars, XX-585 pp., 1941.

146. Król, Rev. John T., J.C.D., The Defendant in Ecclesiastical Trials, XII-207 pp., 1942.

147. Comyns, Rev. Joseph J., C.SS.R., A.B., J.C.D., Papal and Episcopal Administration of Church Property, XIV-155 pp., 1942.

148. Barry, Rev. Garrett Francis, O.M.I., J.C.D., Violation of the Cloister XII-260 pp., 1942.

149. Bolduc, Rev. Gatien, C.S.V., A.B., S.T.L., J.C.D., Les Études dans les Religions Cléricales, VIII-155 pp., 1942.

150. Boyle, Rev. David John, M.A., J.C.D., The Juridic Effects of Moral Certitude on Pre-Nuptial Guarantees, XII-188 pp., 1942.

151. Canavan, Rev. Walter Joseph, M.A., Litt.D., J.C.D., The Profession of Faith, XII-143 pp., 1942.

152. Desrochers, Rev. Bruno, A.B., Ph.L., S.T.B., J.C.D., Le Premier Concile Plénier de Québec et le Code de Droit Canonique, XIV-186 pp., 1942.

153. Dillon, Rev. Robert Edward, A.B., J.C.D., Common Law Marriage, X-148 pp., 1942.

154. Dodwell, Rev. Edward John, Ph.D., S.T.B., J.C.D., The Time and Place for the Celebration of Marriage, X-156 pp., 1942.

155. Donnellan, Rev. Thomas Andrew, A.B., J.C.D., The Obligation of the Missa pro Populo, VII-131 pp., 1942.

156. Eltz, Rev. Louis Anthony, A.B., J.C.D., Cooperation in Crime, XII-208 pp., 1942.

157. Gass, Rev. Sylvester Francis, M.A., J.C.D., Ecclesiastical Pensions, XI-206 pp., 1942.

158. Guiniven, Rev. John Joseph, C.SS.R., J.C.D., The Precept of Hearing Mass, XIV-188 pp., 1942.

159. Gulczynski, Rev. John Theophilus, J.C.D., The Desecration and Violation of Churches, X-126 pp., 1942.

160. Hammill, Rev. John Leo, M.A., J.C.D., The Obligations of the Traveler According to Canon 14, VIII-204 pp., 1942.

161. Haydt, Rev. John Joseph, A.B., J.C.D., Reserved Benefices, XI-148 pp., 1942.

162. Huser, Rev. Roger John, O.F.M., A.B., J.C.D., The Crime of Abortion in Canon Law, XII-187 pp., 1942.

163. Kearney, Rev. Francis Patrick, A.B., S.T.L., J.C.D., The Principles of Canon 1127, X-162 pp., 1942.

164. LINAHEN, REV. LEO JAMES, S.T.L., JC.D., De Absolutione Complicis in Peccato Turpi, V-114 pp., 1942.

165. McCLOSKEY, REV. JOSEPH ALOYSIUS, A.B., J.C.D., The Subject of Ecclesiastical Law According to Canon 12, XVII-246 pp., 1942.

166. O'NEILL, REV. FRANCIS JOSEPH, C.SS.R., J.C.D., The Dismissal of Religious in Temporary Vows, XIII-220 pp., 1942.

167. PRINCE, REV. JOHN EDWARD, A.B., S.T.B., J.C.D., The Diocesan Chancellor, X-136 pp., 1942.

168. RIESNER, REV. ALBERT JOSEPH, C.SS.R., J.C.D., Apostates and Fugitives from Religious Institutes, IX-168 pp., 1942.

169. STENGER, REV. JOSEPH BERNARD, J.C.D., The Mortgaging of Church Property, 186 pp., 1942.

170. WALDRON, REV. JOSEPH FRANCIS, A.B., J.C.D., The Minister of Baptism, XII-197 pp., 1942.

171. WILLETT, REV. ROBERT ALBERT, J.C.D., The Probative Value of Documents in Ecclesiastical Trials, X-124 pp., 1942.

172. WOEBER, REV. EDWARD MARTIN, M.A., J.C.D., The Interpellations, XII-161 pp., 1942.

173. BENKO, REV. MATTHEW ALOYSIUS, O.S.B., M.A., J.C.D., The Abbot *Nullius*, XVI-148 pp., 1943.

174. CHRIST, REV. JOSEPH JAMES, M.A., S.T.L., J.C.D., Dispensation from Vindicative Penalties, XIV-285 pp., 1943.

175. CLANCY, REV. PATRICK M. J., O.P., A.B., S.T.Lr., J.C.D., The Local Religious Superior, X-229 pp., 1943.

176. CLARKE, REV. THOMAS JAMES, J.C.D., Parish Societies, XII-147 pp., 1943.

177. CONNOLLY, REV. JOHN PATRICK, S.T.L., J.C.D., Synodal Examiners and Parish Priest Consultors, X-223 pp., 1943.

178. DRUMM, REV. WILLIAM MARTIN, A.B., J.C.D., Hospital Chaplains, XII-175 pp., 1943.

179. FLANAGAN, REV. BERNARD JOSEPH, A.B., S.T.L., J.C.D., The Canonical Erection of Religious Houses, X-147 pp., 1943.

180. KELLEHER, REV. STEPHEN, A.B., S.T.B., J.C.D., Discussions with Non-Catholics: Canonical Legislation, X-93 pp., 1943.

181. LEWIS, REV. GORDIAN, C.P., J.C.D., Chapters in Religious Institutes, XII-169 pp., 1943.

182. MARX, REV. ADOLPH, J.C.D., The Declaration of Nullity of Marriages Contracted Outside the Church, X-151 pp., 1943.

183. MATULENAS, REV. RAYMOND ANTHONY, O.S.B., A.B., J.C.D., Communication, a Source of Privileges, XII-225 pp., 1943.

184. O'LEARY, REV. CHARLES GERARD, C.SS.R., J.C.D., Religious Dismissed After Perpetual Profession, X-213 pp., 1943.

185. POWER, REV. CORNELIUS MICHAEL, J.C.D., The Blessing of Cemeteries, XII-231 pp., 1943.

186. SHUHLER, REV. RALPH VINCENT, O.S.A., J.C.D., Privileges of Religious to Absolve and Dispense, XII-195 pp., 1943.

187. ZIOLKOWSKI, REV. THADDEUS STANISLAUS, A.B., J.C.D., The Consecration and Blessing of Churches, XII-151 pp., 1943.

188. HENEGHAN, REV. JOHN JOSEPH, S.T.D., J.C.D., The Marriages of Unworthy Catholics: Canons 1065 and 1066, XVI-213 pp., 1944.

189. CARROLL, REV. COLEMAN FRANCIS, M.A., S.T.L., J.C.L., Charitable Institutions.

190. CIESLUK, REV. JOSEPH EDWARD, PH.B., S.T.L., J.C.D., National Parishes in the United States, VI-178 pp., 1944.

191. COBURN, REV. VINCENT PAUL, A.B., J.C.D., Marriages of Conscience, XII-172 pp., 1944.

192. CONNORS, REV. CHARLES PAUL, C.S.SP., A.B., J.C.D., Extra-Judicial Procurators in the Code of Canon Law, X-94 pp., 1944.

193. COYLE, REV. PAUL RAYMOND, A.B., J.C.D., Judicial Exceptions, X-142 pp., 1944.

194. FAIR, REV. BARTHOLOMEW FRANCIS, A.B., S.T.L., J.C.D., The Impediment of Abduction, XII-122 pp., 1944.

195. GALLAGHER, REV. THOMAS RAPHAEL, O.P., A.B., S.T.L8., J.C.D., The Examination of the Qualities of the Ordinand, X-166 pp., 1944.

196. GANNON, REV. JOHN MARK, S.T.L., J.C.D., The Interstices Required for the Promotion to Orders, XII-100 pp., 1944.

197. GOLDSMITH, REV. J. WILLIAM, B.C.S., S.T.L., J.C.D., The Competence of Church and State Over Marriages—Disputed Points, X-128 pp., 1944.

198. GOODWINE, REV. JOSEPH GERARD, A.B., S.T.B., J.C.D., The Reception of Converts, XIV-326 pp., 1944.

199. KOWALSKI, REV. ROMUALD EUGENE, O.F.M., A.B., J.C.D., Sustenance of Religious Houses of Regulars, X-174 pp., 1944.

200. MCCOY, REV. ALAN EDWARD, O.F.M., J.C.D., Force and Fear in Relation to Delictual Imputability and Penal Responsibility, XII-160 pp., 1944.

201. MCDEVITT, REV. VINCENT JOHN, PH.B., S.T.L., J.C.L., Perjury.

202. MARTIN, REV. THOMAS OWEN, PH.D., S.T.D., J.C.D., Adverse Posession, Prescription and Limitation of Actions: The Canonical "Praescriptio," XX-208 pp., 1944.

203. MIKLOSOVIC, REV. PAUL JOHN, A.B., J.C.L., Attempted Marriages and Their Consequent Juridic Effects.

204. MUNDY, REV. THOMAS MAURICE, A.B., S.T.L., J.C.D., The Union of Parishes, X-164 pp., 1944.

205. O'DEA, REV. JOHN COYLE, A.B., J.C.D., The Matrimonial Impediment of Nonage, VIII-126 pp., 1944.

206. OLALIA, REV. ALEXANDER AYSON, S.T.L., J.C.D., A Comparative Study of the Christian Constitution of States and the Constitution of the Philippine Commonwealth, XII-136 pp., 1944.

207. POISSON, REV. PIERRE-MARIE, C.S.C., A.B., PH.L., TH.L., J.C.L., Droits Patrimoniaux des Maisons et des Églises Religieuses.

208. STADALNIKAS, REV. CASIMIR JOSEPH, M.I.C., J.C.D., Reservation of Censures, X-141 pp., 1944.

209. SULLIVAN, REV. EUGENE HENRY, S.T.L., J.C.D., Proof of the Reception of the Sacraments, X-165 pp., 1944.

210. VAUGHAN, REV. WILLIAM EDWARD, J.C.D., Constitutions for Diocesan Courts, X-210 pp., 1944.

211. Paro, Rev. Gino, S.T.D., J.C.L., The Right of Apostolic Legation.

212. Balzer, Rev. Ralph Francis, C.P., J.C.D., The Computation of Time in a Canonical Novitiate, X-227 pp., 1945.

213. Dougherty, Rev. John Whelan, A.B., S.T.L., J.C.D., De Inquisitione Speciali, XII-195 pp., 1945.

214. Dziob, Rev. Michael Walter, J.C.D., The Sacred Congregation for the Oriental Church, XII-181 pp., 1945.

215. Eidenschink, Rev. John Albert, O.S.B., B.A., J.C.D., The Election of Bishops in the Letters of Pope Gregory the Great, VIII-200 pp., 1945.

216. Gill, Rev. Nicholas, C.P., J.C.D., The Spiritual Prefect in Clerical Religious Houses of Study, X-140 pp., 1945.

217. Hynes, Rev. Harry Gerard, S.T.L., J.C.D., The Privileges of Cardinals, XII-183 pp., 1945.

218. McDevitt, Rev. Gerald Vincent, S.T.L., J.C.D., The Renunciation of an Ecclesiastical Office, XIV-179 pp., 1945.

219. Manning, Rev. Joseph Leroy, J.C.D., The Free Conferral of Offices, VII-116 pp., 1945.

220. Meyer, Rev. Louis G., O.S.B., A.B., S.T.B., J.C.D., Alms-gathering by Religious, XII-163 pp., 1945.

221. O'Donnell, Rev. Cletus Francis, M.A., J.C.D., The Marriage of Minors, XII-268 pp., 1945.

222. Prunskis, Rev. Joseph, J.C.D., Comparative Law, Ecclesiastical and Civil, in Lithuanian Concordat, X-161 pp., 1945.

223. Sweeney, Rev. Francis Patrick, C.SS.R., J.C.D., The Reduction of Clerics to the Lay State, X-199 pp., 1945.

224. Vogelpohl, Rev. Henry John, J.C.D., The Simple Impediments to Holy Orders, XVI-190 pp., 1945.

225. Brockhaus, Rev. Thomas Aquinas, O.S.B., J.C.D., Religious who are known as *Conversi*, X-127 pp., 1945.

226. Griese, Rev. Orville Nicholas, S.T.D., J.C.D., The Marriage Contract and the Procreation of Offspring, XVI-224 pp., 1946.

227. Boudreaux, Rev. Warren Louis, J.C.D., The *"ab acatholicis nati"* of Canon 1099, § 2, XII-110 pp., 1946.

228. Bowe, Rev. Thomas Joseph, A.B., J.C.D., Religious Superioresses, VIII-206 pp., 1946.

229. Diederichs, Rev. Michael Ferdinand, S.C.J., J.C.D., The Jurisdiction of the Latin Ordinaries over their Oriental Subjects, XIV-153 pp., 1946.

230. Dingman, Rev. Maurice John, A.B., S.T.L., J.C.L., The Plaintiff in Contentious Trials.

231. Frison, Rev. Basil, C.M.F., M.Mus., J.C.D., The Retroactivity of Law, X-221 pp., 1946.

232. Galvin, Rev. William Anthony, M.A., J.C.D., The Administrative Transfer of Pastors, XII-288 pp., 1946.

233. Goracy, Rev. Joseph C., J.C.L., The Diriment Matrimonial Impediment of Major Orders.

234. HALE, REV. JOSEPH FRANCIS, M.A., S.T.L., J.C.L., The Pastor of Burial.

235. HENRY, REV. JOSEPH ARTHUR, A.B., J.C.D., The Mass and Holy Communion: Interritual Law, XII-138 pp., 1946.

236. LINENBERGER, REV. HERBERT, C.PP.S., J.C.D., The False Denunciation of an Innocent Confessor, VIII-205 pp., 1949.

237. LOWRY, REV. JAMES MARTIN, A.B., J.C.D., Dispensation from Private Vows, XII-266 pp., 1946.

238. LYNCH, REV. GEORGE EDWARD, A.B., S.T.L., J.C.D., Coadjutors and Auxiliaries of Bishops, X-107 pp., 1947.

239. LYNCH, REV. TIMOTHY, M.S.SS.T., J.C.D., Contracts between Bishops and Religious Congregations, XIII-232 pp., 1946.

240. MCCLUNN, REV. JUSTIN DAVID, A.B., S.T.L., J.C.D., Administrative Recourse, VII-142 pp., 1946.

241. LOHMULLER, REV. MARTIN NICHOLAS, A.B., J.C.D., The Promulgation of Law, XII-140 pp., 1947.

242. MCGRATH, REV. JAMES, A.B., J.C.D., The Privilege of the Canon, XII-156 pp., 1946.

243. MARBACH, REV. JOSEPH FRANCIS, A.B., J.C.D., Marriage Legislation for the Catholics of the Oriental Rites in the United States and Canada, XIV-314 pp., 1946.

244. SHIMKUS, REV. BERNARD ALOYSIUS, A.B., J.C.L., The Determination and Transfer of Rite.

245. SMITH, REV. VINCENT MICHAEL, A.B., S.T.L., J.C.L., Ignorance Affecting Matrimonial Consent.

246. WACHTRLE, REV. PAUL ANTHONY, A.B., J.C.L., The Baptism of the Children of Non-Catholics.

247. CROTTY, REV. MATTHEW M., J.C.D., The Recipient of First Holy Communion, X-142 pp., 1947.

248. EAGLETON, REV. GEORGE, J.C.L., The Quinquennial Faculties, Formula IV.

249. GIBBONS, REV. MARION L., C.M., LL.B., J.C.D., Domicile of the Wife Unlawfully Separated from Her Husband, XIV-171 pp., 1947.

250. KELLY, REV. BERNARD M., S.T.L., J.C.D., The Functions Reserved to Pastors, XII-141 pp., 1947.

251. KILCULLEN, REV. THOMAS J., LL.M., J.C.D., The Collegiate Moral Person as Party Litigant, X-150 pp., 1947.

252. LAFONTAINE, REV. GERMAIN J., W.F., J.C.D., Relations Canoniques entre Le Missionnaire et Ses Superieurs, X-117 pp., 1947.

253. LANE, REV. LORAS THOMAS, B. For. Comm., A.B., S.T.L., J.C.D., Matrimonial Procedure in the Ordinary Courts of Second Instance, XVI-184 pp., 1947.

254. LOVER, REV. JAMES F., C.SS.R., M.A., J.C.D., The Master of Novices, X-168 pp., 1947.

255. MCNICHOLAS, REV. TIMOTHY JOSEPH, J.C.L., The *Septimae Manus* Witness.

256. MAROSITZ, REV. JOSEPH J., M.S.C., J.C.D., Obligations and Privileges of Religious Promoted to the Episcopal or Cardinalitial Dignities, XII-180 pp., 1947.

257. MURPHY, REV. FRANCIS J., A.B., J.C.D., Legislative Powers of the Provincial Council, XII-158 pp., 1947.

258. O'BRIEN, REV. ROMAEUS W., O. Carm., J.C.D., The Provincial Superior in Religious Orders of Men, X-294 pp., 1947.

259. PFALLER, REV. BENEDICT A., O.S.B., J.C.D., The *Ipso Facto* Effected Dismissal of Religious, XII-225 pp., 1947.

260. POPEK, REV. ALPHONSE S., M.A., J.C.D., The Rights and Obligations of Metropolitans, XX-460 pp., 1947.

261. RISTUCCIA, REV. BERNARD JOSEPH, C.M., J.C.L., Quasi-Religious.

262. SONNTAG, REV. NATHANIEL L., O.F.M., Cap., J.C.D., Censorship of Special Classes of Books, XII-147 pp., 1947.

263. STADLER, REV. JOSEPH NICHOLAS, J.C.D., Frequent Holy Communion, X-158 pp., 1947.

264. SZAL, REV. IGNATIUS JOSEPH, J.C.D., The Communication of Catholics with Schismatics, XII-217 pp., 1947.

265. WAGNER, REV. URBAN S., O.F.M. Conv., J.C.D., Parochial Substitute Vicars and Supplying Priests, X-126 pp., 1947.

www.ingramcontent.com/pod-product-compliance
Lightning Source LLC
LaVergne TN
LVHW050236080826
844660LV00012B/543

* 9 7 8 0 8 1 3 2 2 4 3 1 2 *